Selected Papers on SAS

Shaoji Xu

BeAuthor Press

Selected Papers on SAS

ISBN 1-59356-005-2

Written by Shaoji Xu

Cover design by David Zhao

Printed in the United States of America

http://www.BeAuthor.com

Preface

There is an old saying in Chinese: "Indigo comes from blue but is darker than blue; ice comes from water but is colder than water." This means, "The master is surpassed by the apprentice." However, this saying also describes the situation of my two "daughters": *Understanding SAS* and *Selected Papers on SAS*. This new book (*Selected Papers on SAS)* is derived from the older sister (*Understanding SAS)*, but she is prettier and more charming than the older sister because I have concentrated on important and interesting parts rather than discussing every point. Actually, I should say that papers in this book are the essence of the older sister.

In the book *Understanding SAS* I included many new ideas, that is, my own research results. I finished the book, but the labor and delivery process takes a long time. Meanwhile, I decided to write some papers. I have taken some ideas from the book and finished them as separate, independent papers. So now the younger sister makes her debut before her older sister.

The book has 17 papers.

Mainly, there are three kinds of contents: basic, fundamental parts such as names, order of statements and options, end of data set, and operators; hot topics such as CHKLOG, page of, rtf files and special characters, and transmitting between SAS data sets and Excel files; and that are just for fun.

The SAS manual is a great resource for every SAS programmer. However, it is too general in some places. For example, when talking about variable names, it says

You do not assign the names of special SAS automatic variables (such as _N_ and _ERROR_) or variable list names (such as _NUMERIC_, _CHARACTER_, and _ALL_) to variables.

This is far, far from enough. As we know, many computer languages have a determined set of reserved words, such as SQL. But SAS is different. "*The rules are more flexible for SAS variable names than for other language elements. . . . . SAS reserves a few names for automatic variables and variable lists, SAS data set, and librefs.*"

First, what are these "a few names"? Second, this gives users great flexibility. They can use almost any words freely. On the other hand, it brings users some inconvenience, because you don't know how SAS treats a word: Is it treated as a user-defined name or as a keyword? This depends on SAS's interest and SAS's understanding. Sometimes you may think it is OK to use a specified word as a name, but SAS says: No, it is a keyword. Then your programming will be messed up. The following program creates two printouts. Guess what these printouts are.

```
DATA s;
a=5;n=6;
PROC REPORT NOWD;
COLUMN a n;
RUN;
DATA s;
not=0;
yes=not+1;
PROC PRINT;RUN;
```

Therefore, if you don't know how SAS behaves, you may not get the results that you want. We need to know about individual names. We need to know what names are forbidden in SAS and what names and in what situations SAS has its own interpretation of their meanings, and then we can correctly use these names or just avoid them.

Another example is subsetting. We all know that we can use a WHERE statement and an IF statement (subsetting IF) to subset a data set. Also, we know that there are some differences between a WHERE statement and a subsetting IF statement. We know that they will produce different data sets in some situations as the SAS manual mentions in the following:

The WHERE statement can produce a different data set from the subsetting IF when a BY statement accompanies a SET, MERGE, or UPDATE statement.

Then we may ask the question: If there is no BY statement, are there any differences? Some books discuss this, but the discussions do not contain enough details. We need comprehensive comparisons between two statements. Several papers in this book discuss this topic.

END of data set is fundamental in the SAS language. Almost every programmer uses option END=. In the paper [IV] I discuss when we can use this option and how SAS works on this option.

Relationships among the options KEEP (DROP), RENAME, and WHERE are basic. In the paper [III] I discuss relationships among statements and options. You may not care about relationships between options OBS= and WHERE= because you never use them together. However, it is quite possible that you have used options RENAME= and WHERE= together. The SAS online document talks about relationships among the options KEEP=, DROP=, and RENAME=, but not with the WHERE= option. So what is wrong with the following program?

```
DATA s;
a=3;
DATA t;
SET s(WHERE=(a>2) RENAME=(a=b));
RUN;
```

```
3    DATA t;
4    SET s(WHERE=(a>2) RENAME=(a=b));
ERROR: Variable a is not on file WORK.S.
```

```
RUN;

NOTE: The SAS System stopped processing this step because of errors.
```

Some topics are just for fun, for example, the positive prefix operator. Do you know what the printout of the following program is?

```
DATA s;
a=3;OUTPUT;
a=-3;OUTPUT;
DATA t;
SET s;
WHERE +a>0;
PROC PRINT;
RUN;
```

This is a very simple and trivial program, but I believe that no one has ever tried it. If you are interested or curious, you can find this out by yourself (It is very simple.), or you can read this book. This problem is discussed in [V]. Of course, this is not the main topic of that paper. Actually, [V] is my favorite paper. In that paper, I discuss operators in a DATA step (not in a WHERE statement or a WHERE option), in a WHERE statement, in PROC SQL, and in macro facility, and I make a comprehensive comparison. These are fundamental parts of the SAS language and can be a supplement of the SAS manual. They touch a basic and fundamental question: When we learn, use, analyze, and compare operators, what factors do we need to consider? I think it is not very clear for many SAS programmers and in many books. The following program creates three data sets s, t, and p. Do you know the difference between the data set t and the data set p?

```
DATA s;
INPUT a b c;
CARDS;
-3 5 2
2 5 2
;
DATA t;
SET s;
IF a=-3 MAX b MIN c;
PROC PRINT;
DATA p;
SET s;
WHERE a=-3 MAX b MIN c;
PROC PRINT;
RUN;
```

Let's see another example. Do you know what the printouts of the following program are?

```
%MACRO ss(company);
%IF &company EQ GE %THEN %PUT The company is GE;
%MEND;
%ss(GE)
```

```
%MACRO tt(state);
%IF &state EQ OR %THEN %PUT The state is Oregon;
%MEND;
%tt(OR)
```

We can see that the first macro is OK, but the second one is not. This problem has been discussed in many papers and books. There are two questions: Why does this happen and how could we avoid the problem? Many books give the answer to the second question: Use quoting functions. In [V], I give my explanation for the first question.

Every programmer knows about variable lists and more or less uses variable lists. Now I ask the following question: Precisely which statement can use which variable list? I think many people may be not clear about this. This is the purpose of paper [VI]. Many people know statistical functions. You can guess that the function MEAN() returns the mean value of arguments without reading any book. But do you know how to use variable lists in statistical functions? For example, in the following, which statements are OK, and which have problems? Assume that all variables and arrays are defined.

```
A=MEAN(OF x1-x6 p, OF q y1-y5, OF z1 z2,y1+y2);
A=MEAN(OF x1-x6 p q y1-y5 z1 z2);
A=MEAN(OF x1-x6 y1+y2);
A=MEAN(x1 x2 x3);
A=MEAN(OF x1-x5, y2 y3);
A=MEAN(OF x:);
A=MEAN(OF z(1) - z(3));
A=MEAN(OF z(*));
```

In [XIII], I discuss relationships between formats and outputs of statistical procedures. Formats affect not only the appearance of printouts but also the results as well. For example, the following program creates two printouts. Do you know if they are different?

```
DATA s;
a=1.34; b=5;OUTPUT;
a=1.28;b=4;OUTPUT;
a=2;b=5;OUTPUT;
a=2;b=4;OUTPUT;
FORMAT a 5.1;
PROC MEANS;
CLASS a;
PROC SQL;
SELECT a,MEAN(b) FROM s GROUP BY a;
QUIT;
```

A variable has two kinds of values: original (unformatted) values and formatted values. Every SAS programmer knows that if there is a BY statement, the data set should be sorted, but should the data set be sorted by original values or by formatted values? The following program is supposed to have two printouts. Is there any problem for the program? If there is no problem, what printout do you need? This problem is discussed in [XIV].

```
PROC FORMAT;
VALUE aa 1,3,5=odd 2,4=even;
DATA s;
INPUT a b @@;
FORMAT a aa.;
CARDS;
1 1 1 1 3 3 3 3 2 2 2 2 4 4 4 4
;
PROC MEANS;
BY a;VAR b;
PROC SORT;
BY a;
PROC MEANS;
BY a;VAR b;
RUN;
```

PROC SQL is an important part of SAS. Many people have done some work on this topic and advocate using PROC SQL. However, most SAS programmers still prefer DATA step because they are used to it. In this book, I discuss PROC SQL in much detail. Moreover, I present two complete programs using PROC SQL to create two tables that are used in pharmaceuticals companies, so you can compare these programs with those using DATA steps. Will you turn to PROC SQL after reading this book? Well, it is possible.

Is .1+.2 equal to .3? If you ask a math professor, he will say 'Yes'. But if you ask Dr. SAS (Dr. C, Dr. JAVA, or Dr. AWK), she will say 'No'. Moreover, she will tell you that the difference is 2**(-54) or approximately 5.55E-17. In [VIII] I discuss how SAS stores numeric values and does addition so that you can understand why Dr. SAS says No and how SAs's behavior affects your programming.

Some parts of the book are state of the art, most advanced, such as Excel and RTF. I am sure that many SAS programmers will encounter them. This book, I think, could be a good reference.

There are so many ways to move data between SAS and Excel files. In paper [XV], not only do I collect more than thirty methods, but also I indicate how to categorize them and how to compare them. You can then choose the one that best fits your needs. For example, many people know that some methods require the installation of SAS/ACCESS, and some methods do not. Do you know the answers to the following questions? What methods need SAS/ACCESS, and what methods do not? What is the difference between these two kinds of methods? What is the advantage of installing SAS/ACCESS? If there is no difference between them, then why would people waste money purchasing SAS/ACCESS software? (SAS/ACCESS has other functionalities, but here we concentrate on Excel.)

I provide my programs for CHKLOG and Page x of y. My criteria for good programs are that they are easy to use, easy to understand, and easy to modify. I hope my programs meet these criteria.

Finally, I have to emphasize that these results are run on PC Windows using SAS v9. Due to different settings, some conclusions may not apply to your situation. In many cases I will indicate the differences for v8, because so many SAS programmers are still using SAS v8.

No doubt, some conclusions may be inaccurate. The author welcomes readers' criticisms, comments, and suggestions.

I want to thank the SAS institute. Whenever I have questions, I can always get answers from them. I want to thank all the colleagues that I have ever worked with and that I am working with now. Discussions between you and me greatly inspire my thinking and my research.

I want to express my sincere thanks to Mrs. Jenny Brain for her help.

It is my hope that everyone who sees my "daughter" will say, "Your daughter is so charming. I like her." In other words, "I enjoy reading this book. I have learned something from it." Then, I will be happy.

Contents

View a SAS data set

Introduction

If you are a SAS programmer, no doubt, you have to view data sets. There are two commonly used applications to view a data set. One is the SAS Viewtable window, and the other is SAS System Viewer window.

SAS Viewtable window

You create a data set in the work directory, or you virtually move a directory to your SAS by assigning it a libname. Then you can open the data set in SAS. For the sake of illustration, we create the following data set:

```
DATA orsales;
SET SASHELP.orsales;
RUN;
```

PROC PRINT is a commonly used method to look up a data set. PROC PRINT is easy to use, but it has some limitations. If there are too many variables, the printout will be wrapped. Also, since the output is accumulated, if several data sets are printed out, you need to scroll up and down to find the desired results. If the output is known, then we can click the right one in the Results window to see the printout. Comparing two data sets is not easy.

Directly viewing a data set using the VIEWTABLE window brings some convenience and is a commonly used method to view a data set. It will never be wrapped up. When you scroll to any variable(s), you will always see the observation numbers that correspond to the values of the variable(s). The data set is grid lined. Any column or any row can be highlighted, and the data set can be opened and closed easily. Several data sets can be opened at the same time for comparison purposes.

There are several ways to open a data set in the Viewtable window, as follows:

- Type "viewtable data-set-name" in the command box (above the Explorer window);
- Right click the data set in the Explorer window and choose Open.
- Double click the data set in the Explorer window.

Now double click on the data set Orsales in the WORK library. We get a table that has 912 observations and 8 variables, as follows:

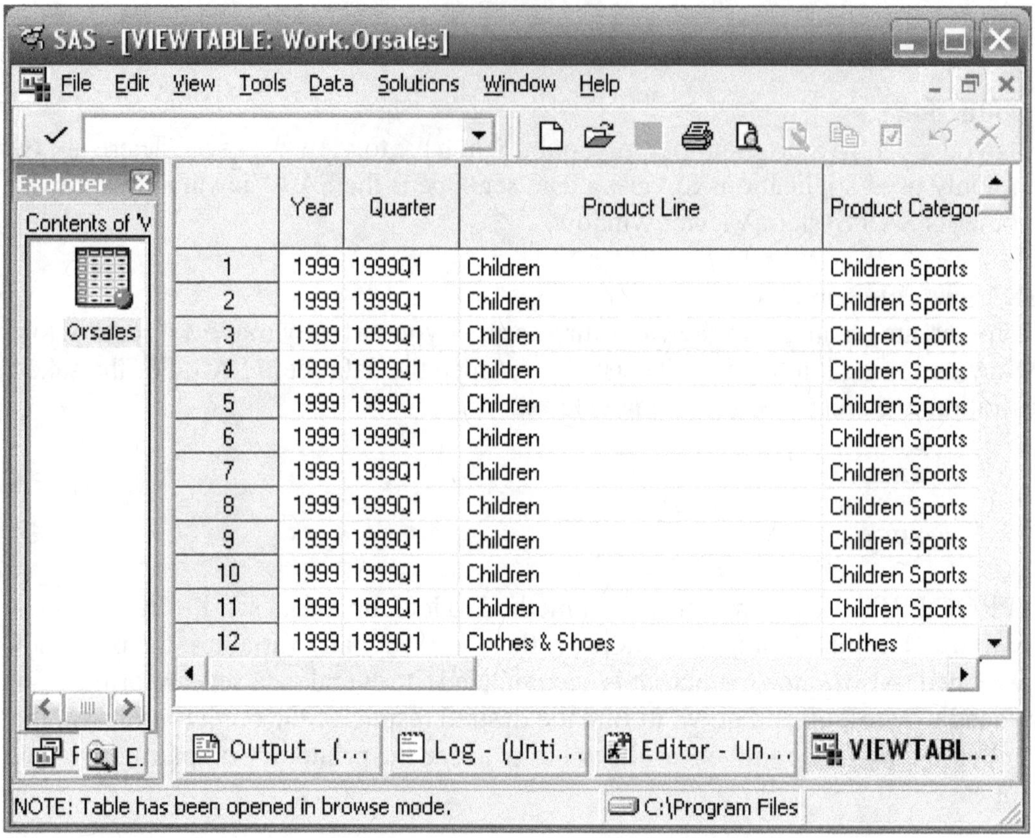

Now we can do the following:

- Scrolling the bar on the bottom allows you to move the table left and right. Scrolling the bar on the right side allows you to move the table up and down.
- You may concentrate on some adjacent columns or on some adjacent rows. They can be highlighted. To do this, click on the column header(s) or observation number(s).
- Columns may be moved. To do this, highlight columns and drag on the column headers. This makes it easy to compare the values of two columns.
- By default, the table shows the labels of columns. In order to see variable names, click View->Column Names. The options View Label and View Names are both very useful. You will learn the meaning of variables by viewing their labels. A programmer needs to know the names of variables.
- Some columns will be too wide, such as Product Line, and you want them to be narrow so that more columns can be seen in the table. To do this, click on the separator of the column headers, and then you can move the cursor to make the column wider or narrower.

Now right click the column header to get a pop-up menu, as the following picture shows:

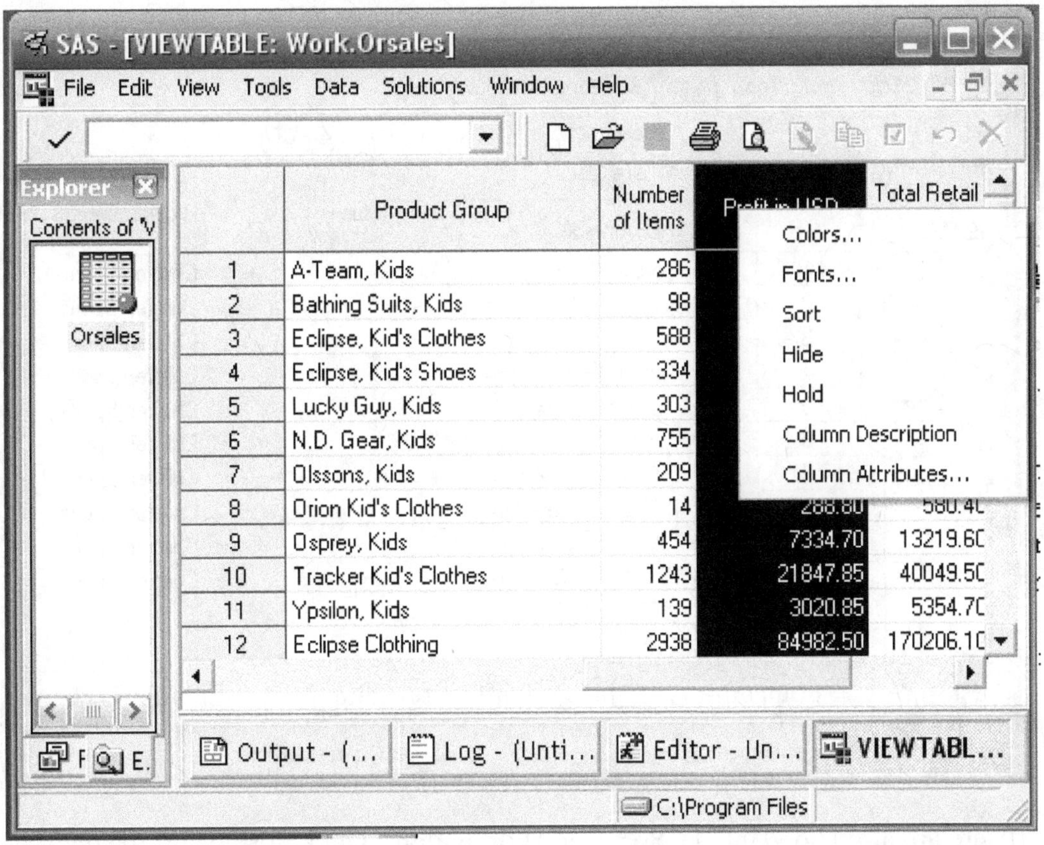

On the pop-up menu there are the following buttons: Colors, Fonts, Sort, Hide, Hold, Column description, and Column attributes. You can change color and font of the column here. In addition, useful and often used choices are Sort, Hide, Hold, and Column Attributes. Now let's highlight one column or several columns. We can do the following:

- Click the Hide button to hide them.
- Click the Hold button to hold them so that when the bottom scroll bar is moved, the hold column will always be there. For example, hold the variable Product Group so that it is easy to compare the variable with other variables.
- Click on the Sort button to sort the data set according to the highlighted column(s). SAS will ask Ascending or Descending; then SAS will ask you to enter a name for the sorted data set. This will result in a sorted data set. From a sorted data set, it is easy to find an observation with a special or specific value in the column, especially the max or min values. The pertinent buttons 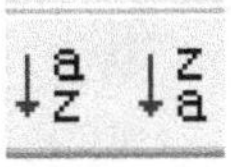 are on the tool bar. Click either of them to sort the data set in ascending or descending order according to highlighted columns.

We can also accomplish these tasks by clicking the Data button on the menu bar. When you click the Data button, you get the following pull-down menu:

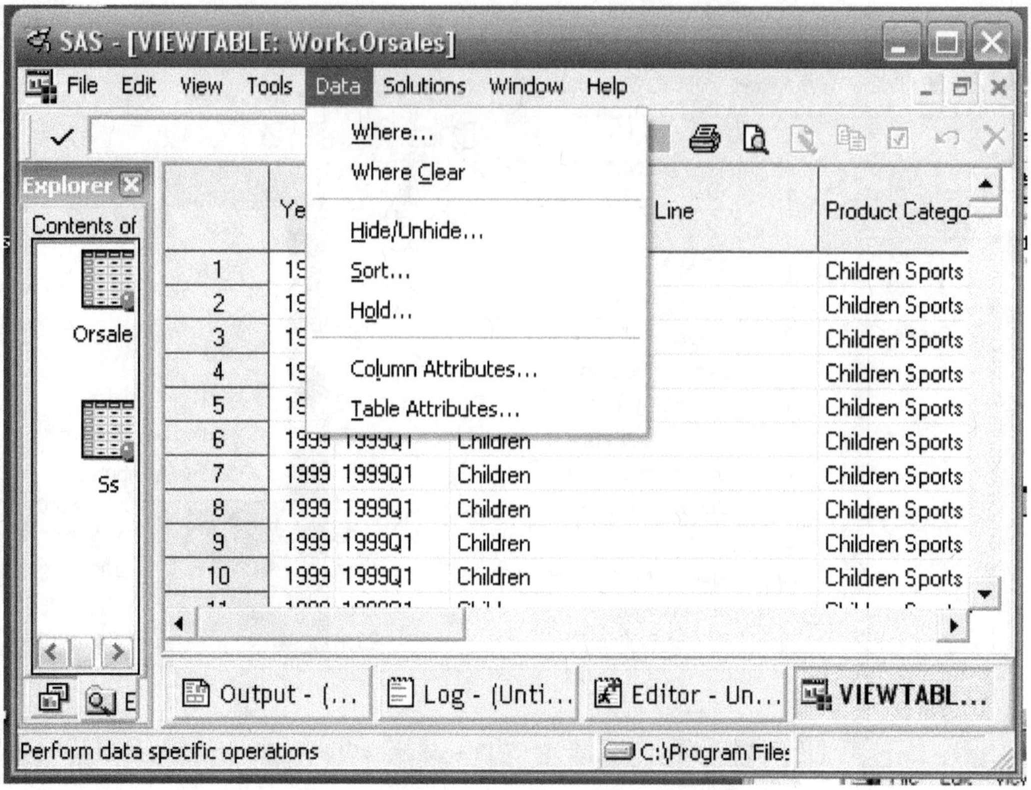

There are also Hide/Unhide, Sort, and Hold buttons. Click Sort to sort the data set, and we will get the following window. Notice that if we click on Sort button on the toolbar without highlighting any column, we will get the same window.

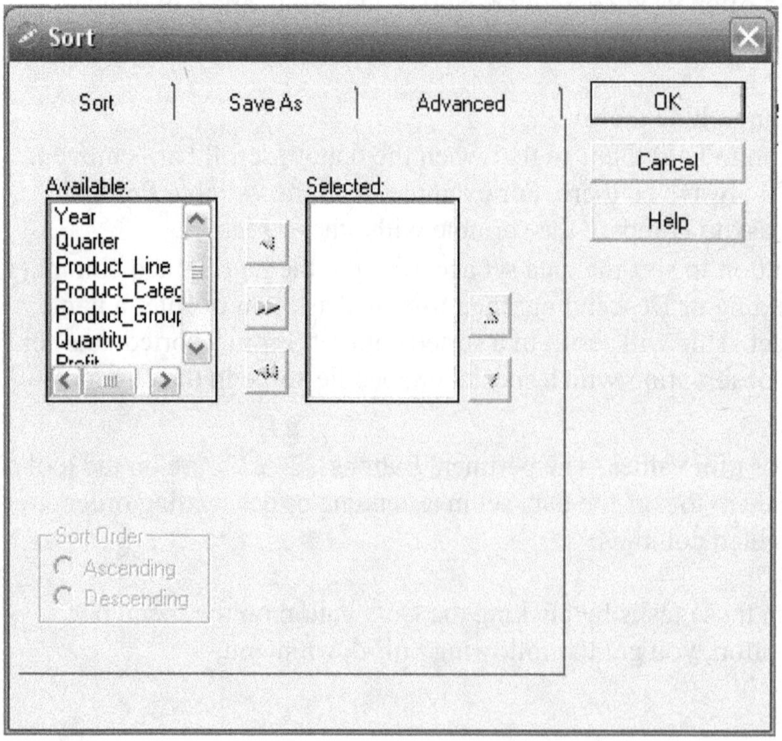

Now we can choose columns to sort. Notice that if we highlight columns and then do sort, it is only for adjacent columns and from left to right, but using Sort table, we can choose any columns and in any order. For example, in the above table, we can choose to order first by Product_Line and then by Year.

When sorting a data set, whatever method is used, SAS will pop up a window to ask you to enter the data set name. This will create a new data set. After you have sorted a data set, it can be sorted again and again, and SAS will never ask for the name again. If you don't want to create a new data set, you can use edit mode (Edit -> Edit Mode).

The Hide/Unhide button has the same functionality as the Hide button when clicking column header. Click on the Hide/Unhide button, and we will see the following similar window:

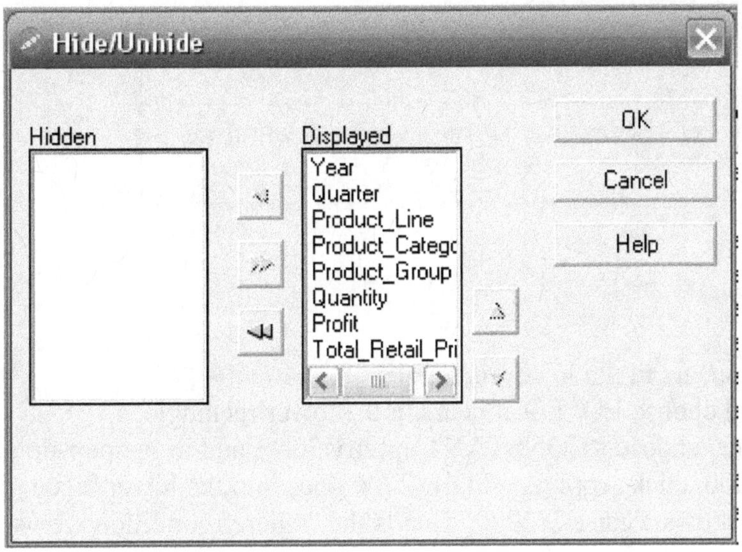

Now we can choose any columns to display. Often we have only a few columns to display. We can first move all columns to the Hidden box and then choose columns to move to the Displayed box. Using this method, not only can we choose which columns to display, but also we can decide their display order as well.

Another useful button is Where. The Hide/Unhide button let us choose columns, and the Where button let us choose rows. Clicking this button will allow us to set selecting condition(s) to get a subset of the data set. Let's click this button. We have the following window:

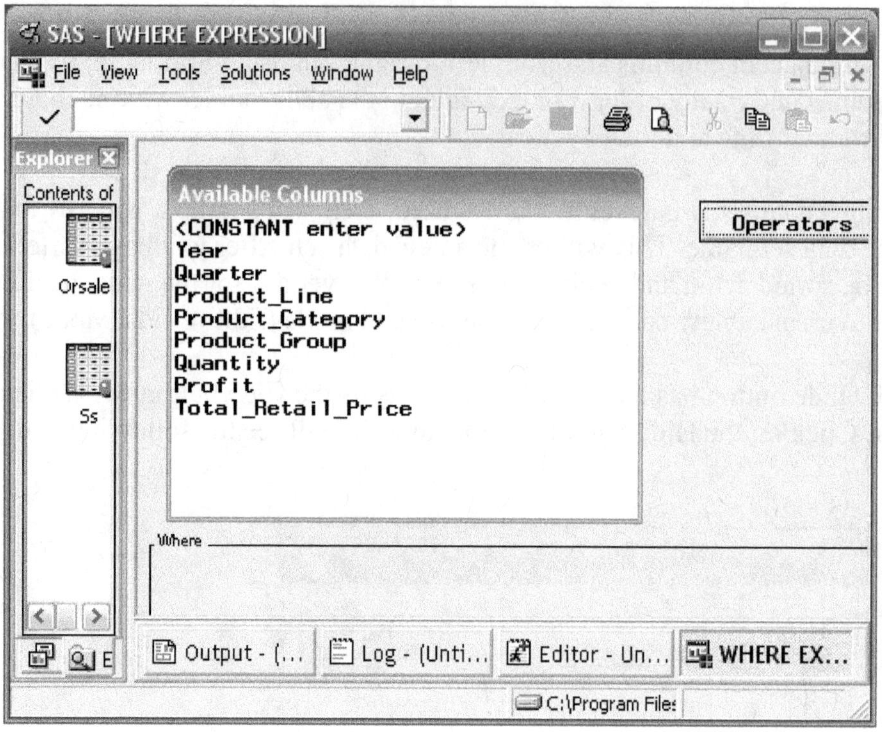

Let's do this.

1. Click Year. Year appears in the lower rectangle.
2. Click Operators and choose EQ. EQ appears in the lower rectangle.
3. In available columns, choose <CONSTANT enter value>, and in the pop-up window, type in 2000, click Apply, and OK. 2000 goes into the lower rectangle.
4. Now the rectangle shows Year EQ 2000. That is the "where" condition we want. Click OK.

Now we get a sub data set for the condition Year=2000.

The WHERE EXPRESSION window is also useful to find different values of a variable. For example, we want to find all the different years in the table. We can do this the following way:

1. Click on the variable Year.
2. Click Operators and choose the operator IN.
3. In the Available Columns window, choose <LOOKUP distinct values>.

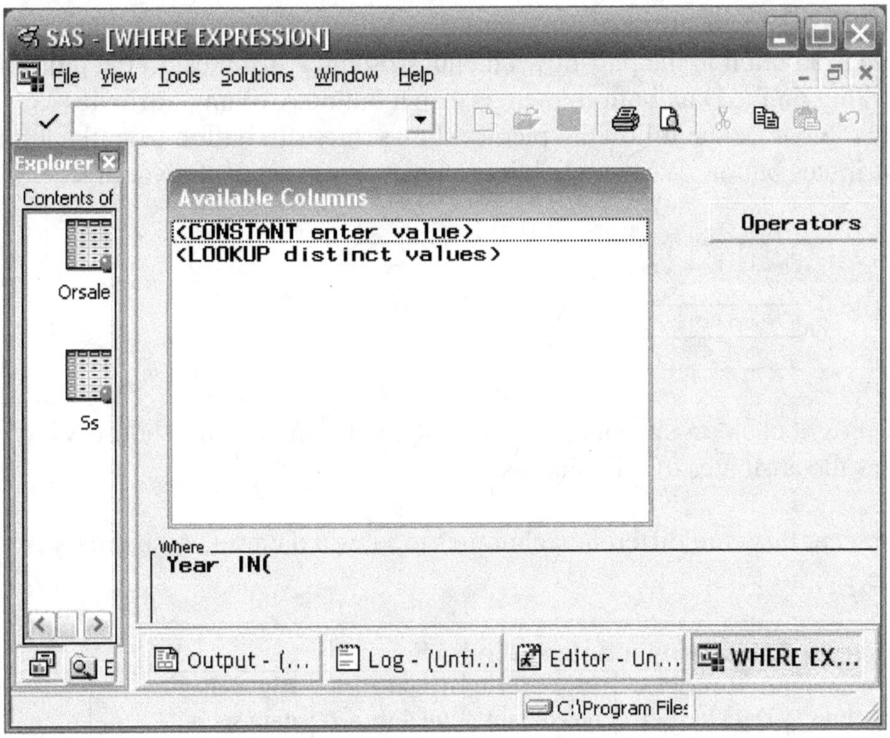

The Lookup Values window contains the different values of the variable Year. Any values can be chosen to filter the data set.

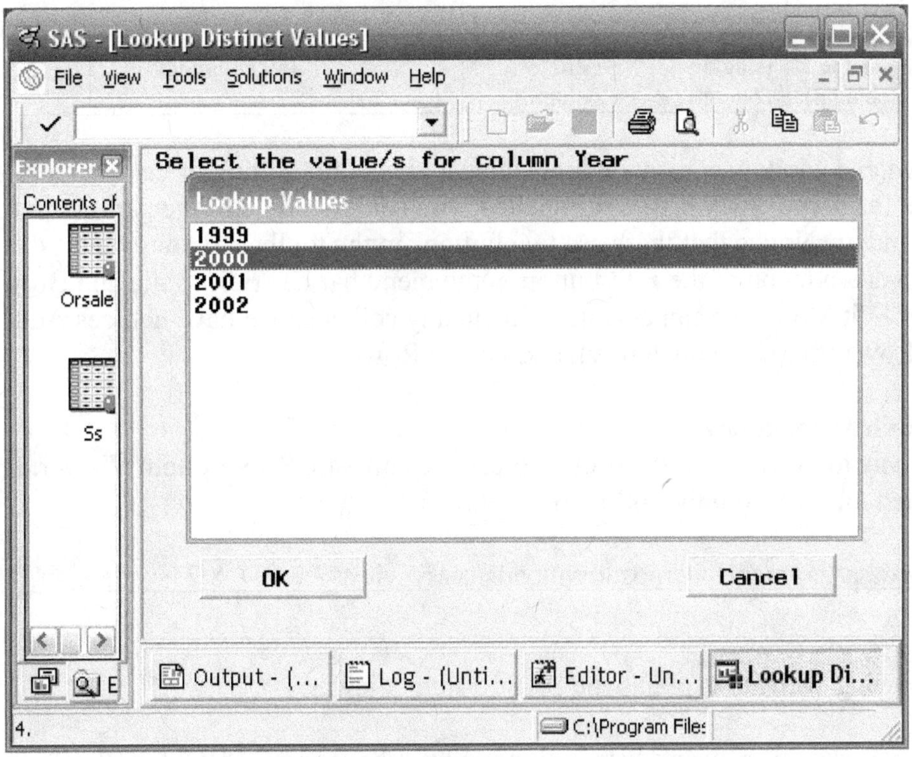

Notice that we can also click Edit->Find to accomplish the same task. Click Data->Where Clear, and the original table comes again.

It is important to view the attributes of a variable. When clicking on a column header, we see that there is a button in the pull-down menu: Column Attributes. In the pull-down menu when clicking on the Data button, there is also a button: Column attributes. However, in the toolbar, as the following picture shows, the fifth button from the left is the Column Attributes button. We can click it to view the attributes of a variable.

You can also right click on the data set in the Explorer window and choose View Columns to view the attributes of all columns.

As we have seen, there are different techniques to view a data set. A summary of them is in Table 1.

Table 1. Techniques for viewing a data set in SAS

Functionality	Toolbar buttons	Left click on Data button in menu bar	Right click on column header	Right click on data set	Right click on data set in Explorer window	Edit->Find
hide		x	x			
hold		x	x			
sort	x	x	x			
where		x		x		x
Column attributes	x (single column)	x (single column)	x (single column)		x (all columns)	

The Viewtable window is for viewing a table and also for editing or creating a table. For example, if a name or address is misspelled, you can directly edit the data set in the Viewtable window. Notice that there are two buttons in the toolbar: Browse and Edit. Also, the pull down menu of the Edit button in the menu bar has Edit Mode and Browse Mode. Under Edit Mode, we can change value in any cell, also we have choices Add Row, Copy Row (after choosing a row), and Delete Row.

SAS System viewer window

Another way to view a SAS data set is to use the software SAS System Viewer. It can be downloaded for free from the following Website:

http://www.sas.com/apps/demosdownloads/sassysview_PROD_8.2_sysdep.jsp?packageID=000176

The following Website explains the SAS System Viewer:

http://www.sas.com/software/distribution/readme/sassysview_PROD_8.2/readme_win.pdf

With the SAS System Viewer, a SAS data set can be viewed without the SAS software being installed. The SAS Viewer is similar to the SAS Viewtable window. For example, we can drag and move columns in both windows. There are still differences between them. In the SAS System Viewer, there is a Find button that is used to search for a specified value, but SAS Viewtable has no such functionality. In the SAS Viewtable window, there is a Find button on the pull-down menu when clicking on Edit button, but it is the same as a WHERE statement.

In the SAS System Viewer, there are two buttons in the menu bar: Edit and View, there are buttons in the toolbar, and also we can right click on data set. We will first talk about buttons in the toolbar. See the following picture:

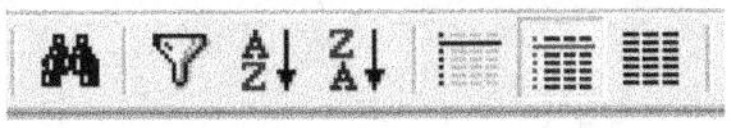

From left to right, they are Find, Filter, Ascending Order, Descending Order, Unformatted View, Formatted View, and Variables View.

Click on the View button in the menu bar to get the following pull-down menu:

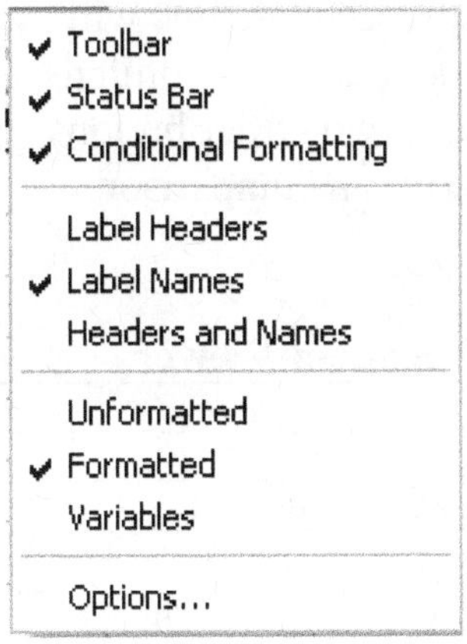

The second block in the menu gives you choices for viewing headers. You can choose to view headers, names, or both. The third block contains three buttons. Therefore, we can either click on the View button in the menu bar or directly click on a button in the toolbar to change the data set view.

Now left click on the Edit button or right click anywhere in the data set, and you will get the following pop-up:

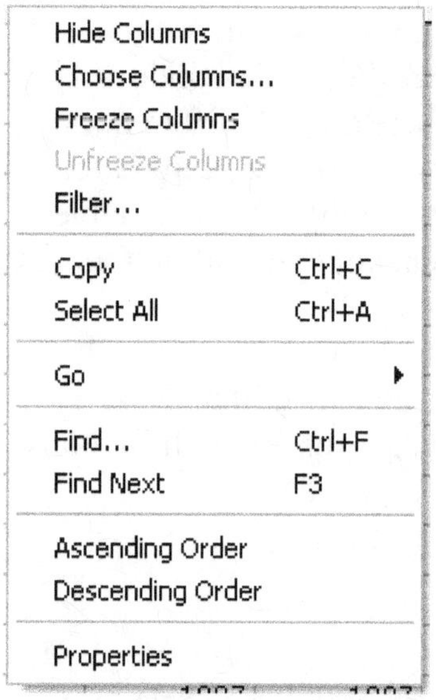

The options Filter, Find, and Order buttons correspond to buttons in the toolbar. The options Hide, Choose, and Freeze work similarly to those in the SAS Viewtable, so I won't say too much. Notice that in the SAS Viewer, although Hide Columns and Choose Columns have the same functionalities, they behave differently. Choose Columns will pop-up a window so you can choose any columns to display or hide, but Hide Columns is only for highlighted columns. It is the same for Freeze Columns and two Order buttons. They are used only for highlighted columns. The following table gives a comparison between the SAS Viewtable and the SAS System Viewer:

Table 2. Comparison between the SAS Viewtable and the SAS System Viewer

	SAS System Viewer	**SAS Viewtable**
Data set	Easy for permanent data set	In WORK or other library
Functionality	Only for display	Can modify the data set if in Edit Mode.
Functionality	Can view SAS program, SAS log, or output (lst file). For csv file, works the same as Notepad.	Only data set.
Header	View label headers (variable label), label name (variable name), or both.	Either label or name, not both.
Format	Only system format, but not user-defined format.	Both system format and user-defined format. Failed if user-defined format cannot be found
Sort	Only for highlighted columns, no new data sets created. One column sort.	Created a new data set (default browse mode) for the first time sort, or sort the original data set (Edit mode) Multiple columns sort.
Copy	Can select a rectangle and copy, you may choose header and/or label, or choose only contents.	In SAS v9, you can copy to the clipboard that is for the whole data set including variable names, title, and footnote.
Find	Search for specified value	Equivalent to WHERE

Names in the SAS Language

Introduction

There are many kinds of names in the SAS language: data set names, variable names, format names, column names in PROC SQL, macro variable names, etc. The rules for these names are simple and similar. They may contain only letters, non-initial numerals, and underscores (_), and they have a length restriction (depending on SAS version).

Many people believe that there are no restrictions on a name as long as the above conditions are satisfied. The SAS manual says, "*The rules are more flexible for SAS variable names than for other language elements. . . . . SAS reserves a few names for automatic variables and variable lists, SAS data set, and librefs.*" This gives users great flexibility. They can use almost any words freely. On the other hand, this brings users some inconvenience, because you don't know how SAS treats a word: Is it treated as a user-defined name or as a keyword? This depends on SAS's interest and SAS's understanding. Sometimes you may think it is OK to use a specified word as a name, but SAS says No, it is a keyword. Then your programming will be messed up. Therefore, we need to investigate the following two problems:

What keywords (or non-keywords) cannot be what kinds of names?

What names may cause confusion, and how does SAS handle the situation in these cases?

Data set names

Four keywords may cause a problem when used as data set names in a DATA statement. These keywords are SET, MERGE, RETAIN, and UPDATE. Whether or not they cause a problem depends on the setting of the option DATASTMTCHK. (SAS System Options in *SAS Language Reference: Dictionary*, 2005; Lora and Slaughter, 2003). To illustrate, run the following program:

```
DATA SET;
   a=3;
RUN;
```

We get the following error message:

```
286  DATA SET;
          ---
          56
ERROR 56-185: SET is not allowed in the DATA statement when option
DATASTMTCHK=COREKEYWORDS.  Check for a missing semicolon in the DATA statement, or use
DATASTMTCHK=NONE.
```

From the message, we can see that the problem is related to option DATASTMTCHK=.

- The purpose of checking keywords is not to forbid you to use them as names but to remind you that maybe you forget to put a semicolon.
- If, however, you were to set DATASTMTCHK=NONE, then SAS would accept SET as a valid data set name and would not return an ERROR.
- The default value of the option DATASTMTCHK= is COREKEYWORDS. It checks four keywords: UPDATE, MERGE, SET, and RETAIN. You can assume that UPDATE, MERGE, and SET statements always follow a DATA statement. Therefore, when you use them as a data set name, it is possible that there is a missing semicolon. Why RETAIN? I have no idea.
- You can also ask SAS to check more keywords by setting the option DATASTMTCHK=ALLKEYWORDS. Notice that ALLKEYWORDS does not mean "all keywords," but it means keywords that can begin a statement in a DATA step. So with this option, you can use PROC, SORT as dataset names because they do not belong to a DATA step; you can also use AND, DESCENDING as dataset names because they do not begin a statement in a DATA step. But the keywords IF, WHERE, ABORT, ARRAY, INFILE, and BY are not OK because they begin a statement in a DATA step.
- This is only for a one-level name. If you want to use them, you can use a two-level name, such as DATA WORK.set. It is OK no matter how you set the option DATASTMTCHK=, such as in the following program:

```
DATA WORK.retain;
a=4;
RUN;
```

- In contexts other than the DATA statement, you can use SET, MERGE, RETAIN, and UPDATE as data set names with no problem. The following program shows the use of these keywords as data set names in a SET statement, in PROC SQL to create a table, and in PROC FREQ to create an output data set:

```
DATA s;
a=5;
PROC FREQ;
TABLE a/OUT=set;
DATA tt;
SET set;
DROP percent;
PROC SQL;
CREATE TABLE merge (a CHAR(2));
QUIT;
```

SET, MERGE, RETAIN, and UPDATE are examples of what we might call "soft" forbidden data set names, i.e., names that are forbidden in some but not all contexts and that are related to an option setting. There are also "hard" forbidden data set names that are not allowed in *any* context. Examples are CON and COM1-COM9 in PC SAS (These names are allowed on UNIX SAS); there may be others. To illustrate, run the following programs in PC SAS with DATASTMTCHK=NONE:

```
DATA com3;
a=4;
```

```
RUN;

PROC FREQ;
TABLE a/OUT=con;
RUN;

DATA WORK.com8;
a=5;
RUN;

PROC SQL;
   CREATE TABLE com5 (a CHAR(2));
QUIT;
```

All steps return the following error message or its analogues:

```
ERROR: Invalid member name for file WORK.COM3.DATA.
NOTE: The SAS System stopped processing this step because of errors.
```

What happens if you are working on UNIX? For UPDATE, MERGE, SET, and RETAIN, SAS behaves the same way as it does on a PC. However, for version 8, SAS will also set option OBS=0 if you use any of them as a dataset name. Then SAS will check syntax without creating datasets for the following data steps. See the following example:

```
DATA merge;
a=4;
RUN;
```

```
1          data merge;

                -----
                56
ERROR 56-185: MERGE is not allowed in the DATA statement when option
DATASTMTCHK=COREKEYWORDS.  Check for a missing semicolon in
             the DATA statement, or use DATASTMTCHK=NONE.

2          a=4;

NOTE: The SAS System stopped processing this step because of errors.
NOTE: SAS set option OBS=0 and will continue to check statements. This may cause NOTE: No
observations in data set.
WARNING: The data set WORK.MERGE may be incomplete.  When this step was stopped there
were 0 observations and 1 variables.
```

The following reserved keywords have special meaning when used as a data set name: _NULL_, _LAST_, and _DATA_. The statement DATA _NULL_; instructs SAS to execute the data step but create no output data set. The following program illustrates a common usage of DATA _NULL_. It assigns the number of observations in the input data set to a macro variable, but does not create an output data set:

```
DATA S;
   a=3;
DATA _NULL_;
```

```
    SET s NOBS=nobs;
    IF _N_=1 THEN CALL SYMPUT("tot",nobs);
    STOP;
RUN;
```

LAST stands for the data set last created. As we know, we can run some procedures without specifying data set name. The default is the last created data set. Actually SAS refers to the data set _LAST_. In the following program, the data set t created in the second data step is updated in the third data step:

```
DATA s;
   a=3;
DATA t;
   b=5;
DATA _LAST_;
   a=5;
RUN;
```

DATA refers to a data set named DATA*n* where *n* is an integer. The first time it appears in the SAS session, _DATA_ refers to a data set named DATA1; the second time, DATA2; the third time, DATA3; and so on. Try the following program:

```
DATA _DATA_;
a=3;
DATA DATA2;
a=4;
DATA _DATA_;
a=5;
RUN;
```

In this program, two _DATA_ refers to data sets DATA1 and DATA2, respectively. Therefore, the second step creates the data set DATA2, and the third step modifies the data set DATA2.

Variable names

Now we consider variable names. Many SAS keywords (for example, IF, THEN, ELSE, DO, END, SELECT) can serve as a variable name because SAS interprets these words as either a keyword or a name depending on the context and their positions. Thus, both of the following statements are legal in a DATA step:

IF = 3; (assign value 3 to variable IF)
IF IF = 3 … (The first IF is a keyword, and the second IF is variable name)

The keyword NOT differs from the other keywords mentioned above.

- In an expression, it is interpreted as a keyword. Examples are IF, WHERE, SELECT and WHEN statements, UNTIL, WHILE, TO and BY clauses in DO statement, right side of equal sign in an assignment, including that in DO clause, THEN clause, and WHEN clause.

- In statements that need a variable name, it is interpreted as a variable name. Examples are BY, FORMAT, INFORMAT, LENGTH, RENAME, LABEL, KEEP, DROP, and PUT statements.
- In an assignment statement, if it is on the left side of an equal sign, it is a variable name.

There are four steps in the following program. The first three are OK. Well, in the statement c=not+1;, not is interpreted as a keyword. The last one has a problem.

```
DATA s;
not=3;
c=not + 1;
FORMAT not MMDDYY8.;
DATA s2;
INPUT not;
CARDS;
3
;
PROC SORT;
BY not;
RUN;
DATA t2;
   SET s;
   IF not=3;
RUN;
```

```
336  DATA t2;
337     SET s;
338     IF not=3;
             -
             22
ERROR 22-322: Syntax error, expecting one of the following: a name, a quoted string,
              a numeric constant, a datetime constant, a missing value, INPUT, PUT.

339  RUN;

NOTE: The SAS System stopped processing this step because of errors.
```

It also has a different meaning in a sum statement depending on its position. If it is at the beginning of a sum statement, it is interpreted as a variable name; otherwise, it is interpreted as a keyword. In the following data step, there are three sum statements. The first one interprets NOT as a variable name, and the last two interpret it as a keyword. The last one even causes a problem.

```
DATA s;
a=1;
not+a;
b+not a;
c+not;
PROC PRINT;RUN;
```

```
169  c+not;
```

```
      -
      22

ERROR 22-322: Syntax error, expecting one of the following: a name, a quoted string,
              a numeric constant, a datetime constant, a missing value, INPUT, PUT.

NOTE: The SAS System stopped processing this step because of errors.
```

There are many mnemonic operators in DATA step, but only NOT is prefix. Other operators will not cause confusion. There are three WHERE statements in the following. In the first two statements, ne is interpreted as a variable name, and in the last statement, ne is interpreted as an operator.

```
WHERE ne+1;
WHERE 2+ne+1;
WHERE 2 ne+1;
```

There are three options in a BY statement: DESCENDING, NOTSORTED, and GROUPFORMAT. There are no problems using them as variable names in a DATA step, but if they are used in a BY statement, we have to be careful that this may cause confusion. The following table gives a comparison of these options:

Table 1. Options in a BY statement

	Need sorted when using BY statement?	**Where to use as an option?**	**How to set first.byvar and last.byvar?**	**Is treated as a keyword or a variable name in BY statement?**
DESCENDING	Sorted, descending for specified variables(s)	Any BY statement	According to group	Keyword
GROUPFORMAT	Sorted	BY statement in DATA step	Set to 1 when formatted BY value(s) change	Keyword in a DATA step, variable name otherwise
NOTSORTED	Not	Any BY statement except in PROC SORT	Set to 1 when BY value(s) change	Variable name in PROC SORT, keyword otherwise

The following program shows how to use options GROUPFORMAT and NOTSORTED:

```
PROC FORMAT ;
VALUE pp 1-2=abc 3-5=cdf;
DATA s;
INPUT a b;
CARDS;
2 4
3 5
1 3
1 2
;
DATA t;
```

```
SET s;
BY a NOTSORTED;
first=FIRST.a;
last=LAST.a;
PROC PRINT;

PROC SORT DATA=s;
BY a;
DATA p;
SET s;
FORMAT a pp.;
BY a GROUPFORMAT;
first=FIRST.a;
last=LAST.a;
PROC PRINT;RUN;
```

Obs	a	b	first	last
1	2	4	1	1
2	3	5	1	1
3	1	3	1	0
4	1	2	0	1

Obs	a	b	first	last
1	abc	3	1	0
2	abc	2	0	0
3	abc	4	0	1
4	cdf	5	1	1

The following program shows the behavior of the option DESCENDING:

```
DATA s1;
    INPUT ASCENDING DESCENDING; *DESCENDING is a variable
name;
    CARDS;
      3 5
      2 4
      5 1
    ;
PROC SORT DATA=s1 OUT=s2;
    BY DESCENDING ASCENDING;  *DESCENDING is a keyword;
PROC PRINT DATA=s2;
RUN;
```

Obs	ASCENDING	DESCENDING
1	5	1
2	3	5
3	2	4

The following program shows the behavior of the option NOTSORTED:

```
DATA s;
```

```
a=5;OUTPUT;
a=3; OUTPUT;
DATA t;
SET s;
IF _N_=1 THEN notsorted='bb'; *variable name;
IF _N_=2 THEN notsorted='aa';
BY a NOTSORTED ; *keyword;
PROC PRINT;
VAR notsorted a; *variable name;
RUN;
PROC SORT DATA=S;
BY notsorted a; *variable name, causes a problem;
RUN;
```

You will see an output and log message as follows:

Obs	notsorted	a
1	bb	5
2	aa	3

```
109   PROC SORT DATA=S;
110   BY notsorted a; *variable name, causes a problem;
ERROR: Variable NOTSORTED not found.
111   RUN;

NOTE: The SAS System stopped processing this step because of errors.
```

The following program shows the behavior of option GROUPGORMAT.

```
PROC SORT DATA=s;
BY  groupformat a;
RUN;
```

```
112   PROC SORT DATA=s;
113   BY  groupformat a;
ERROR: Variable GROUPFORMAT not found.
```

Four keywords may be used in a PROC SQL ORDER BY clause: ASCENDING, ASC, DESCENDING, and DESC. SAS interprets all four words as either a variable name or an ordering keyword, depending on the context, and there is no confusion.

```
PROC SQL;
    SELECT *
    FROM s1
    ORDER BY ASCENDING, DESCENDING;
            *with comma: both are variable names;
QUIT;
```

ASCENDING	DESCENDING
2	4
3	5
5	1

```
PROC SQL;
    SELECT *
    FROM s1
    ORDER BY ASCENDING DESCENDING;
            *without comma: DESCENDING is keyword;
QUIT;
```

ASCENDING	DESCENDING
5	1
3	5
2	4

We all know the keywords _NUMERIC_, _CHAR_, _ALL_, and _CHARACTER_. They stand for a *list* of variables: all numeric variables, all character variables, and all variables of either type, respectively. However, these keywords behave differently. First, we will try assignments.

```
90   data s;
91    _ALL_=1;
ERROR: Cannot use _ALL_ as a variable name.
92    _NUMERIC_=1;
ERROR: Cannot use _NUMERIC_ as a variable name.
93    _CHAR_=1;
ERROR: Cannot use _CHAR_ as a variable name.
94    _CHARACTER_=1;
95    run;
```

You can see that we cannot use the first three keywords as variable names, but we can use the last one. Next we will try a PUT statement. We will use the following data set:

```
DATA s;
a=4;b='4';
RUN;
```

Then we will try the following four statements:

```
PUT _ALL_;          put all variables.
PUT _NUMERIC_;  ERROR: Cannot use _numeric_ as a variable name.
PUT _CHAR_;  ERROR: Cannot use _char_ as a variable name.
PUT _CHARACTER_;  NOTE: Variable _character_ is uninitialized.
```

You can see that a PUT statement treats _ALL_ as a variable list, it does not recognize _NUMBERIC_ and _CHAR_ as variable lists, and it treats _CHARACTER_ as a variable name.

Now we consider their behaviors in other statements. _NUMERIC_, _CHAR_, and _ALL_ work the same way: They cannot be used as variable names, so we only need to consider _CHARACTER_. For an IF statement and a WHERE statement, it is treated as a variable name, the same as if it were in an assignment. For a DROP, KEEP, BY, FORMAT, INFORMAT, or LENGTH statement, it is treated as a variable list, the alias of _CHAR_. Let's see the following example:

```
DATA a1;
   _CHARACTER_=8;   *variable name, not _CHAR_ alias;
   b='b';
   KEEP _CHARACTER_;   *_CHAR_ alias, not variable name;
RUN;
```

Data set a1 contains *one* variable b, because SAS interprets _CHARACTER_ in the KEEP statement as an alias of _CHAR_. In the following program, the DATA step is OK, but the PROC SORT step has a problem:

```
DATA a1;
   _CHARACTER_=8;
PROC SORT;
BY _character_;
RUN;
```

```
318   PROC SORT;
319   BY _character_;
WARNING: No character variables found in data set WORK.A1.
320   RUN;

ERROR: No BY statement used or no BY variables specified. A BY statement must be used
with variable names to sort on.
```

Notice that if there is no numeric variable and there is statement KEEP _NUMERIC_; or there is no character variable and there is statement KEEP _CHAR_; or KEEP _CHARACTER_; you may feel the message in the log file strange. See the following program.

```
DATA a;
_character_=5;b=3;
KEEP _char_;
RUN;
```

```
439   DATA a;
440   _character_=5;b=3;
441   KEEP _char_;

WARNING: The variable _CHARACTER_ in the DROP, KEEP, or RENAME list has never been
referenced.
NOTE: The data set WORK.A has 1 observations and 0 variables.
```

The system variables _N_, _ERROR_, _FILE_, _INFILE_, and _IORC_ are generated by SAS in a DATA step. _N_ is a sequence number of iterations. _ERROR_ shows if any iteration has a problem. _INFILE_ is for file input or instream input. It refers to an input record text buffer. The following program shows how to use it:

```
DATA s;
INPUT a b $;
PUT _infile_;
CARDS;
3 r
2 ttt
;
RUN;
```

You will see the following printout in the log file:

```
3 r
2 ttt
```

It is created only if there is an INFILE statement or a DATALINES (CARDS) statement. Otherwise, you will get an ERROR message.

```
DATA t;
SET s;
PUT _infile_;
RUN;
ERROR: The _INFILE_ variable has been referenced, but no DATALINES or INFILE statement
was found.
```

FILE is similar to _INFILE_. It is related to a FILE statement and represents that in an output buffer. See the following program:

```
DATA s;
    INPUT a b $;
    FILE PRINT;
    PUT a b @;
    c= _file_;
    PUT c=;
CARDS;
1 ab
2 4
;
RUN;
```

You will see the following output in the output window (not the log window because of the statement FILE PRINT):

```
1 ab c=1 ab
2 4 c=2 4
```

The system variable _IORC_ is created for error checking when you use the MODIFY statement or the SET statement with the KEY= option.

They have a commonality in that they cannot be used as user-defined variables. The following program creates a data set that has only three variables, a, b, and c:

```
DATA s;
```

```
INPUT a b;
_file_='ab';_infile_='bc';
_n_=3;_error_=0;_iorc_=4;
c=5;
CARDS;
1 3
2 4
;
RUN;
```

```
564  DATA s;
565  INPUT a b;
566  _file_='ab';_infile_='bc';
567  _n_=3;_error_=0;_iorc_=4;
568  c=5;
569  CARDS;

ab
NOTE: The data set WORK.S has 2 observations and 3 variables.
```

But you can print out their values.

```
DATA s;
INPUT a b;
_file_='ab';_infile_='bc';
_n_=3;_error_=0;_iorc_=4;
c=5;
PUT _ALL_;
CARDS;
1 3
2 4
;
RUN;
```

```
a=1 b=3 c=5 _ERROR_=0 _FILE_=a= _INFILE_=bc _N_=3
a=2 b=4 c=5 _ERROR_=0 _FILE_=a= _INFILE_=bc _N_=3
```

Here the value for _FILE_ is strange, and there is no printout for _IORC_ because _ALL_ does not include _IORC_. You can print it separately using the statement PUT _IORC_;.

In addition, _IORC_, _FILE_, and _INFILE_ also have their own characteristics.

FILE cannot be in a PUT statement;
INFILE can be in a PUT statement, but _INFILE_= (named output) cannot be in a PUT statement.

```
DATA s;
INPUT a b $;
FILE PRINT;
PUT _FILE_;
PUT _FILE_=;
PUT _INFILE_;
PUT _INFILE_=;
```

```
CARDS;
1 ab
2 4
;
RUN;
```

```
372  DATA s;
373  INPUT a b $;
374  FILE PRINT;
375  PUT _FILE_;
ERROR: The _FILE_ variable cannot be referenced by the INPUT/PUT statement.
376  PUT _FILE_=;
ERROR: The _INFILE_ and _FILE_ variables cannot be referenced when using named I/O.
377  PUT _INFILE_;
378  PUT _INFILE_=;
ERROR: The _INFILE_ and _FILE_ variables cannot be referenced when using named I/O.
```

CMD, _MSG_, and _I_ are all system variables. They have a commonality in that they can be used as user-defined variables.

The WINDOW statement creates two system variables: _CMD_ and _MSG_. If there is no WINDOW statement, it is OK to define them as variable names.
The system variable _I_ is created when an implicit array is defined. If you don't use an implicit array definition, it is OK to use _I_ as a variable name. See the following program:

```
DATA s;
    _cmd_='abc';_msg_=5;a=3;_i_=5;
RUN;
```

```
575  DATA s;
576    _cmd_='abc';_msg_=5;a=3;_i_=5;
577    RUN;

NOTE: The data set WORK.S has 1 observations and 4 variables.
```

The following program shows that if there is an implicit array defined, _I_ will not be a dataset variable name:

```
DATA s;
   ARRAY test t1-t5;
   DO _i_=1 to 5;
      test=_i_;
   END;
   _i_=3;
   PUT test=;
PROC PRINT;
RUN;
```

You will see in the log file that

T3=3

and _I_ is not in the data set.

Array names

An array can be defined with any valid SAS name, but there are two things to be aware of. First, the array name cannot also be used as a variable name in the same DATA step:

```
DATA s;
   ARRAY ab(*) ab1-ab3;
   ab=5;
RUN;
```

```
62    DATA s;
63    ARRAY ab(*) ab1-ab3;
64    ab=5;
ERROR: Illegal reference to the array ab.
65    RUN;

NOTE: The SAS System stopped processing this step because of errors.
```

Second, if the array name is also the name of a function, SAS will interpret it as an array name so that the function will not be accessible in the DATA step:

```
DATA s;
   ARRAY int(*) int1-int3;
   DO i=1 TO 3;
      a=int(i);
   END;
RUN;
```

```
66    DATA s;
67    ARRAY int(*) int1-int3;
WARNING: The array int has the same name as a SAS-supplied or user-defined function.
         Parenthesized references involving this name have been treated as array
references and not function references.
68    DO i=1 TO 3;
69    a=int(i);
70    END;
71    RUN;

NOTE: The data set WORK.S has 1 observations and 5 variables.
```

Format names and informat names

For format names and informat names, SAS forbids using SAS defined format names and informat names. If you go to the SAS manual, you will see that there is an informat BITS but no format with this name. Let's run the following program. You will see that the format bits is OK, the informat $bits is OK, but the informat bits is not OK:

```
PROC FORMAT;
   VALUE bits 1=5;
   INVALUE $bits 1='5';
   INVALUE bits 1=5;
RUN;
```

```
1      PROC FORMAT;
2      VALUE bits 1=5;
NOTE: Format BITS has been output.
3      INVALUE $bits 1='5';
NOTE: Informat $BITS has been output.
4      INVALUE bits 1=5;
NOTE: Informat BITS could not be written because it has the same name as an Institute-
supplied
       informat.
5      RUN;
```

Names in PROC SQL

There are many keywords in PROC SQL, such as AS, ON, FULL, JOIN, LEFT, FROM, WHEN, WHERE, ORDER, GROUP, RIGHT, and INNER. Mostly you can use them as table names or column names. For table names, _NULL_, _DATA_, and _LAST_ have the same meaning as they have in a DATA step. You can run the following statements and get the same results as in a DATA step. The first statement creates no data set, the second statement creates the data set DATA1, and the third statement overwrites the data set DATA1:

```
CREATE TABLE _null_ (a CHAR(2));
CREATE TABLE _data_ (a CHAR(2));
CREATE TABLE _last_ (a CHAR(2));
```

```
2     CREATE TABLE _null_ (a CHAR(2));
3        CREATE TABLE _data_ (a CHAR(2));
NOTE: Table WORK.DATA1 created, with 0 rows and 1 columns.
4        CREATE TABLE _last_ (a CHAR(2));
NOTE: Table WORK.DATA1 created, with 0 rows and 1 columns.
```

Also, as we discussed previously, we can use UPDATE, MERGE, SET, and RETAIN as table names, but we cannot use con and com1-com9 as table names.

Now we will talk about column names. The keywords _NUMERIC_, _CHAR_, _ALL_, and _CHARACTER_ are no longer being treated as lists of variables, and other system variables in a DATA step have no special meaning here. The following code shows that you can use system variable names as column names in a table:

```
PROC SQL;
CREATE TABLE p
          (_character_ CHAR(2),
            _numeric_ NUM ,
            _char_ NUM,_all_ NUM,
            _file_ CHAR(2),
            _infile_ NUM ,
            _n_ NUM,
            _error_ NUM);
INSERT INTO p
      VALUES ('ab',1,4,7,'e',5,.,7);
SELECT * FROM p;
QUIT;
```

character	_numeric_	_char_	_all_	_file_	_infile_	_n_	_error_
ab	1	4	7	e	5	.	7

PROC SQL has its own keyword set. Most keywords can be column names in a table. But some keywords cannot be referenced as such in some clauses where the keyword has a special meaning. Let us consider the following keywords:

- USER has its own meaning in the SELECT statement that is the user's login name.
- DISTINCT and UNIQUE cannot be used in a SELECT clause, but they can be used in other clauses.
- NOT, CALCULATED, CASE, and EXISTS cannot be used in any clause in a SELECT statement.
- ALL cannot be used in a SELECT clause.
- ANY and ALL cannot be used in a WHERE clause after a comparison operator.
- However, although we cannot use these names directly, we can use a table name as their prefix, and then all of them will be OK.

Try the following program:

```
PROC SQL;
CREATE TABLE s(NOT num , CALCULATED num, CASE num, EXISTS num, UNIQUE
num, ALL  num, any num,distinct num, user num);
INSERT INTO s SET not=1 , CALCULATED=1, case=1,exists=1, unique=1,
all=1, any=1,distinct=1,user=1;
/* The above statements are all OK.*/
SELECT * FROM s;
SELECT * FROM s WHERE DISTINCT >0;
SELECT * FROM s ORDER BY distinct;
SELECT  ANY FROM s;
SELECT * FROM s ORDER BY ALL;
SELECT * FROM s WHERE ANY<3;
SELECT * FROM s WHERE unique=1;
SELECT * FROM s WHERE ALL>0;
SELECT * FROM s WHERE DISTINCT=1;
/* The above statements are all OK.*/
/*Guess what is the printout of the following statement*/
SELECT USER FROM s;
/* The following statements have problems.*/
SELECT not FROM s ;
SELECT calculated FROM s ;
SELECT case FROM s ;
SELECT exists FROM s ;
SELECT unique FROM s ;
SELECT all FROM s ;
SELECT distinct FROM s;
SELECT * FROM s WHERE 3> any;
SELECT * FROM s WHERE 0<all;
SELECT * FROM s ORDER BY calculated;
/* The following statements are all OK.*/
SELECT s.not FROM s ;
SELECT s.calculated FROM s ;
SELECT s.case FROM s ;
```

```
SELECT s.exists FROM s ;
SELECT s.unique FROM s ;
SELECT s.all FROM s ;
SELECT s.distinct FROM s;
SELECT * FROM s WHERE 3> s.any;
SELECT * FROM s WHERE 0<s.all;
SELECT * FROM s ORDER BY s.calculated;
/*The value of column user in the following statement is from table.*/
SELECT s.user FROM s;

QUIT;
```

The following are partial messages from the log file:

```
379  SELECT not FROM s ;
                    -
                    79
ERROR 79-322: Expecting a FROM.

380  SELECT calculated FROM s ;
                           -
                           79
ERROR 79-322: Expecting a FROM.

381  SELECT case FROM s ;
                ----
                22
                76
ERROR 22-322: Syntax error, expecting one of the following: a name, a quoted string,
              a numeric constant, a datetime constant, a missing value, (, +, -, BTRIM,
CALCULATED,
              CASE, EXISTS, INPUT, LOWER, NOT, PUT, SELECT, SUBSTRING, TRANSLATE, UPPER,
USER,
              WHEN, ^, ~.

ERROR 76-322: Syntax error, statement will be ignored.

382  SELECT exists FROM s ;
                  ----
                  22
                  76
ERROR 22-322: Syntax error, expecting one of the following: (, SELECT.

ERROR 76-322: Syntax error, statement will be ignored.

383  SELECT unique FROM s ;
                        -
                        79
ERROR 79-322: Expecting a FROM.

384  SELECT all FROM s ;
                    -
                    79
ERROR 79-322: Expecting a FROM.

385  SELECT distinct FROM s;
                         -
```

```
                         79
ERROR 79-322: Expecting a FROM.

386   SELECT * FROM s WHERE 3> any;
                                -
                                22
                                76
ERROR 22-322: Syntax error, expecting one of the following: (, SELECT.

ERROR 76-322: Syntax error, statement will be ignored.

387   SELECT * FROM s WHERE 0<all;
                               -
                               22
                               76
ERROR 22-322: Syntax error, expecting one of the following: (, SELECT.

ERROR 76-322: Syntax error, statement will be ignored.

388   SELECT * FROM s ORDER BY calculated;
                                        -
                                        22
ERROR 22-322: Expecting a name.
```

PROC REPORT: variable names or statistics?

Now let's talk about PROC REPORT. We have to talk about statistics. As we know, we can calculate in PROC REPORT the following statistics:

```
CSS, CV, MAX, MEAN, MIN, N, NMISS, PCTN, PCTSUM, RANGE, STD, STDERR,
SUM, SUMWGT, USS, VAR,
P1, P5, P10, Q1|P25, MEDIAN|P50, Q3|P75, P90, P95, P99, QRANGE,
PRT, T.
```

Notice that STD has an alias STDDEV, but it is only for PROC MEANS and PROC TABULATE, not for PROC REPORT. PROC REPORT does not recognize STDDEV as a statistic. The following program is OK:

```
DATA s;
   a=5;OUTPUT;a=6;OUTPUT;
PROC TABULATE;
   VAR a;
   TABLE a,stddev;
RUN;
PROC MEANS STDDEV;
RUN;
```

But the following two procedures are not OK.

```
PROC REPORT NOWD;
   COLUMN a,stddev;
PROC REPORT NOWD;
   DEFINE a/stddev;
RUN;
```

```
415   PROC REPORT NOWD;
```

```
416  COLUMN a,stddev;

ERROR: There is more than one ANALYSIS usage associated with
       the column defined by the following elements.
       Name                              Usage
       --------------------------------  --------
       a                                 ANALYSIS
       stddev                            COMPUTED
NOTE: The SAS System stopped processing this step because of errors.
NOTE: PROCEDURE REPORT used (Total process time):
      real time           0.10 seconds
      cpu time            0.00 seconds



417  PROC REPORT NOWD;
418  DEFINE a/stddev;
              ------
              1
WARNING 1-322: Assuming the symbol STD was misspelled as stddev.
419  RUN;

NOTE: There were 2 observations read from the data set WORK.S.
```

As we know, among these statistics, the statistic N is different from others in the sense that in a COLUMN statement, N can be an independent item, but other statistics should be used together with an analysis variable.

Now my question is: What is the relationship between variable names and statistics in PROC REPORT? Let's see the following program:

Using statistics as variable names in a data step is OK, such as in the following program:

```
DATA s;
a=3;
n=4;
min=2;
max=5;
mean=6;
pctn=3;
nmiss=5;
sum=4;
sumwgt=4;
uss=3;
css=5;
std=4;
stderr=3;
RUN;
```

Now we run PROC REPORT. Let's try the following program first:

```
PROC REPORT NOWD;
RUN;
```

You can see that it is OK.

```
a          n          min          max          mean          pctn          nmiss
3          4            2            5             6             3              5

      sum        sumwgt          uss          css          std        stderr
        4             4            3            5            4             3
```

Next let us run the following program:

```
PROC REPORT NOWD;COLUMN a n;RUN;
```

The following is a printout:

```
a          n
3          1
```

Although both printouts have the header n, they are different. In the previous program, n is a variable, and in this program, n is a statistic. Now let's try the following program:

```
PROC REPORT NOWD;
COLUMN a n min max mean pctn nmiss sum sumwgt uss css std stderr;
RUN;
```

There is no printout. In the log file, you can see that there are ERRORs. The following is part of an error message:

```
216  COLUMN a n  min max mean pctn nmiss sum sumwgt uss css std stderr ;
217  RUN;

ERROR: There is a statistic but no ANALYSIS usage associated
       with the column defined by the following elements.
       Name                              Usage
       --------------------------------  --------
       min                               STATISTIC
ERROR: There is a statistic but no ANALYSIS usage associated
       with the column defined by the following elements.
       Name                              Usage
       --------------------------------  --------
       max                               STATISTIC
ERROR: There is a statistic but no ANALYSIS usage associated
       with the column defined by the following elements.
       Name                              Usage
       --------------------------------  --------
       mean                              STATISTIC
ERROR: There is a statistic but no ANALYSIS usage associated
       with the column defined by the following elements.
```

I.e., SAS treats them as statistics, rather than variables. Statistics, except N, must be used together with analysis variable. That causes the problem.

Notice that you cannot combine these names with statistics in COLUMN statement. The following program does not work.

```
PROC REPORT NOWD;
   COLUMN n,sum mean,sum;
RUN;
```

```
PROC REPORT NOWD;
COLUMN n,sum mean,sum;
RUN;

ERROR: There is more than one statistic associated
       with the column defined by the following elements.
       Name                            Usage
       ------------------------------- --------
       n                               STATISTIC
       sum                             STATISTIC
ERROR: There is more than one statistic associated
       with the column defined by the following elements.
       Name                            Usage
       ------------------------------- --------
       mean                            STATISTIC
       sum                             STATISTIC
NOTE: The SAS System stopped processing this step because of errors.
```

But you can specify statistics in a DEFINE statement. The following program is OK.

```
PROC REPORT NOWD;
   COLUMN n mean;
   DEFINE n/sum;
   DEFINE mean/mean;
RUN;
```

Names in Macro

In the Macro facility, there are five categories for macro variables. They are _ALL_, _GLOBAL_, _LOCAL_, _AUTOMATIC_, and _USER_. There are three kinds of elements in Macro facility: text, variable name(without ampersand as prefix), and variable reference (with ampersand as prefix). Variable names can only appear in %LET statement (left side of equal sign), %SYMDEL, %LOCAL and %GLOBAL statements. Therefore, these categories will not be confused with variables in statement other than %SYMDEL and %PUT. In %SYMDEL statement, there is no text. So the question is that %SYMDEL treats them as variable names or categories. The answer is: variable names. See the following program:

```
%LET _global_=4;
%LET a=3;
%PUT _user_;
%SYMDEL _global_;
%PUT _user_;
%SYMDEL _global_;
```

```
%LET _global_=4;
%LET a=3;
%PUT _user_;
GLOBAL _GLOBAL_ 4
```

```
GLOBAL A 3
18    %SYMDEL _global_;
19    %PUT _user_;
GLOBAL A 3
20    %SYMDEL _global_;
WARNING: Attempt to delete macro variable _GLOBAL_ failed. Variable not found.
```

But many times we want to do a clean up to delete global variables. You can use other ways to fulfill this. See Dante (2003) and Perry (2003).

In a %PUT statement, we can put text and reference, but not variable name. So the question is that %PUT treats them as text or categories. SAS has the following rule: If a category is together with text or a macro variable reference, %PUT treats it as text. If it is used independently, %PUT treats it as a category. See the following example:

```
%LET a=3;
%LET b=4;
%PUT _user_;
%PUT a=&a;
%PUT _user_ a=&a;
```

```
13    %PUT _user_;
GLOBAL A 3
GLOBAL B 4
14    %PUT a=&a;
a=3
15    %PUT _user_ a=&a;
_user_ a=3
```

However, there are many system macro variables. Of course, you have to avoid using them as your own macro variables. Most of them begin with SYS, AF, etc. You can run %PUT _AUTOMATIC_; to find out. However, it is hard to remember these system variable names. As a simple way to do this, don't use variable names beginning with AF, SYS, SQL, and DMS. You don't see any automatic variable names beginning with SQL in the printout from %PUT _AUTOMATIC_;, but if you run PROC SQL and then run %PUT _ALL_;, you will see them.

Although SQLOBS, SQLOOPS, SQLXOBS, and SQLRC show as GLOBAL variables, I think they should be categorized as system variables. After you run PROC SQL, they are created.

Now come to macro names. Notice that when using a macro variable reference, we put the ampersand sign before the variable name, and when calling a macro, we put the percent sign before the macro name. In macro facility, what begins with a percent sign? Macro functions and macro auto calls. Therefore, in general, you have to avoid using them as macro names. Actually, SAS forbids you to use a macro function name as a macro name. See the following example:

```
%MACRO quote;
   DATA s;
   a=4;
```

```
    RUN;
%MEND;
```

```
237  %MACRO quote;
ERROR: Macro QUOTE has been given a reserved name.
ERROR: A dummy macro will be compiled.
```

By its nature, SAS does not forbid you to use macro auto call names as macro names, but by search order, you cannot use the corresponding auto call anymore. See the following example:

```
%MACRO lowcase;
    DATA s;
    a=4;
    RUN;
%MEND;
%LET a=%lowcase(ABC);
```

```
237  %LET a=%lowcase(ABC);
NOTE: Line generated by the invoked macro "LOWCASE".
1     DATA s; a=4; RUN;
              -
              180
ERROR 180-322: Statement is not valid or it is used out of proper order.
```

Finally, I put the conclusion of this paper in the following table:

Table 2. Names forbidden or not good

	Forbidden	May cause problem or confusion in some usage
Data set	SET, MERGE, RETAIN, and UPDATE are related to option DATASTMTCHK=. Con, com1-com9	_NULL_, _DATA_, _LAST_
Variable	_NUMERIC_, _CHAR_, _ALL_, _N_, _ERROR_, _FILE_, _INFILE_, _IORC_	_CHARACTER_ (KEEP, DROP, BY, FORMAT, INFORMAT, LENGTH), NOT (depends on situation), DESCENDING, NOTSORTED, GROUPGORMAT (BY statement), _MSG_ and _CMD_ (If WINDOW statement defined), _I_ (If implicit array defined)
Array	Variable names	Function names
Libref	SASHELP, WORK	LIBRARY has special functionality. SASCAT, SASMSG, SASUSER
Informat	System informat names	
Format	System format names	
Table name in SQL	Con, com1-com9	
Column name in SQL		USER has special meaning; DISTINCT, UNIQUE (in SELECT clause) NOT, CASE, CALCULATED, EXISTS (in SELECT statement);

		ALL (in SELECT and WHERE clause) ANY (in WHERE clause)
Macro variable		System macro variable names
Macro	Macro function names	Macro auto call names

Acknowledgements

Thanks to Mr. Gregory Smith for his helpful comments and suggestions.

References

diTommaso, Dante. (2003). "Taking Control of Macro Variables." *Proceedings of the Twenty-eighth Annual SAS Users Group International Conference*, Paper 095-28, Cary, NC: SAS Institute Inc.
http://www2.sas.com/proceedings/sugi28/095-28.pdf

"Names in the SAS Language" in *SAS Language Reference: Concepts*, 2005. Cary, NC: SAS Institute Inc.
http://support.sas.com/onlinedoc/913/getDoc/en/lrcon.hlp/a000998953.htm

Delwiche, Lora D. and Susan J. Slaughter (2003). "ERRORS, WARNINGS, AND NOTES (OH MY) A PRACTICAL GUIDE TO DEBUGGING SAS® PROGRAMS" *Proceedings of the Twenty-eighth Annual SAS Users Group International Conference*, Paper 059-28, Cary, NC: SAS Institute Inc.
http://www2.sas.com/proceedings/sugi28/059-28.pdf

Watts, Perry. (2003). "Advanced Programming Techniques for Working with Color in SAS Software." *Proceedings of the Twenty-ninth Annual SAS Users Group International Conference*, Paper 091-29, Cary, NC: SAS Institute Inc.
http://www2.sas.com/proceedings/sugi29/091-29.pdf

"PROC SQL and the ANSI Standard" in *SAS Procedures Guide*, 2006. Cary, NC: SAS Institute Inc.
http://support.sas.com/documentation/onlinedoc/91pdf/sasdoc_913/base_proc_8977.pdf

Statements, Options, and Their Order

Introduction

According to the SAS manual, DATA step statements are those that can appear in the DATA step. They can be either executable or declarative. *Executable statements* result in some action during individual iterations of the DATA step; *declarative statements* supply information to SAS and take effect when the system compiles program statements.

The following two tables are copied from the SAS manual.

Executable Statements in the DATA Step				
Executable Statements				
ABORT	DO While	INPUT, Column	Null	REPLACE
Assignment	ERROR	INPUT, Formatted	OUTPUT	RETURN
CALL	EXECUTE	INPUT, List	PUT	SELECT
CONTINUE	FILE	INPUT, Named	PUT, Column	SET
DELETE	FILE, ODS	LEAVE	PUT, Formatted	STOP
DESCRIBE	GO TO	LINK	PUT, List	Sum
DISPLAY	IF, Subsetting	LIST	PUT, Named	UPDATE
DO	IF-THEN/ELSE	LOSTCARD	PUT, _ODS_	
DO, Iterative	INFILE	MERGE	REDIRECT	
DO Until	INPUT	MODIFY	REMOVE	

Declarative Statements in the DATA Step				
Declarative Statements				
ARRAY	CARDS4	END	Labels, Statement	WINDOW
Array Reference	DATA	FORMAT	LENGTH	
ATTRIB	DATALINES	INFORMAT	RENAME	
BY	DATALINES4	KEEP	RETAIN	
CARDS	DROP	LABEL	WHERE	

However, these two tables are not so accurate. For example, an END statement is related to a DO statement, an IF statement, or a SELECT statement. Each time SAS executes a DO, IF, or SELECT statement, SAS executes an END statement once. Therefore, it should be categorized as an executable statement.

When discussing executable statements and declarative statements, we have to be aware that these are not black and white situations – either this or that, no middle road. For some statements we cannot categorize them so clearly. From one point of view, they may seem executable, but from another point of view, they may seem declarative. The most important thing is to know their behaviors rather than categorizing them. Actually, when people do programming, they may not care whether a specific statement is executable or declarative, but they do have to know how the statement works. Below, I will analyze some specific statements.

As we know, executable statements are executed according to their order in each iteration. But what properties does a declarative statement have? Usually it has the following properties, but it may not have all of them. An executable statement may also have some properties in the following except 1.

1. It is executed only once for the whole DATA step.
2. You can put it anywhere in a DATA step, and it has the same effect.
3. It cannot be the action of an IF statement. In other words, either it cannot be the action of an IF statement or it will be executed no matter whether the IF condition is true.
4. If there is more than one of the same statement, only one is in effect. It may have different effects: not allowed, overwrite, or combine, depending on situations.

Let's look at a RETAIN statement. It is executed only once in the compilation phase. It cannot be an action of an IF statement; otherwise, SAS will give an error message. The following program shows that we can put it any place in a DATA step:

```
DATA s;
   INPUT a;
   IF _N_=1 THEN b=0;
   b=b+a;
   RETAIN b;
CARDS;
1
2
;
PROC PRINT;RUN;
```

Obs	b	a
1	1	1
2	3	2

Let's look at the following example. Although usually we put an INFORMAT statement before an INPUT statement, it can be put anywhere. In the following program there are two INFORMAT statements. One is before INPUT, and the other is after INPUT. You can see that only the last one is effective.

```
DATA s;
   INFORMAT a DDMMYY8.;
   INPUT a;
```

```
   INFORMAT a MMDDYY8.;
CARDS;
04052007
;
PROC PRINT;
   FORMAT a YYMMDD10.;
RUN;
```

```
Obs          a

  1    2007-04-05
```

Definition statements

What does it mean to define a variable? To define a variable means to assign a variable physical place, to determine its position, name, type, and length attribute if it is a character variable. The following statements can be used to define variables and are called *definition statements*:

Assignment, DO, DO/WHILE, DO/UNTIL, IF, INPUT, SET, MERGE, UPDATE, MODIFY, sum, PUT, ARRAY, ATTRIB(LENGTH, FORMAT, INFORMAT, not LABEL), LENGTH, FORMAT, INFORMAT, RETAIN, and SELECT/WHEN.

If a variable var is defined but has no value assigned, then we will get the following message:

```
NOTE: Variable var is uninitialized.
```

Notice that among them, SET, MERGE, UPDATE, and MODIFY statements implicitly define variables, and others explicitly define variables. For statements that explicitly define variables, of course, variable names must appear in the statement, but a statement that has a variable is not necessary a definition statement. The following statements are non-definition statements:

WHERE, BY, RENAME, LABEL, KEEP, and DROP.

Here BY statement and WHERE use only variables existed in previous SET statement.

It is very possible for a variable to appear in more than one definition statement in a DATA step. Which one defines the variable? SAS's rule is simple:

- Only the first one in the data step that has the variable defines it.

Notice if a statement defines a variable, it has no relation to an IF condition. In the following, variable b is defined in an IF statement with a length attribute of $2. Therefore, in the following assignment, b gets the value 'ab' instead of 'abcd'.

```
%LET a=0;
DATA s;
   IF &a THEN b='12';
```

```
    b='abcd';
PROC PRINT;RUN;
```

Among explicit definition statements, the sum statement defines only numeric variables, and other statements define both types of variables. The following are some examples of how they define variables. From a definition point of view, the difference between numeric variables and character variables is that character variables also need to define their length attribute. Therefore, I use character variables in these examples to show you how they define variable and length attributes for character variables. Notice that the length attribute of numeric variables can only be defined in a LENGTH statement or an ATTRIB/LENGTH statement.

Also notice that any format or informat has a width or a default width if not specified. FORMAT statements and INFORMAT statements use width to determine the variable length attribute. The following program shows how a FORMAT statement defines a variable:

```
PROC FORMAT;
   VALUE $aa abcd='cd' ab='ef';
   INVALUE $bb 1='ab';
DATA s;
   FORMAT b $aa. ;
   INFORMAT c $bb.;
   b='abcd';
   c='abcd';
PROC PRINT;RUN;
```

```
Obs    b     c

 1    ef    ab
```

In this program, both the informat $bb and the format $aa have a default width of 2. They define variables b and c with a length attribute of 2. Therefore, both variables b and c get the value 'ab' instead of 'abcd,' and the printout is 'ef' for variable b. The following program uses a DO statement to define a variable:

```
DATA s;
   DO i='ab', 'abc';
      OUTPUT;
   END;
PROC PRINT;RUN;
```

```
Obs    i

 1    ab
 2    ab
```

You may wonder why both values for variable i are `'ab'`. This is because here i=`'ab'` defines the length attribute for variable i, which is 2. In the following program, variable a is defined in a WHILE clause:

```
DATA s;
DO i=1 TO 5 WHILE (a^='abc');
OUTPUT;
a=SUBSTR('abcde',1,i);
END;
PROC CONTENTS;
RUN;
```

```
Alphabetic List of Variables and Attributes

        #    Variable    Type    Len

        2    a           Char      3
        1    i           Num       8
```

The following program uses an IF statement to define a variable:

```
DATA s;
   IF a='ab' THEN b=1;
   a='abc';
PROC PRINT;RUN;
```

```
Obs    a     b

 1     ab    .
```

Here the value of variable a is 'ab' because the IF statement defines variable a, which has a length attribute of 2.

Using a RETAIN statement to define a variable, either it is defaulted to numeric or there is an initial character value that determines the length attribute of the variable. See the following example:

```
DATA s;
RETAIN a 'abc' c;
a='1234';c=1234;
PROC PRINT;RUN;
```

```
Obs    a       c

 1     123    1234
```

A variable in a PUT statement has the following cases:

- It is already defined.
- If it is defined in the PUT statement and there is no format specified, then it is defaulted as a numeric variable.
- If it is defined in the PUT statement with a character format, its length attribute is equal to the width of the format.

Let's look at the following example:

```
PROC FORMAT;
```

```
   VALUE $aa abcd='cd';
DATA s;
   PUT b $aa. c $3.;
   b='abcd';
   c='abcd';
PROC PRINT;RUN;
```

Obs	b	c
1	ab	abc

In this program the length attribute of variables a and c are 2 and 3 respectively because of the definition statement PUT. So actually, they get values 'ab' and 'abc.'

An ARRAY statement does not specify format or width for a variable. The default width is 8. See the following example:

```
DATA s;
   ARRAY a(*) $ a1-a3;
PROC CONTENTS;
RUN;
```

#	Variable	Type	Len
1	a1	Char	8
2	a2	Char	8
3	a3	Char	8

The following program shows that SELECT/WHEN statements can define variables:

```
DATA s;
SELECT (a='r');
WHEN (1) b=3;
OTHERWISE;
END;
PROC CONTENTS;
DATA t;
SELECT ;
WHEN (a='r') b=3;
OTHERWISE;
END;
PROC CONTENTS;RUN;
```

There are two printouts as follows:

#	Variable	Type	Len
1	a	Char	1
2	b	Num	8

There may be more than one data set in a SET statement, and a MERGE statement has at least two data sets. So if there is a variable appearing in more than one data set and it has never been defined before, which data set defines the variable? The first one.

Notice that in an assignment, not only does the left side define a variable, but also the right side defines variable(s), too. However, if the right side defines variable(s), the type is numeric. See the following example:

```
DATA s;
   b=c||'abc';   e=f+3;
PROC CONTENTS;
RUN;
```

#	Variable	Type	Len
1	b	Char	15
2	c	Num	8
3	e	Num	8
4	f	Num	8

In this program, variables c, e, and f are all numeric. Variable b is character with a length attribute of 15 since SAS uses BEST12 to convert numeric value to character here.

The following program shows that RENAME, LABEL, KEEP, and DROP statements do not define variables:

```
DATA s;
a=3;
RENAME b=c; LABEL d='abd';KEEP a d f b c;
PROC CONTENTS;
RUN;
```

#	Variable	Type	Len
1	a	Num	8

However notice the LABEL statement. Even if it does not define variable d, there is an "uninitialized" message.

```
NOTE: Variable d is uninitialized.
```

BY statement

We will now talk about BY statement.

- It must be after a SET (or MERGE, MODIFY, or UPDATE) statement.
- If there is more than one SET statement before it, it affects only the last one.
- Only one BY statement is allowed between two SET statements.

The following points are for SET, MERGE, and UPDATE statements. MODIFY statement does not need the data sets to be sorted according to the following BY statement. The rules of BY statement after MODIFY statement is different from that after other statements.

- It is executed in each iteration to check if the data set is sorted.

- It is executed after the SET statement but before other executable statements, no matter where it is put.
- If there is more than one data set in a SET statement, SAS will check each data set to see if it is sorted. This is called an *interleaving operation.*

The following program has a problem:

```
DATA t;
   BY a;
   SET s;
RUN;
```

```
ERROR: No SET, MERGE, UPDATE, or MODIFY statement is present.
```

The following program shows that if a BY statement is an action of an IF statement, it is executed no matter whether the IF condition is true:

```
%LET con=1;
DATA s;
   INPUT a;
CARDS;
3
2
;
DATA t;
   SET s;
   IF &con=2 THEN BY a;
RUN;
```

```
ERROR: BY variables are not properly sorted on data set WORK.S.
a=3 FIRST.a=1 LAST.a=1 _ERROR_=1 _N_=1
NOTE: The SAS System stopped processing this step because of errors
```

The following program is OK. It shows that the BY statement is only responsible for data set s:

```
DATA s;
   INPUT a @@;
CARDS;
1 1 2
;
DATA t;
   INPUT a @@;
CARDS;
2 2 1
;
DATA p;
   SET t;
   SET s;
   BY a;
PROC PRINT;RUN;
```

The following program is OK. It shows that a BY statement is always executed immediately after the SET statement that comes before it.

```
DATA set2 ;
   INPUT c d;
CARDS;
1 3
2 4
3 5
4 6
;
DATA t;
   SET set2;
   IF _N_=2 THEN c=6;
   BY c;
PROC PRINT;
RUN;
```

The following program shows that SAS first executes the BY statement and then sets FIRST.byvar:

```
DATA s;
INPUT a @@;
CARDS;
1 1 2
;
DATA t;
SET s;
IF FIRST.a THEN a=3;
BY a;
PROC PRINT;RUN;
```

Obs	a
1	3
2	1
3	3

However, if we say that a BY statement supplies information to SAS and takes effect when the system compiles the program, I'd rather say that it asks SAS to check in each iteration to see if the input data set is sorted by the BY variables. Notice that a BY statement has two functionalities: sorting and grouping. Many people (at least previous I) used to think that a BY statement tells SAS that the data set is sorted. Actually, this is not the case. SAS does not care if the data set is already sorted or not. If there is a BY statement, SAS will compare values of BY variables in the current observation with those in the next observation in each iteration. If it is OK, then continue; otherwise, SAS gives an ERROR message. The following program shows that SAS first executes four iterations and then stops during the fourth iteration (_N_=4). Actually, the data set pp is partially built. It has three observations. However, if the data set pp already existed, it will not be replaced because of errors.

```
DATA t;
```

```
    INPUT a b ;
CARDS;
2 1
2 2
3 3
3 4
1 5
2 6
;
DATA pp;
    SET t;
    BY a;
    PUT _N_= a=  FIRST.a= LAST.a=;
PROC PRINT;RUN;
```

```
_N_=1 a=2 FIRST.a=1 LAST.a=0
_N_=2 a=2 FIRST.a=0 LAST.a=1
_N_=3 a=3 FIRST.a=1 LAST.a=0
ERROR: BY variables are not properly sorted on data set WORK.T.
a=3 b=4 FIRST.a=1 LAST.a=0 _ERROR_=1 _N_=4
NOTE: The SAS System stopped processing this step because of errors.
NOTE: There were 5 observations read from the data set WORK.T.
WARNING: The data set WORK.PP may be incomplete.  When this step was stopped there were 3
         observations and 2 variables.
```

For the first three iterations, it is OK. At the fourth iteration, there is a problem. Why? Because at the fourth iteration, SAS reads in the fifth observation, compares it with the fourth observation and finds that the data set is not sorted properly. (NOTE: There were 5 observations read from the data set WORK.T.) Therefore, SAS stops at the fourth iteration before the PUT statement, so SAS executes the PUT statement only three times, and the data set created has only three observations. In the log we can see printout a=3 b=4 FIRST.a=1 LAST.a=0, because FIRST and LAST values have not been updated yet.

A BY statement works in PROCs the same way as it works in a DATA step. Let's see the following example:

```
DATA s;
    DO i=1 TO 5;
    DO j=1 TO 3;OUTPUT;
    END;
    END;
DATA s;
    SET s;
    IF _n_=12 THEN i=0;
PROC MEANS;
    BY i;
RUN;
```

```
ERROR: Data set WORK.S is not sorted in ascending sequence. The current by-group has i =
4 and the next by-group has i = 0.
NOTE: The SAS System stopped processing this step because of errors.
NOTE: There were 12 observations read from the data set WORK.S.
```

Suppose there is more than one data set in a SET statement. If there is no BY statement, SAS first reads from the first data set. After it is finished, SAS begins to read the next data set, and so on. If there is a BY statement, it is called an *interleaving operation*. In each iteration, SAS keeps one value for each data set, knows which one is smallest, and also knows which one is the first if there is a tie. Then SAS reads one observation from this data set and makes a comparison with the reserved one to see if the data set is sorted. If it is sorted, SAS continues the process and otherwise gives the ERROR message. For the case of interleaving option, you can still use FIRST.byvar and LAST.byvar. See the following program:

```
DATA s1;
   INPUT a b;
CARDS;
1 1
1 3
2 4
2 5
;
DATA s2;
   INPUT a c;
CARDS;
0 3
;
DATA s3;
   INPUT a d;
CARDS;
1.5 6
2.5 7
;
DATA p;
   SET s1(in=s1) s2(in=s2) s3(in=s3);
   BY a;
   IF s1=1 THEN pp='s1';
   IF s2=1 THEN pp='s2';
   IF s3=1 THEN pp='s3';
   PUT _N_= a= FIRST.a= LAST.a= 'obs come from ' pp ;
RUN;
```

```
_N_=1 a=0 FIRST.a=1 LAST.a=1 obs come from s2
_N_=2 a=1 FIRST.a=1 LAST.a=0 obs come from s1
_N_=3 a=1 FIRST.a=0 LAST.a=1 obs come from s1
_N_=4 a=1.5 FIRST.a=1 LAST.a=1 obs come from s3
_N_=5 a=2 FIRST.a=1 LAST.a=0 obs come from s1
_N_=6 a=2 FIRST.a=0 LAST.a=1 obs come from s1
_N_=7 a=2.5 FIRST.a=1 LAST.a=1 obs come from s3
```

If there is more that one SET statement, then the FIRST.byvar and LAST.byvar are set according to different BY statements. See the following example:

```
DATA s1;
INPUT a ;
CARDS;
1 1
1 3
```

```
2 4
;
DATA s2;
INPUT a c;
CARDS;
1 2
2 3
2 4
;
DATA p;
SET s1;
BY a;
PUT _N_= 'in s1  ' FIRST.a= LAST.a=;
SET s2;
BY a;
PUT _N_= 'in s2  ' FIRST.a= LAST.a=;
RUN;
```

```
_N_=1 in s1  FIRST.a=1 LAST.a=0
_N_=1 in s2  FIRST.a=1 LAST.a=1
_N_=2 in s1  FIRST.a=0 LAST.a=1
_N_=2 in s2  FIRST.a=1 LAST.a=0
_N_=3 in s1  FIRST.a=1 LAST.a=1
_N_=3 in s2  FIRST.a=0 LAST.a=1
```

So should I say that a BY statement is an executable statement or a declarative statement? Although it has some characteristics as declarative statements, it is still an executable statement, because it is executed for each iteration.

If SET, MERGE, MODIFY, and UPDATE statements are all executable and a BY statement is responsible for one of them, it is not suitable to categorize BY as a declarative statement.

Let's emphasize here again: (1) a BY statement must come after a SET statement; (2) it is responsible for the last SET statement before it; (3) a BY statement is always executed no matter whether it is an action of an IF statement and if the IF condition is true.

Now consider a SET statement. As we know, it is executable. Different form BY statement, it can be an action of an IF statement for conditional execution. This means that if the IF condition is not true, SAS will not execute the SET statement. However, as we said, SET statement is a definition statement, so in the compilation phase, SAS uses variables in data set(s) specified in the SET statement. The following program creates a data set p that is the same as data set s, but it also has the variable b that comes from data set t and has a missing value.

```
DATA s;
   a=3;
DATA t;
   b=4;
%LET con=0;
DATA p;
```

```
   SET s;
   IF &con THEN SET t;
RUN;
```

Now we have questions.

1. Suppose that there is a SET statement that is an action of an IF statement, which is followed by a BY statement. Is the BY statement always responsible for this SET statement, or may be responsible for the previous SET statement depending on the trueness of the IF condition? Let's build the following two data sets:

```
DATA s;
   a=5;OUTPUT;
   a=4;OUTPUT;
DATA t;
   a=3;OUTPUT;
   a=2;OUTPUT;
RUN;
```

Let's run the following program:

```
%LET con=0;
DATA p;
   SET s;
   IF &con THEN SET t;
   BY a;
RUN;
```

2. If both a SET statement and a BY statement are actions of an IF condition, what happens if the IF condition is false? Let's run the following program:

```
%LET con=0;
DATA p;
   SET s;
   IF &con THEN do;
      SET t;
      BY a;
   END;
RUN;
```

Both programs are OK. Although set s is not sorted, it is not followed by a BY statement. The BY statement is for set t, and because the condition is false, the statement SET t; will be falsely executed. The following is a message in the log file for both programs:

```
NOTE: There were 2 observations read from the data set WORK.S.
NOTE: There were 1 observations read from the data set WORK.T.
NOTE: The data set WORK.P has 2 observations and 1 variables.
```

For both questions, the BY statement is always responsible for the previous SET statement, no matter whether it is an action of an IF statement and whether the IF condition is true. We have the following conclusions:

- If the IF condition is true, as you can imagine, both statements work as usual.
- If the IF condition if false, the SET statement will be falsely executed, and the BY statement has no effect. (SAS gives the message `1 observations read` but actually does nothing.)

WHERE statement

You may not think that we can compare a WHERE statement with a BY statement. Actually, they are very similar in syntax, although they are total different in functionalities. They are executed in each iteration. Table 1 gives a comparison between them.

Table 1. Comparison between a BY statement and a WHERE statement

<table>
<tr><th>BY statement</th><th>WHERE statement</th></tr>
<tr><td colspan="2">Must be after a SET (MERGE, UPDATE, or MODIFY) statement</td></tr>
<tr><td>Only one BY statement is allowed between two SET statements.</td><td>Only the last WHERE statement between two SET statements is effective.</td></tr>
<tr><td colspan="2">Only responsible for the last SET statement before it, no matter if the SET statement is conditional and if the IF condition is false.</td></tr>
<tr><td colspan="2">No matter where it is put between two SET statements, it will always be executed immediately after the the last SET statement before it.</td></tr>
<tr><td colspan="2">It is always executed, no matter if it is an action of an IF statement or if the IF condition is true</td></tr>
<tr><td colspan="2">If the previous SET statement is an action of an IF statement, and if the IF condition is false, the BY/WHERE statement will be falsely executed (BY) or not executed (WHERE).</td></tr>
<tr><td colspan="2">Variables in the statement must be in the data set(s) specified in the SET statement.</td></tr>
<tr><td colspan="2">Read two observations in the first iteration, and then read the next observation (compare to iteration) in each iteration.</td></tr>
<tr><td>Check the BY condition.</td><td>Set the END= value [IV].</td></tr>
<tr><td>Read one observation in each iteration.</td><td>Read observations until one that satisfies the WHERE condition [IV].</td></tr>
</table>

Now we discuss detail characteristics of a WHERE statement. Mainly we compare it with a subsetting IF statement, because they have similar functionalities.

- Similar to BY statement, WHERE statement must be after a SET (MERGE, MODIFY, or UPDATE) statement. If there is more than one SET statement before it, it affects only the last one. If there is more than one data set in the same SET statement, it affects them all.

```
DATA t;
  a=2;
DATA p;
  where a=2;
  set t;
RUN;
```

```
1017  DATA p;
1018  where a=2;
ERROR: No input data sets available for WHERE statement.
1019  set t;
1020  RUN;

NOTE: The SAS System stopped processing this step because of errors.
```

In the following example, the WHERE statement affects only data set t. Notice that if we replace the statement WHERE a=2; by the statement WHERE b=2;, the program does not work.

```
DATA s;
   INPUT a b;
CARDS;
2 5
3 6
2 4
;
DATA t;
   INPUT a c;
CARDS;
1 3
2 4
2 5
;
DATA p;
   SET s;
   SET t;
   WHERE a=2;
PROC PRINT;
RUN;
```

```
Obs    a    b    c

  1    2    5    4
  2    2    6    5
```

- If there is more than one WHERE statement between two SET statements, only the last one is effective. The following example shows that each IF statement is executed independently, but only the last WHERE statement is executed.

```
DATA sa;
   INPUT a $ b c;
CARDS;
a 1 5
b 2 3
a 2 7
;
DATA t;
   SET sa;
   IF c=3;IF b=2;
DATA Q;
   SET sa;
   WHERE c=3;WHERE b=2;
PROC PRINT DATA=t;
PROC PRINT DATA=q;RUN;
```

```
Obs    a    b    c

  1    b    2    3

Obs    a    b    c
```

```
1    b    2    3
2    a    2    7
```

The following message is in the log file:

```
NOTE: There were 2 observations read from the data set WORK.SA. WHERE b=2;
```

- It is always executed immediately after a SET statement, no matter where you put it. The following program shows our claim.

```
DATA t;
   SET sa;
   b+2;IF b<4;
DATA q;
   SET sa;
   b+2;WHERE b<4;
PROC PRINT DATA =t;
PROC PRINT DATA=q;RUN;
```

```
Obs    a    b    c

 1     a    3    5


Obs    a    b    c

 1     a    3    5
 2     b    4    3
 3     a    4    7
```

- It is always executed, no matter if it is an action of an IF conditions and if the IF condition is true, as the following program shows:

```
%LET con=1;
DATA s;
   INPUT a;
CARDS;
3
2
;
DATA t;
   SET s;
   IF &con=2 THEN WHERE a<3;
PROC PRINT;
RUN;
```

The following is the log message:

```
NOTE: There were 1 observations read from the data set WORK.S.
      WHERE a<3;
NOTE: The data set WORK.T has 1 observations and 1 variables.
```

```
Obs    a

  1    2
```

- In each iteration, the subsetting IF statement, which is executable, is executed only once. When SAS comes to an IF statement, it determines if the observation should be processed according to the IF condition. A WHERE statement will be executed until SAS finds an observation that satisfies the WHERE condition. The following program uses an IF statement and a WHERE statement in two DATA steps, respectively. You can see that although they create the same data set, two statements run in different iterations. For the second DATA step, SAS reads the first observation in the first iteration (_N_=1), the WHERE condition is not true, SAS continues to read the second observation, and the WHERE condition is true. Then SAS goes to the second iteration. For the third DATA step, SAS reads in the first observation in the first iteration and reads the second observation in the second iteration no matter if SAS continues processing or stops processing the observation.

```
DATA s;
   INPUT a @@;
CARDS;
1 3 5 4 2 6 1
;
DATA t;
   SET s;
   WHERE a>2;
   i=_N_;
TITLE 'where output';
PROC PRINT;RUN;
DATA p;
   SET s;
   IF a>2;
   i=_N_;
TITLE 'if output';
PROC PRINT;RUN;
```

```
where output
Obs    a    i

  1    3    1
  2    5    2
  3    4    3
  4    6    4

   if output
Obs    a    i

  1    3    2
  2    5    3
  3    4    4
  4    6    6
```

- As we know, a SET statement is an executable statement. We often use it as an action of an IF statement when we merge the original data set with its grand total. A WHERE statement depends on a SET statement. Notice that no matter whether a SET statement is an action of an IF condition, WHERE statement always depends on the SET statement. In other words, WHERE is responsible only for the last SET statement before it. This has two meanings: It uses only variables in data set(s) in the previous statement, and it gets the subset of data set(s) in the previous statement. This behavior is the same as that of a BY statement. Suppose we have the following two data sets:

```
DATA s;
   INPUT a b;
CARDS;
1 2
1 3
2 3
2 4
;
DATA t;
   INPUT a c;
CARDS;
1 3
2 4
2 5
3 5
;
```

The following program works OK:

```
DATA p;
   SET s;
   SET t;
   IF b+c>5;
RUN;
```

But the following program does not work:

```
DATA p;
   SET s;
   SET t;
   WHERE b+c>5;
RUN;
```

Now suppose that the SET statement before a WHERE statement is conditional, or both the SET statement and the WHERE statement are conditional. The situation is the same as that of a BY statement. A WHERE statement is responsible only for this SET statement. If the condition is false, both the SET statement and the WHERE statement will not be executed. Let's see the following example:

```
%LET a=0;
DATA p;
   SET S;
```

```
    IF &a THEN SET t;
    WHERE c<6;
RUN;
DATA p;
    SET s;
    IF &a THEN DO;
    SET t;
    WHERE c<6;
    END;
RUN;
```

There are two DATA steps in the program. Both steps have the following log messages:

```
NOTE: There were 4 observations read from the data set WORK.S.
NOTE: The data set WORK.P has 4 observations and 3 variables.
```

Now, both the WHERE statement and the BY statement are executed after a SET statement but before other executable statements. So if there are both a WHERE statement and a BY statement, which one will be executed first? The answer is the WHERE statement. The following program is OK:

```
DATA t;
    INPUT a b ;
CARDS;
2 1
2 2
3 3
3 4
1 5
;
DATA pp;
    SET t;
    BY a;
    WHERE b<5;
    PUT _N_= a=  FIRST.a=;
PROC PRINT;RUN;
```

Effectiveness of declarative statements

Probably you have never written a KEEP statement twice in the same DATA step, but this is OK for syntax. The following table gives the effectiveness of attributes, declarative statements, and BY and WHERE statements. We allow repeated declarative statements. Some of them have already been discussed. A SET statement means one of SET, MERGE, MODIFY, or UPDATE statements.

Table 2. Effectiveness of attributes and declarative statements

Attribute or statement	Which is effective (if more than one statement on the same object)	When it is effective
Length (character)	First definition statement.	Beginning of data step
Length (numeric)	The last statement that defines it if it is explicitly defined;	End of data step
Format		

Informat	or first data set in a SET statement and has it	Beginning of data step
Label	defined; or otherwise null for label, format, and informat, and default 8 for length of numeric variable. Unformat is effective only for a FORMAT statement that is after a SET statement.	
WHERE	Last one between two SET statements	Immediately after the SET statement
BY	Only one is allowed between two SET statements	Immediately after the SET statement (after WHERE)
DROP	Combine	End of data step (before KEEP)
KEEP	Combine	End of data step (before RENAME)
RENAME	Last one	End of data step

To illustrate Table 2, let's run the following program:

```
DATA s;
RENAME c1=c2; /*This will not be effective.*/
RENAME c1=c3; /*This will be effective.*/
INFORMAT a1 $5. b1 5.; /*The length of a1 will be $5.*/
INFORMAT a1 $4. b1 4.; /*The informat of a1 and b1 will be $4. and 4.
respectively.*/
FORMAT a2 $5. b2 5.; /*This determines format of a2 and b2, length of
a2*/
c3='abcde';d3=123; /*The length of c3 will be $5*/
LENGTH a3 c3 $4 b3 d3 4; /*The length of a3 will be 4*/
LENGTH a3 c3 $5 b3 d3 5; /*The length of b3 and d3 will be 5*/
INPUT a0 $4. a1 a2 b0 3. b1 b2 c1; /*The length of a0 is 4*/
FORMAT a3 $6.;
LABEL a1='abc'; /*This will not be effective.*/
LABEL a1='abcd'; /*This will be effective.*/
a5='1234';a3='12';
b5=1234;b3=12;
CARDS;
ab0  ab1 ab2 12 13 14 11
;
PROC CONTENTS;RUN;
```

Alphabetic List of Variables and Attributes

#	Variable	Type	Len	Format	Informat	Label
9	a0	Char	4			
1	a1	Char	5		$4.	abcd
3	a2	Char	5	$5.		
7	a3	Char	4	$6.		
12	a5	Char	4			
10	b0	Num	8			
2	b1	Num	8		4.	
4	b2	Num	8	5.		
8	b3	Num	5			
13	b5	Num	8			
11	c1	Num	8			

```
5    c3        Char    5
6    d3        Num     5
```

The following program shows the situation when we merge data sets that defined label, informat, and format:

```
DATA s;
a=5;b=5;c=5;d=5;
LABEL a='abc'; c='abc';
DATA t;
a=5;b=5;c=5;
LABEL a='aaa' b='aaa';
DATA p;
MERGE s t;
LABEL d='aaa';
PROC CONTENTS;
RUN;
```

```
Alphabetic List of Variables and Attributes

 #    Variable    Type    Len    Label

 1    a           Num       8    abc
 2    b           Num       8    aaa
 3    c           Num       8
 4    d           Num       8    aaa
```

Now you can write the following style of program:

```
DATA s;
/*code to calculate variable a*/
   a=1;
   KEEP a;
   /*code to calculate variable b*/
   b=3;
   KEEP b;
PROC PRINT;RUN;
```

```
Obs    a    b

  1    1    3
```

The following program creates a data set. Guess what are the length attribute and the format of the variable a. Its length is 3, and its format is $tt. The length 3 comes from format $ss because the FORMAT statement defines it, and the format $ss has a default width of 3. It gets the format $tt because the statement FORMAT s $tt.; is the last one to define its format. Notice that format $tt has a default width of 4.

```
PROC FORMAT;
   VALUE $ss a=abc;
   VALUE $tt a=abcd;
DATA s;
   FORMAT a $ss.;
```

```
   a='a';
   FORMAT a $tt.;
PROC CONTENTS;
RUN;
```

#	Variable	Type	Len	Format
1	a	Char	3	$TT.

In the following program, the format for variable b and variable c are both effective. Unformat is effective only for variable a, not for variable d, because unformat for variable a is after the SET statement.

```
DATA s;
   FORMAT a 6. b 6. c 6. d 6.;
   a=4;b=4;c=4;d=4;
DATA t;
   FORMAT c 4. d;
   SET s;
   FORMAT b 4. a;
RUN;
PROC CONTENTS;
RUN;
```

#	Variable	Type	Len	Format
3	a	Num	8	
4	b	Num	8	4.
1	c	Num	8	4.
2	d	Num	8	6.

Order of DROP, KEEP, and RENAME – statements and options

First, we will talk about how SAS executes these statements and options. In order to explain clearly what I am saying, I have to talk about system options DKRICOND= and DKROCOND=. They specify the level of error detection to report when something is wrong in DROP, DEEP, or RENAME, either statements or options, where the option DKRICOND= is for an input data set, and the option DKROCOND= is for an output data set. Therefore, option DKRICOND= affects options in a SET statement, and option DKROCOND= affects options in a DATA statement as well as in independent statements. Both of them take values ERROR|WARN (WARINING)| NOWARN(NOWARNING) that, when something is wrong, decide to give an ERROR message and stop, a WARNING message, or no message. Let's see the following example:

```
OPTION DKROCOND=WARN;
DATA s;
a=1;b=2;
RENAME a=b;
RUN;
OPTION DKROCOND=ERROR;
DATA s;
a=1;b=2;
RENAME a=b;
RUN;
```

We will see the following message:

```
36    OPTION DKROCOND=WARN;
37    DATA s;
38    a=1;b=2;
39    RENAME a=b;
40    RUN;

WARNING: Variable b already exists on file WORK.S.
NOTE: The data set WORK.S has 1 observations and 1 variables.
NOTE: DATA statement used (Total process time):
      real time           0.03 seconds
      cpu time            0.00 seconds


41    OPTION DKROCOND=ERROR;
42    DATA s;
43    a=1;b=2;
44    RENAME a=b;
45    RUN;

ERROR: Variable b already exists on file WORK.S.
NOTE: The SAS System stopped processing this step because of errors.
WARNING: The data set WORK.S may be incomplete.  When this step was stopped there were 0
         observations and 0 variables.
```

It is possible that your settings and my settings are different. If this is the case, then you may not feel comfortable about what I am explaining. Also, if the settings for two options are different, it not good to make a comparison between statements and options. Therefore, in our discussion, we will first run the following statement:

```
OPTION DKROCOND=WARN DKRICOND=WARN;
```

Now let's see the order between a KEEP statement and a DROP statement. Run the following program and look at the log message:

```
DATA s;
   a=1;b=2;c=3;
   KEEP a b;DROP a;
RUN;
```

```
WARNING: The variable a in the DROP, KEEP, or RENAME list has never been referenced.
NOTE: The data set WORK.S has 1 observations and 1 variables.
```

From this message we can see that SAS first executes the statement DROP a;, then the statement KEEP a b;, and SAS finds that there is no variable a (It has already been dropped.), so SAS gives the message: "`The variable a in the DROP, KEEP, or RENAME list has never been referenced.`" The following program is OK because SAS first executes DROP statement, and then executes KEEP statement:

```
DATA s;
   a=1;b=1;c=1;
```

```
    KEEP a; DROP b;
RUN;
```

In other words, if we use both a DROP statement and a KEEP statement, they should not have common variables. However, people do not usually write a DROP statement and a KEEP statement in one DATA step. However, many people do write a KEEP (DROP) statement and a RENAME statement in the same DATA step. Let us consider the order between KEEP and RENAME. Try the following program:

```
DATA s;
    a=1;b=2;c=3;
    RENAME a=d; KEEP b d;
RUN;
```

We get the following messages:

```
WARNING: The variable d in the DROP, KEEP, or RENAME list has never been referenced.
WARNING: The variable a in the DROP, KEEP, or RENAME list has never been referenced.
NOTE: The data set WORK.S has 1 observations and 1 variables.
```

To understand the message, you have to know that SAS executes the KEEP statement before the RENAME statement. When SAS executes the KEEP statement, there is no variable d, so SAS gives the first message, and the data set has only variable b after the KEEP statement. Then SAS executes the RENAME statement, and there is no variable a, so SAS gives the second message.

Changing two statements to either of the following will be OK:

```
RENAME a=d; KEEP a b;
KEEP a b; RENAME a=d;
```

Now we will look at the case that they are options. We have the following conclusions:

- If both DROP= and KEEP= are options in a SET statement for the same data set and they have common variables, there is no WARNING message, and the variable set read in is (KEEP variables\DROP variables). See the following example:

```
DATA s;
INPUT a b @@;
cards;
1 2 3 4 5 6
;
DATA k;
SET s(DROP=b KEEP=a b );
RUN;
```

```
DATA k;
SET s(DROP=b KEEP=a b );
RUN;
```

```
NOTE: There were 3 observations read from the data set WORK.S.
NOTE: The data set WORK.K has 3 observations and 1 variables.
```

- If both DROP= and KEEP= are options in a DATA statement, SAS behaves the same as they are independent statements. See the following example:

```
DATA p(KEEP=a b DROP=b);
SET s;
RUN;
```

```
258  DATA p(KEEP=a b DROP=b);
259  SET s;
260  RUN;

WARNING: The variable b in the DROP, KEEP, or RENAME list has never been referenced.
NOTE: There were 3 observations read from the data set WORK.S.
NOTE: The data set WORK.P has 3 observations and 1 variables.
```

- If both KEEP=(DROP=) and RENAME= are options in DATA statement or in SET statement for the same data set, SAS first executes KEEP= (DROP=) option, then executes RENAME= option.

RENAME statement and RENAME= option

The case in which SAS executes RENAME statements is quite complicated. As we know, a RENAME statement consists of several equations, and for each equation, the left side is a name to be renamed and the right side is a name to rename. We can use one RENAME statement or several RENAME statements in one DATA step. As long as equations and their orders are the same, using one RENAME statement or using several RENAME statements makes no difference. The following two steps have the same effect.

```
DATA s;
a=1;b=2;
RENAME a=b b=c;
DATA s;
a=1;b=2;
RENAME a=b; RENAME b=c;
RUN;
```

Therefore, for the simplicity of discussion, we suppose that there is only one RENAME statement. Now, we will talk about rules that SAS executes RENAME statement.

RENAME statement, of course, is a declarative statement. In compilation phase, SAS determines how to rename variables, but they will be effect at the end of DATA step. Therefore in the data step, we have to use original variable names. RENAME statement is closely related to the order of physical position of variables. Hence we suppose variables' positions are from high to lower. (to avoid confusion with left side and right side of an equation) See the following program and output. In the log file, SAS first gives warning message for RENAME statement (in compilation phase), then prints out a= in execution phase. Also we know RENAME will be effective at the end of the DATA step.

```
2605  data s;
```

```
2606  a=3;
2607  put a=;
2608  rename p=a a=b;
2609  run;

WARNING: The variable p in the DROP, KEEP, or RENAME list has never been referenced.
   a=3
```

The following are rules how SAS executes RENAME statement.

- For each equation in the RENAME statement, the left side must be a name of an original variable. Otherwise SAS will give a WARNING message, and the equation will be dropped. In the following example, variable a is renamed to c and the equation c=b is dropped:

```
DATA s;
a=4;
RENAME a=c c=b;
RUN;
```

```
WARNING: The variable c in the DROP, KEEP, or RENAME list has never been referenced.
NOTE: The data set WORK.S has 1 observations and 1 variables.
```

- If a variable appears on the left side in more than one equation, then only the last one is in effect. In the following two steps, variable a is renamed to b and the equation a=c is dropped. Notice that there is no WARNING message. In other words, no matter how we set option DKROCOND=, SAS will continue processing. SAS does not think there is anything wrong.

```
DATA s;
a=4;
RENAME a=c a=b;
RUN;
```

- If a variable name appears more than once at the right side, the equation that the left side with the highest position may be effective. All others will be dropped. SAS will give WARNING message(s). See the following example:

```
DATA s;
a=1;b=2;c=3;
RENAME b=p a=p;
PROC PRINT;
RUN;
```

```
Obs    p    b    c

 1     1    2    3
```

```
WARNING: Variable b cannot be renamed to p because p already exists.
NOTE: The data set WORK.S has 1 observations and 3 variables.
```

- From the above points, we can suppose that each variable appears at most once at left side of equations, and each variable appear at most once at right side of equations. If we assign a point for each name and draw an arc from left side to right side for each equation, there is at most one arc coming out, and at most one arc coming in for each point. This graph can divided into directed cycles and directed paths. Moreover, for each path, only the last point may be a new name, all others must be original names.

- Directed cycles are OK, SAS renames variable according to the cycle.

```
DATA s;
a=1; b=2;c=3;
RENAME a=c c=b b=a;
RUN;
```

- If the last point on the path is a new name, then all equations are in effect, and there is no WARNING message. The following code is OK.

```
DATA s;
a=1; b=2;c=3;
RENAME c=b b=a a=d;
RUN;
```

- Suppose the last point is an original name. SAS will give a WARNING message and we can find the last point on the path such that its previous point is higher than it. This point is called a *pivot point*. It will be renamed (overwritten) and all points before it will be renamed. However points after it will not be renamed. Let's see the following example:

```
DATA s;
a=1; b=2;c=3;d=4;e=5;f=6;g=7;h=8;i=9;k=10;l=11;
RENAME a=c c=b b=g g=f f=e i=k l=e;
PROC PRINT;
RUN;
```

```
Obs    c    g    b    d    e    f    h    k     l

 1     1    2    3    4    5    6    8    9    11

WARNING: Variable f cannot be renamed to e because e already exists.
WARNING: Variable g cannot be renamed to f because f already exists.
WARNING: Variable g already exists on file WORK.S.
WARNING: Variable k already exists on file WORK.S.
WARNING: Variable l cannot be renamed to e because e already exists.
NOTE: The data set WORK.S has 1 observations and 9 variables.
```

The RENAME statement can be divided into three paths. The path l=e have no pivot point, the path i=k has pivot point k, and the path a=c=b=g=f=e has pivot point g. We can understand the output. Notice the order of WARNING messages. Notice that the final data set has 9 variables.

However, the behavior of the RENAME= option in a SET statement is totally different from that of a RENAME statement. The cycle equations are OK in a RENAME= option.

```
DATA s;
a=1;b=2;c=3;d=4;e=5;f=6;
DATA t;
SET s(RENAME=(c=a a=d d=c));
PROC PRINT;
RUN;
```

Otherwise, SAS executes equations from left to right according their order in the program. A point (variable name) has two statuses: available or unavailable. At beginning, all original variables are unavailable and all new names are available. After executing previous equations, if the left side of the equation is available or the right side is unavailable, SAS gives warning message and the equation will be dropped. Otherwise the left side becomes available and the right side becomes unavailable. Let's see the following example.

```
DATA s;
a=1;b=2;c=3;d=4;e=5;f=6;
DATA t;
SET s(RENAME=(p=q c=p e=d d=r f=c));
PROC PRINT;
RUN;
```

```
Obs    a    b    p    r    e    c

  1    1    2    3    4    5    6
```

```
2637  data t;
2638  set s(rename=(p=q c=p e=d d=r f=c));
WARNING: Variable p is not on file WORK.S.
WARNING: Variable d already exists on file WORK.S.
WARNING: The variable p in the DROP, KEEP, or RENAME list has never been referenced.
```

For the first equation p=q, p is available, the equation is dropped. The second equation is OK, and c becomes available. For the third equation e=d, d is unavailable, and the equation is dropped. The fourth equation d=r is OK. The fifth equation is OK because c is available. Now run the following program:

```
DATA s;
a=4;
RENAME a=c c=b;
RUN;
DATA s1;
a=4;
DATA t;
SET s1(RENAME=( a=c c=b));
RUN;
```

In the first DATA step, SAS gives a WARNING message and variable a is renamed to c. However, in the third DATA step, there is no WARNING message, and variable a is renamed to b.

When a RENAME= option is in a DATA statement, SAS executes it as an independent statement.

WHERE= option

The relationship between options DEEP= (DROP=), RENAME= and WHERE= is simple. SAS executes WHERE= option after executing other options. The following program is OK:

```
DATA s;
   a=5;b=3;
DATA p1;
   SET s(WHERE=(c=5) RENAME=(a=c) KEEP=a);
RUN;
```

But two DATA steps in the following program are not OK:

```
DATA t1;
   SET s(WHERE=(a=5) RENAME=(a=c) );
RUN;
DATA t3;
   SET s(WHERE=(b=3) KEEP=a);
RUN;
```

When talking about WHERE= option, we have to talk about options OBS= and FIRSTOBS= in a SET statement. We can think that SAS first executes a WHERE= option or an independent WHERE statement, and then executes FIRSTOBS= and OBS= options. Let's see the following example:

```
DATA s;
INPUT a @@;
CARDS;
2 7 3 5 3 6 8 4 3 9 6 6 6
;
DATA t;
SET s(FIRSTOBS=2 OBS=6 WHERE=(a>3));
PROC PRINT;
DATA t;
SET s(FIRSTOBS=2 OBS=6 );
WHERE a>3;
PROC PRINT;
PROC PRINT DATA =s(FIRSTOBS=2 OBS=6 WHERE=(a>3));
PROC PRINT DATA =s(FIRSTOBS=2 OBS=6 );
WHERE a>3;
RUN;
```

The program creates four printouts. All printouts are the same, as shown below. The difference is Obs column.

```
Obs    a

  3    5
  5    6
  6    8
  7    4
```

```
9  9
```

Although we put the options FIRSTOBS= and OBS= before the option WHERE=, SAS first executes the WHERE= option, gets values 7 5 6 8 4 9 6 6 6, and then executes options FIRSTOBS= and OBS= from which SAS gets the values 5 6 8 4 9.

This order is the same even if we use FIRSTOBS= and OBS= as a system option. The following program creates the same output:

```
OPTION OBS=6 FIRSTOBS=2;
PROC PRINT DATA =s(WHERE=(a>3));
RUN;
```

Notice that in *SAS Language Reference: Dictionary (v8)*, the following statement is not accurate:

FIRSTOBS must be set to 1 in order to use a WHERE statement or a WHERE= data set option. By default, FIRSTOBS=1.

However, we have to talk about OBS= and FIRSTOBS= options from one point of view. Here we use instream input or INFILE input with double trailing at sign (@@). You have to know how options OBS= and FIRSTOBS= affect this kind of input. Let's run the following code:

```
OPTIONS FIRSTOBS=2 OBS=3;
DATA s;
   INPUT a @@;
CARDS;
1 2 3
4 5 6
7 8 9
10 11 12
;
PROC PRINT;RUN;
```

```
Obs    a

 2     5
 3     6
```

For the instream input, options OBS= and FIRSTOBS= do not mean observations; they mean lines. Therefore, the example means to input the following data:

```
4 5 6
7 8 9
```

Actually, you can find the following message in the log file:

```
NOTE: The data set WORK.S has 6 observations and 1 variables.
```

When coming to the step PROC PRINT, SAS uses the options OBS= and FIRSTOBS= again. Now you can understand the printout.

Usually options OBS= and FIRSTOBS= are used to test a program. Notice that these options affect each step in the program. For example, in the above example, they affect both DATA step and PROC PRINT step. So many times we need to set them to default values.

Now we talk about relationship between WHERE= option and WHERE statement. For DROP, KEEP and RENAME, statements and options are independent, but WHERE= option and WHERE statement are not independent.

- The WHERE (option or statement) used to control reading data and that (option) to control output data are independent. To control reading data, you can only use variables in the input data set. To control output data, you can use all variables in PDV. See the following program:

```
DATA s;
   INPUT a @@;
CARDS;
1 5 15 24 30
;
DATA t(WHERE=(b>20));
   SET s;
   b=a+5;
   WHERE MOD(a,5);
PROC PRINT;RUN;
```

```
                    Obs    a    b

                     1     1    6
                     2    24   29
```

- In a DATA step, if there is an independent WHERE statement and a WHERE= option in a SET statement, only the option is effective. See the following program:

```
DATA s;
   a=5;b=3;
DATA t;
   SET s(WHERE=(a=5));
   WHERE b=3;
PROC PRINT;
RUN;
```

```
778  SET s(WHERE=(a=5));
779  WHERE b=3;
WARNING: The WHERE statement cannot be applied to a data set on the last
SET/MERGE/UPDATE/MODIFY statement.  Either the data sets listed failed with open errors
or they already specify a WHERE data set option.

NOTE: There were 1 observations read from the data set WORK.S.
```

```
WHERE a=5;
```

A WHERE statement appears to be redundant if we use a WHERE option, but sometimes we may still want to use both of them. See the following example:

```
DATA s;
   INPUT a b;
CARDS;
2 5
3 6
2 4
;
DATA t;
   INPUT a c;
CARDS;
1 3
2 4
;
DATA p;
   SET s t(WHERE=(a>1));
   WHERE a>2;
PROC PRINT;RUN;
```

The following is the message in the log file. It shows that the option for data set t overwrites a WHERE statement, so a WHERE statement only applies to data set s.

```
NOTE: There were 1 observations read from the data set WORK.S.
      WHERE a>2;
NOTE: There were 1 observations read from the data set WORK.T.
      WHERE a>1;
```

- For PROC, if there is an independent WHERE statement and a WHERE= option in a PROC statement for an input data set, SAS will combine the option and statement. See the following program:

```
PROC COMPARE DATA=s COMPARE=t(WHERE=(a<4));
   WHERE a>1;
RUN;
```

The following is the message in the log file:

```
NOTE: There were 3 observations read from the data set WORK.S.
      WHERE a>1;
NOTE: There were 1 observations read from the data set WORK.T.
      WHERE (a>1 and a<4);
```

Order of statements and options

Although it is not suitable to compare the order of executable statements with declarative statements or between declarative statements, because declarative statements are executed in the compilation phase, and executable statements are executed in each iteration. However, when writing programs, we can consider that SAS processes according to the some order in a DATA step, so we can use variables and their names correctly. The following are rules for a DATA step:

1. There may be more than one SET statement.
2. SAS divides a program into several parts according to SET statements. We call the part of a DATA step from one SET statement up to the next SET statement a *sector*.
3. SAS executes statements before any sector (pre-sector) first. Then SAS executes sector by sector according to their order.
4. In each sector, SAS executes statements according to some order as shown in Figure 1.

The following program shows that SAS first executes statements in pre-sector, then those in sectors.

```
DATA set1;
   a=4;b=3;OUTPUT;
   a=6;b=4;OUTPUT;
   a=5;b=4;OUTPUT;
DATA t;
   c+1;
   PUT _N_= 'pre-sector ' a= c=;
   SET set1 ;
   WHERE a<6;
   PUT _N_= 'first sector  ' a= c=;
RUN;
```

```
_N_=1 pre-sector a=. c=1
_N_=1 first sector  a=4 c=1
_N_=2 pre-sector a=4 c=2
_N_=2 first sector  a=5 c=2
_N_=3 pre-sector a=5 c=3
NOTE: There were 2 observations read from the data set WORK.SET1.
      WHERE a<6;
```

Figure 1. Pseudo flow of options and statements in DATA steps

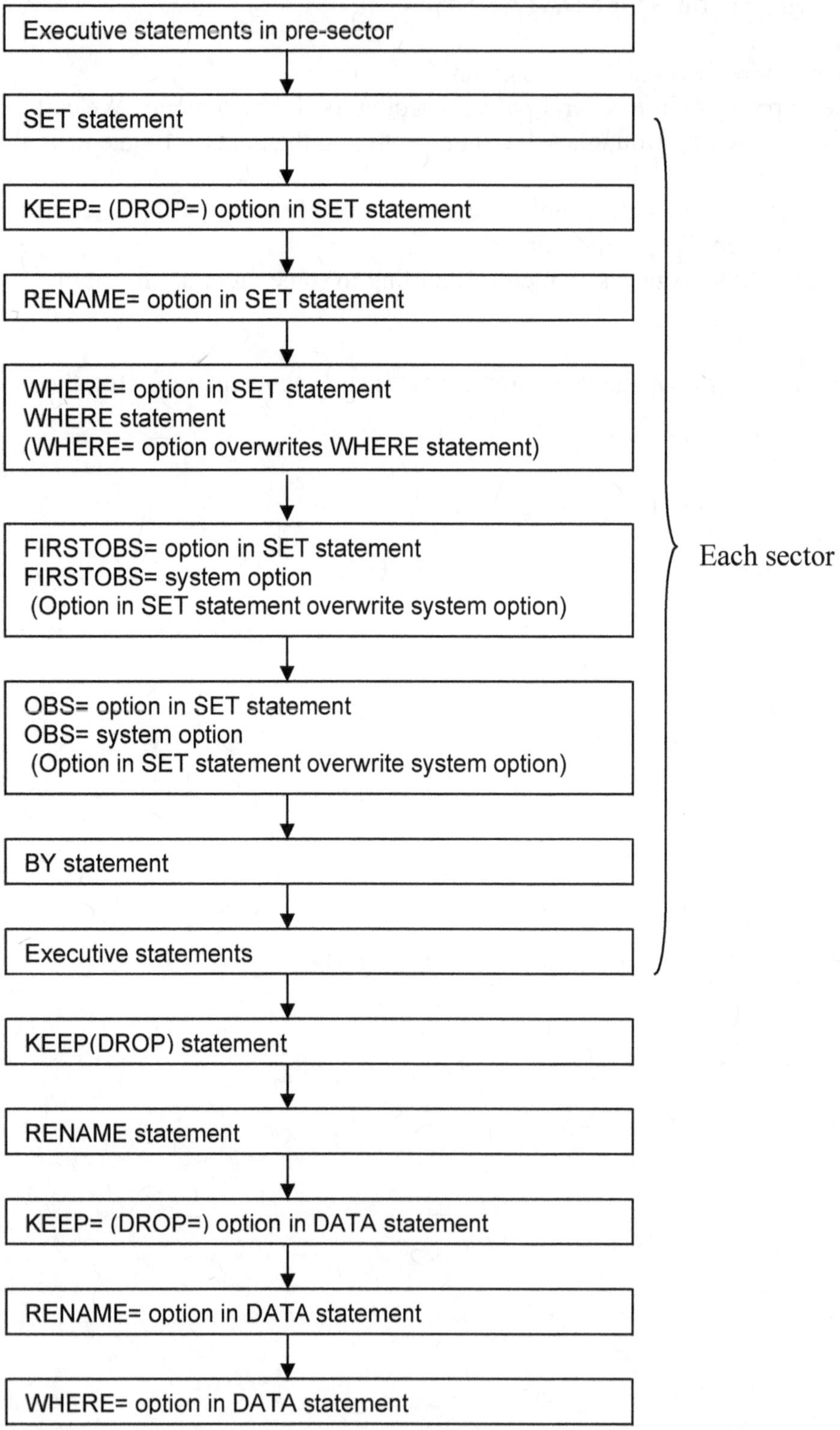

The following program shows the behaviors of the RENAME option and statement.

```
DATA s;
```

```
   a=8;
DATA t(RENAME=(c=d));
   SET s(RENAME=(a=b));
   RENAME b=c;
   IF b=8;
PROC PRINT;RUN;
```

These options can also be used in some PROCs. The order among them is similar to that in a DATA step. The following figure is for PROCs:

Figure 2. Pseudo flow of options and statements in some PROC steps

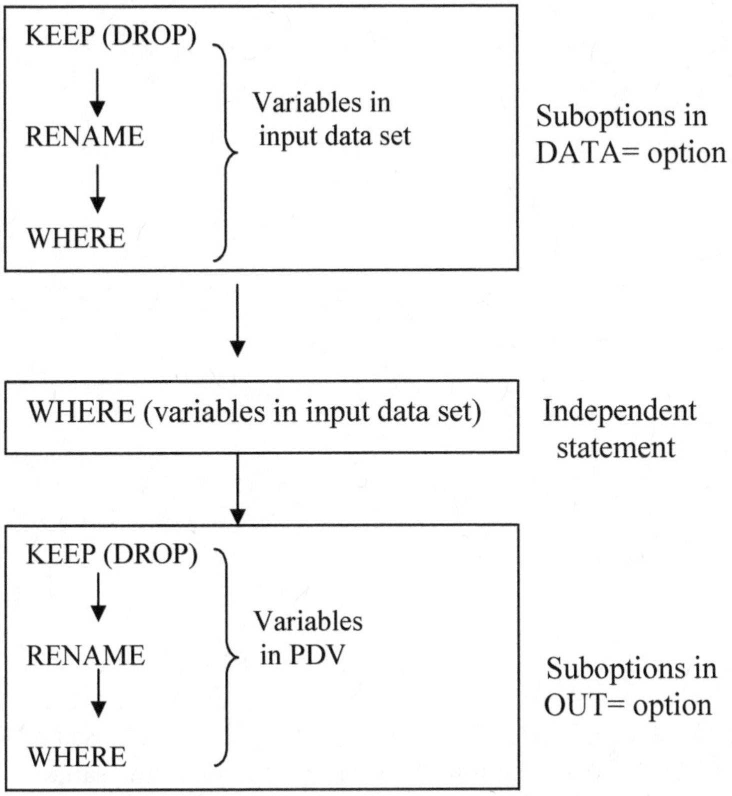

Order in PROC SQL

First notice that in PROC SQL, we can put KEEP=, DROP=, RENAME= and WHERE = options following a table name. This gives us some flexibility. For example, after dropping some columns or renaming some columns, we can use SELECT * (wildcard) from two tables, and there is no conflict. Notice the following:

- A WHERE= option and a WHERE clause are independent as the following example shows:

```
OPTIONS FIRSTOBS=1 OBS=MAX;
DATA s;
INPUT a @@;
```

```
CARDS;
4 2 1 2 7 6 8
;
PROC SQL;
SELECT * FROM s(WHERE=(a>3)) WHERE MOD(a,3)=1;
```

a
4
7

- A WHERE= option and a WHERE clause follow different rules as we discussed in [V]. See the following example:

```
DATA s;
INPUT a b;
CARDS;
3 5
0 2
1 0
;
PROC SQL;
SELECT * FROM s WHERE ^a*b;
SELECT * FROM s(WHERE =(^a*b));
```

a	b
0	2
1	0

a	b
0	2

Notice that in PROC SQL, there are no option OBS= and FIRSTOBS=, but the system options OBS= and FIRSTOBS= still work. The conclusion we discussed in the last section are also true for PROC SQL, i.e., SAS first executes the WHERE clause and then system options OBS= and FIRSTOBS=. The following program creates the same printout as the example in the last section (DATA step with WHERE statement):

```
DATA s;
   INPUT a @@;
CARDS;
2 7 3 5 3 6 8 4 3 9 6 6 6
;
OPTION OBS=6 FIRSTOBS=2;
PROC SQL;
   SELECT a FROM s WHERE a>3;
RUN;
```

In PROC SQL, there are options INOBS= and OUTOBS=. The option INOBS= determines how many observation to read and OUTOBS= determines how many observations to output. If you think that SAS first executes INOBS=, then a WHERE clause, and then OUTOBS=, that is wrong. Actually, a WHERE clause is executed before INOBS=. See the following program:

```
OPTIONS FIRSTOBS=1 OBS=MAX;
DATA s;
   INPUT a @@;
CARDS;
2 7 3 5 3 6 8 4 3 9 6 6 6
;
PROC SQL INOBS=4;
   SELECT a FROM s WHERE a>3;
RUN;
```

```
       a
--------
       7
       5
       6
       8
```

When comparing the options INOBS= and OUTOBS= with the system options OBS= and FIRSTOBS=, SAS executes the system option first. As the following example shows, SAS first executes the WHERE clause, then system option FIRSTOBS=, and then option INOBS=:

```
OPTIONS FIRSTOBS=1 OBS=MAX;
DATA s;
   INPUT a @@;
CARDS;
2 7 3 5 3 6 8 4 3 9 6 6 6
;
OPTION OBS=MAX FIRSTOBS=2;
PROC SQL INOBS=3;
   SELECT a FROM s WHERE a>3;
RUN;
```

```
       a
--------
       5
       6
       8
```

Now we will concentrate on order of clauses in a SELECT statement. There are the following clauses: WHERE, GROUP BY, ORDER BY, and HAVING. Also, there are calculations of summary functions. They have the following order for the syntax:

```
SELECT *,AVG(a) FROM s WHERE b>3 GROUP BY a HAVING b<=AVG(b) ORDER BY
a;
```

For the executing order, they have the following order:

GROUP BY clause (in SELECT clause and in HAVING clause)

Calculation of summary functions
HAVING clause
ORDER BY clause

Let's see the following example:

```
OPTIONS FIRSTOBS=1 OBS=MAX;
DATA s;
   INPUT a b;
CARDS;
1 3
1 4
1 5
2 4
2 5
;
PROC SQL ;
   SELECT *,AVG(b) FROM s GROUP BY a HAVING b>3;
QUIT;
```

a	b	
1	5	4
1	4	4
2	5	4.5
2	4	4.5

Therefore, it is reasonable to guess the executing order in a SELECT statement:

WHERE clause
System options FIRSTOBS= and OBS=
PROC SQL option INOBS=
GROUP BY clause
Calculation of summary functions
HAVING clause
ORDER BY clause
PROC SQL option OUTOBS=

Let's see the following example:

```
OPTION FIRSTOBS=2 OBS=14;
DATA s;
   DO i=1 TO 5;
   DO j=1 TO 5;
      OUTPUT;
   END;
   END;
PROC SQL INOBS=8 OUTOBS=7;
SELECT *,AVG(j) FROM s HAVING j>3;
SELECT * FROM S HAVING j>AVG(j);
SELECT * FROM s WHERE i IN (2 3 4) GROUP BY i HAVING COUNT(*)=4 ;
QUIT;
```

i	j	
1	4	3
1	5	3
2	4	3

i	j
1	4
1	5
2	4

i	j
2	4
2	2
2	3
2	5
3	3
3	2
3	1

For the first SELECT statement, options FIRSTOBS= and OBS= determine that the set of j is (2,3,4,5,1,2,3,4,5,1,2,3,4), and option INOBS= determines the set to be (2,3,4,5,1,2,3,4), whose average is 3. The second SELECT statement has the same results because AVG(j)=3. For the last SELECT statement, SAS first executes the WHERE clause, then system options, then PROC SQL option INOBS=, then the HAVING clause, and finally the PROC SQL option OUTOBS=. Therefore, we get the following flow:

Figure 3. Pseudo flow in a PROCSQL SELECT statement

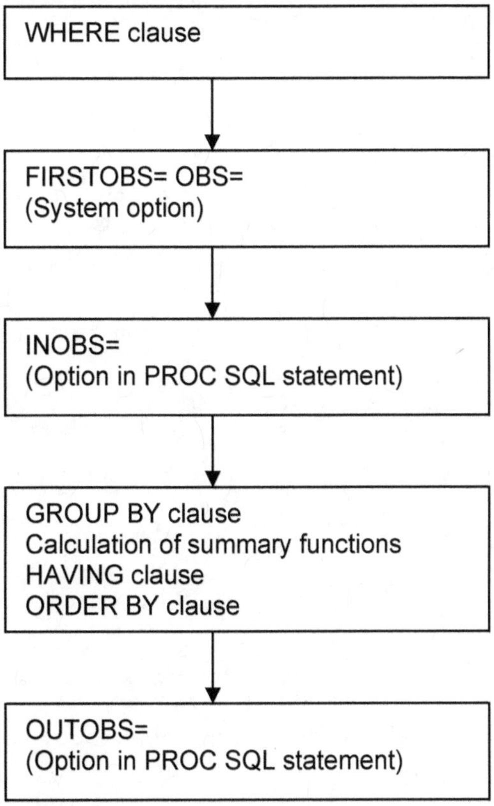

However, there are some exceptions. First in the above examples, there are summary functions. When there is no summary function, a HAVING clause works the same as a WHERE clause. Notice that in the above example, AVG(j)=3. Let's run the following program:

```
OPTION FIRSTOBS=2 OBS=14;
PROC SQL INOBS=8 OUTOBS=7;
SELECT * FROM s HAVING j>3;
SELECT * FROM s WHERE j>3;
QUIT;
```

Both statements have the same printout as the following:

i	j
1	5
2	4
2	5
3	4
3	5
4	4
4	5

Let's try another example:

```
OPTIONS FIRSTOBS=1 OBS=MAX;
DATA s;
   INPUT a @@;
CARDS;
2 2 7 6 6 8 8 8
;
OPTION OBS=MAX FIRSTOBS=2;
PROC SQL INOBS=3;
   SELECT * FROM s WHERE a>5;  ❶
   SELECT * FROM s HAVING a>5;  ❷
   SELECT *,AVG(a),COUNT(a) FROM s WHERE a>5;  ❸
   SELECT *,AVG(a),COUNT(a) FROM s HAVING a>5;  ❹
QUIT;
```

a
6
6
8

a
6
6
8

a		
6	6.666667	3
6	6.666667	3

```
8  6.666667         3

a
-------------------------------
7             5     3
6             5     3
```

Let's analyze the above program in detail:

❶ and ❸ are the same. They work the following way: WHERE a>5 (7 6 6 8 8 8), FIRSTOBS=2 (6 6 8 8 8), INBOS=3 (6 6 8), calculates AVG (=6.67), and COUNT (=3).

❹ is different from ❶ and ❸ because it has summary functions. It works as follows: FIRSTOBS=2 (2 7 6 6 8 8 8), INBOS=3 (2 7 6), AVG=5, and COUNT=3, HAVING a>5 (5 from inquery) (7 6).

❷ has no summary function, so it is the same as ❶, but not ❹.

Now we consider a WHERE clause again. As we know, a WHERE clause cannot have a summary function, but it can have a subquery. Also for a subquery, SAS first picks a row from an outer query, and then SAS executes the subquery and checks the WHERE condition to decide if the row should be displayed. So there is a difference from what we discussed earlier. Let's see the following example:

```
OPTIONS FIRSTOBS=1 OBS=MAX;
DATA s;
INPUT a @@;
CARDS;
2 2 7 6 6 8 8 8
;
RUN;
OPTIONS FIRSTOBS=2;
PROC SQL INOBS=3;
SELECT *,AVG(a) AS where_avg,COUNT(a) AS where_count
   FROM s WHERE a>(SELECT AVG(a) FROM s); ❺
SELECT *,AVG(a) AS having_avg,COUNT(a) AS having_count
   FROM s HAVING a>(SELECT AVG(a) FROM s); ❻
```

a	where_avg	where_count
7	6.5	2
6	6.5	2

a	having_avg	having_count
7	5	3
6	5	3

In this example, ❻ is the same as ❹ in the above example, but ❺ is different from any of them. It works as follows: FIRSTOBS=2 (2 7 6 6 8 8 8), INBOS=3 (2 7 6), WHERE a>5 (5 from inquery)(7 6), AVG=6.5 and COUNT=2.

Mystery of PROC SORT

Let's talk about PROC SORT. We know that it has the option NODUPLICATES|NODUPREC|NODUP, which removes identical adjacent rows. Also in a DATA= option and an OUT= option, we have KEEP= and DROP= (WHERE=, RENAME= as well) suboptions. Let's see the following example:

```
DATA s;
   INPUT a b;
CARDS;
1 1
1 2
1 2
1 3
1 2
;
RUN;
PROC SORT DATA =s(KEEP=a) OUT=t NODUP;BY a;
PROC PRINT;
RUN;
```

In the program, SAS does three things: KEEP, SORT and NODUP (removes identical adjacent rows). So what is their order? I think that you must be thinking the same thing that I am: SAS first does KEEP, then does SORT and NODUP. So how many observations are there in the printout? It should be one. But let's see the printout:

Obs	a
1	1
2	1
3	1
4	1

It is different from the following program:

```
DATA t;
   SET s;
   KEEP a;
PROC SORT DATA=t NODUP;
   BY a;
RUN;
```

It looks like SAS first does NODUP SORT and then does KEEP. I don't know how to explain this. Anyway, the important point is to know how SAS works. Even if I don't know why, at least I know how. In the above program, if we use the option NODUPKEY, the results will be different.

Let's see the following program:

```
PROC SORT DATA =s(KEEP=a) NODUP;BY a;
RUN;
PROC SORT NODUP;BY a; RUN;
```

Now how many observations are left in the data set? Four. When SAS runs first SORT, there are four observations left as the above example shows. When SAS runs the second SORT, since the data set is already sorted, SAS does not run sort again. Therefore, the final data set still has four observations. This may seem strange to you. Try to understand SAS. However, the following program behaves differently:

```
PROC SORT DATA =s(KEEP=a) NODUP;BY a;
RUN;
PROC SORT NODUP FORCE;BY a; RUN;
```

WHERE statement, BY statement, and LENGTH statement

As we know, both a WHERE statement and a BY statement are executed immediately after a SET statement, and the WHERE statement is executed before the BY statement. Now we will talk about their relationship to a LENGTH statement.

As we know, a LENGTH statement must be put before a SET statement if you want it to be effective, and a SET statement must be before a WHERE statement. This is the order in the program. But when SAS executes a WHERE statement, it does not care about the length setting. In other words, the length setting affects variables in PDV, but a WHERE statement concerns only variables in the original data set. The following program creates the two data sets t and p from data set s. However, data set t has two observations because an IF statement takes values from PDV, and the LENGTH statement is already in effect, so the value of a becomes 'ab' in both observations. But data set p has one observation because the WHERE statement does not care about LENGTH setting, and the values of variable a are still 'abc' and 'ab,' respectively. So it is not suitable to write order as LENGTH -> SET -> WHERE. Anyway, the most important thing is understanding.

```
DATA s;
a='abc';OUTPUT;
a='ab';OUTPUT;
DATA t;
LENGTH a $2;
SET s;
IF a='ab';
DATA p;
LENGTH a $2;
SET s;
WHERE a='ab';
PROC PRINT;RUN;
```

```
NOTE: There were 2 observations read from the data set WORK.S.
NOTE: The data set WORK.T has 2 observations and 1 variables.

NOTE: There were 1 observations read from the data set WORK.S.
      WHERE a='ab';
NOTE: The data set WORK.P has 1 observations and 1 variables.
```

Now what happens for a BY statement? It is different from a WHERE statement, i.e., it uses values in PDV. Let's see the following example:

```
DATA x;
LENGTH a $2;
SET s;
BY a;
RUN;
```

We can see that SAS gives a WARNING message, but the program is OK because when it comes to the BY statement, the LENGTH statement is already in effect.

Let us see one more thing. Suppose we want to do the following three things:

1. Get data set s from data set t;
2. Change the variable's length attribute;
3. Rename the variable name.

Since we want to change the length attribute, we have to use a LENGTH statement before the SET statement. Now the question is, in a LENGTH statement, should we use the old variable name or the new variable name? For a RENAME statement, we use the old variable name, and for option RENAME= in a SET statement, we use the new variable name. Otherwise, it does not work. See the following program:

```
DATA s;
var='ab'; var1='ab';
DATA t;
LENGTH var $1 var2 $1;
SET s(RENAME=(var1=var2));
RENAME VAR=var3;
PROC PRINT;
RUN;
```

Reference

"DKRICOND= System Option", *SAS 9.1.3 Language Reference: Dictionary* 2006. Cary, NC: SAS Institute Inc.
http://support.sas.com/documentation/onlinedoc/91pdf/sasdoc_913/base_lrdictionary_10307.pdf

"DKROCOND= System Option", *SAS 9.1.3 Language Reference: Dictionary* 2006. Cary, NC: SAS Institute Inc.
http://support.sas.com/documentation/onlinedoc/91pdf/sasdoc_913/base_lrdictionary_10307.pdf

"Dropping, Keeping, and Renaming Variables", in *SAS 9.1.3 Language Reference: Concepts* 2006. Cary, NC: SAS Institute Inc.
http://support.sas.com/documentation/onlinedoc/91pdf/sasdoc_913/base_lrconcept_9196.pdf

Options NOBS=, END=, and EOF=

Introduction

In a DATA step, sometimes we need to know the end of the data set that we are reading. We have several ways to do this, as Table 1 shows.

Table 1. Options to indicate the end of a data set

Statement	END=	NOBS=	EOF=
SET	x	x	
MERGE	x		
UPDATE	x		
MODIFY	x	x	
INFILE	x		x

We can see that these options can be used in different statements. We can use them to control the end of a data set although their usages are slightly different. As long as we don't take a subset of an input data set, usually we can use any of them. However, the difference will appear when we take a subset of an input data set. We are going to discuss how SAS works on them and how to use these options.

NOBS= option

NOBS= value gives the number of observations in an input data set. SAS sets the NOBS= value at the compilation phase. Usually people use it for two purposes: to get the number of observations in the input data set or to check the last observation. In the following program there are three DATA steps. The second DATA step assigns the number of observations in the input data set to a macro variable and the third DATA step output information to a new data set after reading the last observation.

```
DATA set1;
INPUT a b;
CARDS;
 1 3
 1 4
 2 3
 2 4
 ;
DATA _NULL_;
SET set1 NOBS=obs;
IF _N_=1 THEN CALL SYMPUT('s_ttl',obs);
STOP;
DATA t;
SET set1 NOBS=obs;
s+a;
IF _N_=obs THEN OUTPUT;
RUN;
```

Let's see what the SAS manual says about the NOBS= option.

NOBS=variable

creates and names a temporary variable whose value is usually the total number of observations in the input data set or data sets. If more than one data set is listed in the SET statement, NOBS= the total number of observations in the data sets that are listed.

At compilation time, SAS reads the descriptor portion of each data set and assigns the value of the NOBS= variable automatically. Thus, you can refer to the NOBS= variable before the SET statement.

Therefore, the value of a NOBS= variable is fixed. It comes from the input data set or data sets. The value of the NOBS= variable does not change, no matter how you manipulate the data. It is independent with a subsetting IF statement or a WHERE statement, even with option OBS= and FIRSTOBS=. See the following example. In this case we cannot use its value to determine the end of the data set since we don't have the number of iterations that reaches the value.

```
DATA t;
SET set1(OBS=1) NOBS=tot;
s+a;
PUT _N_= tot=;
RUN;
```

```
_N_=1 tot=4
```

END= option

However, most programmers use END= to determine if the last observation is reached. The following is a typical usage:

```
DATA t;
SET set1 END=end;
s+a;
IF end THEN OUTPUT;
RUN;
```

Compared to NOBS=, END= is more useful and more complicated. Let's first look at what is said in the SAS manual.

END=variable

creates and names a temporary variable that contains an end-of-file indicator. The variable, which is initialized to zero, is set to 1 when SET reads the last observation of the last data set listed.

END=variable

names a variable that SAS sets to 1 when the current input data record is the last in the input file. Until SAS processes the last data record, the END= variable is set to 0.

From the description, END= values are set by the SET statement during the execution of a program. The following program shows the difference between the NOBS= value and the END= values. The former is not affected by the OBS= option, but the latter is.

```
DATA s;
DO i=1 TO 4;
OUTPUT;
END;
DATA t;
SET set1(OBS=2) NOBS=tot END=end;
PUT _N_= tot= end=;
RUN;
```

```
_N_=1 tot=4 end=0
_N_=2 tot=4 end=1
```

Now compare the following two pieces of code. The first piece of code gives a summary data set, but the second piece of code gives an empty data set because _N_ only takes value 1, 2 and 3, and _N_=tot never happens.

```
DATA t;
SET set1(OBS=3) END=end;
s+a;
IF end THEN OUTPUT;
RUN;

DATA t;
SET set1(OBS=3) NOBS=tot;
s+a;
IF _N_=tot THEN OUTPUT;
RUN;
```

You can see in this case that we can use the END= value to control the end of a data set, but we cannot use the NOBS= value to do this.

Now we consider relationship between END= values and a subsetting IF statement. Let's run the following program:

```
DATA s;
SET set1 END=end1;
IF a<2;
PUT 'In data set s ' _N_= end1=;
RUN;
DATA t;
SET set1 END=end2;
IF a>1;
PUT 'In data set t ' _N_= end2=;
RUN;
```

```
In data set s _N_=1 end1=0
In data set s _N_=2 end1=0

In data set t _N_=3 end2=0
```

```
In data set t _N_=4 end2=1
```

In this program there are two DATA steps. The first DATA step reads in observations 1 and 2. The second DATA step reads in observations 3 and 4, where observation 4 is the last observation in the input data set. Therefore, in data set s, there is no observation with an END= value of 1, but in data set t, the last observation has the END= value of 1. In other words, in the first DATA step, we cannot control the end of the data set, but in the second DATA step, we can. In other words again, whether or not we can control the end of a data set depends on whether the IF condition is true for the last observation.

For data set s, although we cannot use an END= setting since they are all 0, it is also reasonable. For data set t, when SAS reads the fourth observation, SAS knows that it is the last observation in the input data set, so SAS sets the END= value to 1. However, for data set s, when SAS reads in the second observation, there are still observations in the input data set that will be read by later iteration. How does SAS know if they will be processed (satisfy the IF condition)? Therefore it is reasonable for SAS to set the END= value to 0 for the second iteration, the last observation that is being processed.

It is reasonable, but you can see that it may not be useful because we cannot control the last observation that satisfies the IF condition. All END= values are 0. However, a WHERE statement has different behaviors. Try the following program:

```
DATA p;
SET set1 END=end1;
WHERE a<2;
PUT _N_= end1= ;
RUN;
```

```
_N_=1 end1=0
_N_=2 end1=1
```

This also applies to the WHERE= option in a SET statement. See the following example:

```
DATA p;
SET set1(WHERE=(a<2)) END=end1;
PUT _N_= end1= ;
RUN;
```

Here we have a similar situation. For a WHERE statement, when SAS did the second iteration and set the END= value to 1, SAS must know that there are no more observations satisfying the WHERE condition. It is hard for an IF statement to do so, but it is easy for a WHERE statement. As we know, an IF statement is executed after an observation is read in, and then SAS decides if the observation is needed to continue the process. In each iteration, SAS reads only one observation. But a WHERE statement reads data until an observation satisfies the WHERE condition. Therefore, to determine END= values, the only thing needed is to read the next observation in each iteration. We have already seen that a BY statement does this [III], and we know that a BY statement and a WHERE statement are very similar. Therefore, we can conclude that WHERE statement reads the next observation too, and that observation is used to set END= value for the current observation. Precisely, if the WHERE statement reads in the next observation, then the END= value of the current observation is set to 0, and otherwise to 1.

So we can say that when there is a WHERE statement, the END= values are set by the WHERE statement. In other words, END= values are set in a SET statement if there is no WHERE statement, and they are set in a WHERE statement otherwise.

As we know, we can use END= values in an IF statement but not in a WHERE statement. Therefore, we have the following conclusion:

An IF statement can read END= values but cannot set them;
A WHERE statement will set END= values but cannot read them.

At beginning of this paper, we see that an OBS= option affects the END= value setting. As we know, a WHERE statement is executed before an OBS= option [III]. Therefore, we can say that SAS uses a SET statement, a WHERE statement, and an OBS= options to determine END= values. See the following example.

```
DATA s;
DO i=1 TO 10;
OUTPUT;
END;
OPTION OBS=3;
DATA t;
SET s END=end;
WHERE i>3;
PUT end= _n_=;
RUN;
```

```
end=0 _N_=1
end=0 _N_=2
end=1 _N_=3
```

If there is more than one data set in the same SET statement, END= treats them as one set that results from concatenation. The rule is the same for the case in which there is only one data set.

If there is more than one SET statement in a DATA step, each SET statement can have an END= setting. The above rules apply for each SET statement. Let's see the following example. For data set p, SAS reads three observations from set3, and the last one has END1=1. SAS reads two observations from set4, and the latter one has END2=1. The final data set has min(3,2) observations and end1=0, end2=1.

```
DATA set3;
INPUT a b;
CARDS;
1 3
```

```
2 4
3 5
;
DATA set4 ;
INPUT c d;
CARDS;
1 3
2 4
3 5
4 6
;
DATA p;
SET set3 END=end1;
WHERE a<4;
PUT end1=;
SET set4 END=end2;
PUT end1= end2= a= b= c= d=;
WHERE c<3;
RUN;
```

```
end1=0
end1=0 end2=0 a=1 b=3 c=1 d=3
end1=0
end1=0 end2=1 a=2 b=4 c=2 d=4
end1=1
NOTE: There were 3 observations read from the data set WORK.SET3.
      WHERE a<4;
NOTE: There were 2 observations read from the data set WORK.SET4.
      WHERE c<3;
NOTE: The data set WORK.P has 2 observations and 4 variables.
```

Therefore, if we want to do something for the last observation, we have to write the statement as

IF end=1 or end2=1 then *action*;

EOF= option

Finally, we will talk about the EOF= option. As Table 1 shows, this is only for an INFILE statement. Its value, the right side of the equal sign, is a label of a statement. Notice that END= has some restriction for an INFILE statement as is stated in the SAS manual.

> **Restriction:** You cannot use the END= option with
>
> - the UNBUFFERED option
> - the DATALINES or DATALINES4 statement
> - an INPUT statement that reads multiple input data records.
>
> **Tip:** Use the option EOF= when END= is invalid.

People may think that options EOF= and END= have the same effect if the END= option is valid. This is not true. Notice that we cannot use a WHERE statement here. The difference appears when a subsetting IF statement is used. Let's see the following example. Suppose we have a file temp1.txt in directory c:\temp with the following contents:

```
1
2
3
4
5
6
7
8
9
```

Now run the following program:

```
DATA s1;
INFILE 'c:\temp\temp1.txt' EOF=g;
INPUT i;
*PUT _n_= i= a=;
*IF i<5;
a+1;
OUTPUT;
RETURN;
g:PUT "total obs read in with EOF option: " a;
RUN;

DATA s2;
INFILE 'c:\temp\temp1.txt' END=end;
INPUT i;
*PUT _n_= i= a=;
*IF i<5;
a+1;
IF end THEN PUT "total obs read in with END option: " a;
RUN;
```

The following is the printout in the log file.

```
total obs read in with EOF option: 9
total obs read in with END option: 9
```

Now we recover the statement IF i<5; in both steps, although the data sets created in two steps are the same, in the log file there is no printout from the second DATA step. As we have already discussed, the END= value will never be 1, but the first DATA step will eventually reach EOF.

Another difference appears when there is a double trailing at sign (@@) in the INPUT statement. Suppose we have the following data in c:\temp\temp2.txt.

1 2 3 4 5

We run the following program:

```
DATA s1;
INFILE 'c:\temp\temp2.txt' EOF=g;
INPUT i @@;
a+1;
OUTPUT;
RETURN;
g:PUT "total obs read in with EOF option: " a;
RUN;

DATA s2;
INFILE 'c:\temp\temp2.txt' END=end;
INPUT i @@;
a+1;
IF end THEN PUT "total obs read in with END option: " a;
RUN;
```

We see the following printouts in the log file:

```
total obs read in with EOF option: 5

total obs read in with END option: 1
total obs read in with END option: 2
total obs read in with END option: 3
total obs read in with END option: 4
total obs read in with END option: 5
```

We can see that SAS sets the END= value to 1 for every observation. We can also run the following program

```
DATA s2;
INFILE 'c:\temp\temp2.txt' END=end;
INPUT i @@;
abc=end;
PROC PRINT;
RUN;
```

Obs	i	abc
1	1	1
2	2	1
3	3	1
4	4	1
5	5	1

Therefore, in this case if we want to use the END= option, we have to separate the DATA step into two DATA steps.

Now we make a comparison of these settings from the program point of view.

The option NOBS= assigns to the specified variable the number of observations in an input data set. It is set in compilation phase and will not change in the DATA step. You can use it before a SET statement.

For the option END=, SAS uses a SET statement, a WHERE statement, and an OBS= option to determine END= values. Don't use it in an INFILE statement if you use double trailing at signs (@@) in the INPUT statement.

The right side of an option EOF= is a label, not a variable. This tells SAS to check when executing the INFILE statement if it is the end of the input file. If it is, SAS goes to the label assigned to EOF= option.

Notice that options END= and EOF= are also slightly different. You can use END= to modify the last observation, but you cannot do this by using EOF=.

Reference

SAS 9.1.3 Language Reference: Dictionary 2006. Cary, NC: SAS Institute Inc. http://support.sas.com/documentation/onlinedoc/91pdf/sasdoc_913/base_lrdictionary_10307.pdf

Operators in the SAS language

Introduction

Expressions are often used in SAS programming. In SAS programming, they are used in assignments, IF statements, WHERE statements etc. An expression consists of values (variables), operators and functions. In this paper we talk about operators. Every SAS programmer knows operators and uses them in his/her programming. However, there are some details or tricky parts that people may not notice. We need to discuss operators in detail. That is the purpose of this paper.

There are four kinds of operators: arithmetic, comparison (We categorize MAX and MIN as comparison), logic, and concatenation. We suppose that readers already know how SAS does operations when there is only one operator, especially a comparison operator between two numeric values and that between two character values.

In SAS, there are four places to use operators. Most operators are similar in these four places, but their usage may be different.

- A DATA step, except in a WHERE statement and a WHERE option; (Sometimes we say: in an IF statement)
- A WHERE statement in a DATA step or in some PROC, including a WHERE option for a specified data set
- PROC SQL
- Macro language, in an implicit or explicit function %EVAL and in a function %SYSEVALF.

We will give four tables to show what operators SAS have in each place and how they work.

When we talk about operators, what factors do we need to consider?

First, we have to consider precedence. I suppose that people know the operators ^ (NOT) and + (plus), so what is the value of ^3+4? In other words, is it evaluated as ^(3+4) or (^3)+4? Comparing ^ and +, which one will be executed first? This is the precedence of operators. In SAS, as in other languages, we give each operator a precedence number. The smaller the number is, the higher the precedence. If two operators with different precedence are put together, SAS will execute the operator with higher precedence first.

The second factor is associativity. If two operators with the same precedence are put together, which one will be executed first? For example, people know exponentiation (**) and 2**3=8. What is the result of 2**3**2? In other words, is it evaluated as 2**(3**2) (from right to left) or (2**3)**2 (from left to right)? We have to consider associativity.

The third factor is operands. An operator needs operands, one or two. When we learned them in school, we rarely asked this question. First we learned integers, then rational numbers, then real numbers, and then complex numbers. We don't have questions for operands. However, SAS has its own characteristics. It has two types of values: numeric and character. Does SAS allow character value as an operand of +? If the answer is yes, how does SAS handle this situation?

For example, conditions in an IF statement, a WHERE statement, a WHERE clause (PROC SQL), and an %IF statement all need a Boolean value. In an IF statement and a WHERE statement either a numeric value or a character value is OK, and it will be converted to a Boolean value, but only a numeric value is allowed in a WHERE clause, and only an integer value is allowed in an %IF statement. In other words, an operator in different places may have different requirements for operand types. Although both an IF statement and a WHERE statement allow a character value as the condition and will convert it to a Boolean value, they have different converting rules. In other words, for operands of an operator in different places, we not only have to consider value types, allowed or not allowed, but have to consider how SAS evaluate the operation for a specific value type if it is allowed as well.

Another factor is the return type of values. This is relatively easy. The last one is position. This is the easiest one. There are two kinds of operators in SAS: prefix and infix. Prefix positive, prefix negative, and NOT are prefix operators that need only one operand on their right side. All others are infix operators that need two operands.

Comparing operators used in four places, there are slight differences on precedence and associativity. However, as we have seen from the above examples, big differences are for operands.

In this paper, we have the following kinds of operands:

- Numeric_c: needs numeric values. Character values will be converted to numeric values;
- Numeric_p: (p means pure) needs numeric values. Character values do not work;
- Integer/Text: Integer comparison if both are integers, text comparison otherwise.
- Character_c: needs character values. Numeric values will be converted to character values;
- Character_p: needs character values. Numeric values do not work;
- Num/Char: Both sides could be numeric value or character value. Numeric operation if at least one is numeric, character operation otherwise;
- Both: either both sides are numeric (numeric operation) or both sides are character (character operation). Mixed types are not allowed;
- Boolean_d: needs Boolean value. Both numeric values and character values are OK and will be converted to Boolean value. Character value will be converted to Boolean values according to the rules in DATA step;
- Boolean_w: needs Boolean value. Both numeric values and character values are OK and will be converted to Boolean value. Character value will be converted to Boolean values according to the rules in WHERE statement;

- Boolean_n: needs Boolean value. Only numeric values are allowed;
- Boolean_i: needs Boolean value. Only integer values are allowed;
- Either: Either type is OK.

DATA step operators

We first talk about operators in a DATA step. They are used for all operations such as assignments, IF conditions, DO statements, and so on, but not for WHERE statements. We summarize these operators in Table 1. Notice that we also put an assignment sign (=) in the table.

Table 1 Operators in a DATA step (sym.=symbol, mne.=mnemonic, pre.=precedence)

Sym.	Mne.	Meaning	Pre.	Operands	Return value	Associativity
()		Parentheses	0			
**		Exponentiation	1	Numeric_c	Numeric	Right-to-left
<>	MAX	Maximum	1	Num/Char	Num/Char	
><	MIN	Minimum	1	Num/Char	Num/Char	
+		Positive prefix	2	Either	Same as operand	
–		Negative prefix	2	Numeric_c	Numeric	
^, ~, ¬	NOT	Logical not	2	Boolean_d	Boolean	
*		Multiplication	3	Numeric_c	Numeric	Left-to-right
/		Division	3	Numeric_c	Numeric	
+		Addition	4	Numeric_c	Numeric	Left-to-right
–		Subtraction	4	Numeric_c	Numeric	
||, !!, ¦¦		Concatenation	5	Character_c	Character	Left-to-right
	IN	Belongs to	6	Left value right set Num/Char	Boolean	
	NOTIN	Does not belong to	6	Left value right set Num/Char	Boolean	
=	EQ	Equal to	7	Num/Char	Boolean	Same time
^=, ~=, ¬=	NE	Not equal to	7			
>	GT	Greater than	7			
<	LT	Less than	7			
>=	GE, NL	Greater than or equal to	7			
<=	LE, NG	Less than or equal to	7			
=:		Truncated equal to	7			
^=:		Truncated not equal to	7			
>=:		Truncated greater than or equal to	7			
>:		Truncated greater than	7			
<=:		Truncated less than or equal to	7			
<:		Truncated less than	7			
&	AND	Logical and	8	Boolean_d	Boolean	
|, !, ¦	OR	Logical or	9	Boolean_d	Boolean	

=		Assignment	10	Left variable right expression		

In the following we give some notes for Table 1:

- The following program shows you that the operator MAX has operands Num/Char:

```
DATA s;
INPUT a1 $ b1 $ a2 b2;
CARDS;
14 6 14 6
;
DATA t;
SET s;
max_ch=a1 MAX b1;
max_num=a2 MAX b2;
max_cn=a1 MAX b2;
max_nc=a2 MAX b1;
PROC PRINT;RUN;
```

```
a1    b1    a2    b2    max_ch    max_num    max_cn    max_nc

14    6     14    6     6           14         14         14
```

You can check that among four new variables, only max_ch (both sides are character) uses character comparison, and all others use numeric comparison. You can also look at the log file. There are conversion messages for max_cn and max_nc.

- The plus (+) and minus (–) signs can be either prefix or arithmetic operators. Notice that when using as a prefix, their operarand are different, as Table 1 shows. The way to decide what operator – is is easy, as declared in SAS Language Reference: Concepts (2005, p. 126),

The minus (-) sign can be either a prefix or arithmetic operator. A minus sign is a prefix operator only when it appears at the beginning of an expression or when it is immediately preceded by a left parenthesis or another operator.

However, the same statement for positive prefix is not true, as we will talk soon.

- For operator IN (NOTIN is similar.).

    - It is equivalent to a series of OR operators with the same variable or expression. The following two statements are equivalent:

```
IF ain ='12' OR ain ='ab' OR ain='.';
IF ain IN ('12' 'ab' '.');
```

    - Its right side is a list of values. They must be constants, either all numeric or all character.

- o We can use either a blank or a comma to separate values in the list, such as the following:

```
Name IN ('Joe','Edward')
A IN (3.5, 4 5)
```

- o Also, we can specify a range of sequential integers. The following two expressions are equivalent:

```
x IN (1,2,5:8)
x IN (1,2,5,6,7,8)
```

Notice that the set is a finite set, so we cannot use an IN operator for an interval like x<3.

- o Its operands are Num/Char. If both sides have the same type, than we don't have any doubt, and this is the common situation. If two sides have different types, then SAS converts the character value(s) to numeric and does comparison. However, when the left value is numeric and the set is character, the converting rule is strange, or we can say that there is a bug. See the following example:

```
DATA s;
     c='   5' in (5);d=5 in ('   5');e=. in ('   5');
proc print;
RUN;
```

```
Obs    c    d    e

 1     1    0    1
```

```
2641  DATA s;
2642  c='   5' in (5);d=5 in ('   5');e=. in ('   5');

NOTE: Character values have been converted to numeric values at the places given by:
(Line):(Column).
      2642:3    2642:19   2642:35
```

In one word, when values in the set are character and SAS converts them to numeric, only a standard numeric value with no leading blanks will be converted to numeric, and others will be converted to missing value.

- For a concatenation operator (||), logical AND, and logical OR, it doesn't matter whether evaluation is from left to right or from right to left; the results are the same. However, SAS evaluates them from left to right.

- In Table 1, we give precedence for each operator. For associativity, notice that there are three operators with precedence 1: **, MAX and MIN. Their associativity is right-to-left. All other arithmetic operators (+,-,* and /) have associativity left-to-right. The operators IN and NOTIN have no associativity because it cannot happen that two consecutive operators have precedence 6. In the following I give some examples to show how SAS applies precedence and associativity:

Expression	evaluates as		result
`2**3 MAX 5`	`2**(3 MAX 5)`	`2**5`	32
`2 MAX 5 ** 3`	`2 MAX (5 ** 3)`		125
`-2 MAX 5 ** 3`	`-(2 MAX(5 **3))`		-125
`2 MAX 3 MIN 1`	`2 MAX (3 MIN 1)`		2
`2 MIN 1 MAX 3`	`2 MIN (1 MAX 3)`	`2 MIN 3`	2
`~3+4`	`(~3)+4`	`0+4`	4
`1<2 IN (1,2)`	`1< (2 IN (1,2))`	`1<1`	0
`5-1 IN (1,2)`	`(5-1) IN (1,2)`	`4 IN (1,2)`	0
`1||'1'<23`	`'11'<23`	`11<23`	1

- Associativity "Same time" means that if there is more than one operator with precedence 8 occurring together, SAS does all the comparisons at the same time, returns the value "true" if all of them are true, and returns the value "false" otherwise. For example, the expression 3<5<7 is equivalent to the expression 3<5 AND 5<7, so the return value is "true." The expression 2=2=2 is equivalent to the expression 2=2 AND 2=2, so it returns the value 1. For the same reason, the expression 3<5>2 returns 1. Now you can safely use the expression 0<A<B<10 that just means 0<A AND A<B AND B<10. The exprcssion A<B>10 means A<B AND B>10 or B>MAX(A, 10). The following program is just for fun:

```
DATA s;
INPUT a $ b $ c;
CARDS;
6 19 6
;
DATA t;
SET s;
IF a>b>c THEN d=1;
PROC PRINT;
RUN;
```

Obs	a	b	c	d
1	6	19	6	1

Checking Table 1, the operands for > are Num/Char. When SAS compares a>b, it uses a character comparison, and the result is "true." When SAS compares b>c, it converts b to a numeric value, uses a numeric comparison, and the result is also "true." Consequently, the IF condition in the program is "true".

- We see that the equal sign (=) has two meanings. It can be a comparison operator or an assignment operator, so how does SAS determine its meaning?
  - There are three places that we can assign a value to a variable: independent assignments, including those as actions in THEN clauses and WHEN clauses, those in DO clause (in DO-TO statement), and sum statements.

- In an assignment (in the independent assignment or following the keyword DO, THEN and WHEN), the leftmost equal sign must be the second token following a name token. This equal sign is treated as assignment operator. Other equal signs, if there are any, will be treated as comparison operators.
- Equal signs in all other places, including those in "expressions" following the keywords IF, WHERE, UNTIL, WHILE, SELECT, WHEN, and TO, are treated as comparison operators.
- Therefore, if the variables a, b, c, and d have values 2, 3, 4, and 5, respectively, then after executing the statement a=b=c=d;, only the value of a is changed to 0 because the condition b=c=d is "false." If you have a background in some other languages, you have to be careful, for such syntax is different from that in some languages. This may also be convenient. For instance, you have a variable, SEX, which takes on the values f and m. Now you want to change them to the numeric values 1 and 0. You can write a statement like

```
Gender=sex='f';
```

That means

```
Gender=(sex='f');
```

which is equivalent to the following statements:

```
IF sex='f' THEN gender=1;
ELSE gender =0;
```

- When you are making a comparison, you have to pay attention to the following points:
  - Type of comparison: numeric or character
  - Upper and lower case letters in the case of character comparisons
  - Leading blanks in the case of character comparisons.

- The operators for truncated comparisons are also Num/Char, i.e. numeric comparison if at least one is numeric and character comparison otherwise. It is the same as a regular comparison for numeric comparison. The difference from regular comparisons is for character comparison. Suppose we have two character values A and B with m and n characters respectively including trilling blanks, where m<=n. For regular comparison, SAS compares n characters and fills blanks in the short one. For truncate comparison, SAS compares the first m characters. See the following example:

```
DATA s;
a='ab';
b='ab ';
c='abcd';
dt_ab=a=:b; dr_ab=a=b;
dt_bc=b=:c; dr_bc=b=c;
```

```
dt_ca=c=:a; dr_ca=c=a;
PROC PRINT NOOBS;RUN;
```

```
a     b     c      dt_ab    dr_ab    dt_bc    dr_bc    dt_ca    dr_ca

ab    ab    abcd     1        1        0        0        1        0
```

The most common usage of truncated comparison is to pick observations based on some first characters. For example, if we want to find a subset that patients' names begin with letter P, we can use the following equivalent statement.

```
IF lastname =:'P';
IF lastname >='P' and lastname <'Q';
IF 'P' <= lastname <'Q';
```

Operators in a WHERE statement

Notice that a WHERE statement can be used in a DATA step and a PROC step, except PROC SQL. Also, we can use WHERE= option in a DATA statement, SET, MERGE, MODIFY, and UPDATE statements or suboptions for a specified data set in a PROC statement, including a FROM clause and a CREATE-AS clause in PROC SQL. Variables must be in the corresponding input data set or PDV. Operations in all these places follow the same rules.

The WHERE statement has similar operators compared to those in Table 1, but the rules are very different. Table 2 gives operators for a WHERE statement.

Table 2. Operators in a WHERE statement
(P.= Precedence)

Symbol	Mnemonic	Meaning	P.	Operands	Return value	Associativity
()		Parentheses	0			
**		Exponentiation	1	Numeric_p	Numeric	Right-to-left
+		Positive prefix	2	Either	Either	
–		Negative prefix	2	Numeric_p	Numeric	
	MAX	Maximum	3	Both	Both	Left-to-right
	MIN	Minimum	3	Both	Both	
^, ~, ¬	NOT	Logical not	4	Boolean_w	Boolean	
*		Multiplication	5	Numeric_p	Numeric	Left-to-right
/		Division	5	Numeric_p	Numeric	
+		Addition	6	Numeric_p	Numeric	Left-to-right
–		Subtraction	6	Numeric_p	Numeric	
||		Concatenation	7	Character_p	Character	
	IN	Belongs to	8L*	Both	Boolean	
	NOTIN	Does not belong to	8L	Both		
	BETWEEN - AND		8L	Both		
?	CONTAINS		8L	Character_p		
	IS MISSING IS NULL		8L	Either		

	IS NOT MISSING IS NOT NULL		8L	Either		
	LIKE		8L	Character_p		
=*		Sounds-like	8L	Character_p		
=	EQ	Equal to	8	Both	Boolean	Same time
^=, ~=, ¬=, <>	NE	Not equal to	8			
>	GT	Greater than	8			
<	LT	Less than	8			
>=	GE	Greater than or equal	8			
<=	LE	Less than or equal	8			
=:		Truncated equal	8			
^=:		Truncated not equal	8			
>=:		Truncated great than or equal	8			
>:		Truncated great than	8			
<=:		Truncated less than or equal	8			
<:		Truncated less than	8			
&	AND	Logical and	9	Boolean_w	Boolean	
|	OR	Logical or	10	Boolean_w	Boolean	

*Operators with precedence 8L cannot be used together with any operator with precedence 8L or 8. In other words, the operator & or | must be between an operator with precedence 8L and any operator with precedence 8L or 8 if there are no parentheses.

Compare Table 2 with Table 1, and notice the following points:

- For arithmetic operators, in Table 1 it is Numeric_c. Character values will be converted to numeric. In Table 2, it is Numeric_p. Character values will cause ERROR and stop processing. See the following example:

```
DATA s;
a='14';
DATA t;
SET s;
IF a+1;
DATA p;
SET s;
WHERE a+1;
RUN;
```

```
NOTE: Character values have been converted to numeric values at the places given by:
      (Line):(Column).
      240:4
NOTE: There were 1 observations read from the data set WORK.S.
```

```
NOTE: The data set WORK.T has 1 observations and 1 variables.

ERROR: Where clause operator requires numeric variables.
NOTE: The SAS System stopped processing this step because of errors.
```

- For a concatenate operator, Table 1 is Character_c, and Table 2 is Character_p. See the following example:

```
DATA s;
a=14;
DATA t;
SET s;
IF 'ab'||a='ab          14';
DATA p;
SET s;
WHERE 'ab'||a='ab          14';
RUN;
```

```
165  IF 'ab'||a='ab          14';

NOTE: Numeric values have been converted to character values at the places given by:
      (Line):(Column).
      165:10
NOTE: There were 1 observations read from the data set WORK.S.

168  WHERE 'ab'||a='ab          14';
ERROR: Where clause operator requires character variables.
NOTE: The SAS System stopped processing this step because of errors.
```

- For comparison operators, operands in Table 1 are Num/Char, i.e. numeric comparison if at least one is numeric, and character comparison if both are character. Operands in Table 2 are Both, i.e., both numeric or both character, mixed cases are not allowed. See the following example:

```
DATA s;
a=2;
DATA t1;
SET s;
WHERE 3<4;
DATA t2;
SET s;
WHERE '3'<'4';
DATA t3;
SET s;
WHERE 3<'4';
RUN;
```

```
NOTE: There were 1 observations read from the data set WORK.S.
      WHERE 3<4;
NOTE: The data set WORK.T1 has 1 observations and 1 variables.

NOTE: There were 1 observations read from the data set WORK.S.
      WHERE '3'<'4';
NOTE: The data set WORK.T2 has 1 observations and 1 variables.
```

```
59    where 3<'4';
ERROR: Where clause operator requires compatible variables.
NOTE: The SAS System stopped processing this step because of errors.
```

- As well as expression itself, for logic operators, operators in Table 1 and those in Table 2 all convert numeric values and character values to Boolean. The rules to convert numeric to Booleans are the same. Missing value and 0 are converted to false and others to true. However, the rules to convert character values to Boolean values are different. The following figure shows when SAS does auto converting:

Figure 1. Conversion rules in a non-WHERE statement and in a WHERE statement

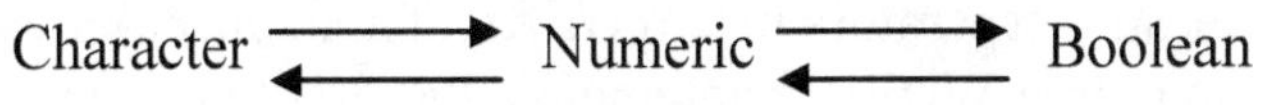

Auto converting in a data step (other than a WHERE statement)

Auto converting in a WHERE statement

The following table shows how SAS does auto converting:

Table 3. Rules to convert character values to Boolean values

	Convert to 0 (false)	Convert to 1 (true)
DATA step operators	Non standard numeric values, 0 and null value	Standard numeric value other than 0
Operators in a WHERE statement	Null value	Non-null value

Let's see the following example.

```
DATA s;
INPUT a $ b;
CARDS;
1 1
a 2
0 3
. 4
;
DATA t;
SET s;
IF a;
PROC PRINT;
DATA t2;
SET s;
WHERE a;
```

```
PROC PRINT;
RUN;
```

```
Obs    a    b

 1     1    1

Obs    a    b

 1     1    1
 2     a    2
 3     0    3
```

Notice that only for the expression (return value of the whole expression) or operands of NOT, AND, or OR in a WHERE statement, SAS will convert a character value to a Boolean value. For operands of other operators in a WHERE statement, SAS will not do this. Therefore, for the following three WHERE statements, the first two are syntax OK, but the last is not OK, where a is a character variable and b is either numeric or character.

```
WHERE a;
WHERE (a & b) +1;
WHERE (a)+1;
```

- The operators IS MISSING or IS NULL (IS NOT MISSING or IS NOT NULL) check to see if a value is a missing value. Either numeric type or character type is OK.

For a character variable CH, the following statements are equivalent:

```
WHERE ch ^=' ';
WHERE ch IS NOT MISSING;
WHERE ch IS NOT NULL;
WHERE ch;
```

For a numeric value NUM, the following statements are equivalent:

```
WHERE num^=.;
WHERE num IS NOT MISSING;
WHERE num IS NOT NULL;
```

Also, the following statements are equivalent:

```
WHERE num^=. AND num^=0;
WHERE num;
```

For two character variables a and b, there are two groups of codes in the following. Statements in each group are equivalent:

```
WHERE a^='' AND b^= ''; WHERE a AND b; WHERE a MIN b;

WHERE a^='' OR b^= '';WHERE a OR b;  WHERE a||b; WHERE a MAX b;
```

- The following program shows that operands of MAX, MIN, and IN, NOTIN in an IF statement are Num/Char but in a WHERE statement are Both:

```
DATA s;
a=3;b='4';
DATA t;
SET s;
IF a MAX b;
IF a IN ('3');
IF b IN (4,0);
DATA p;
SET s;
WHERE a MAX b;
WHERE a IN ('3');
WHERE b IN (4,0);
RUN;
```

```
174  IF a MAX b;
175  IF a IN ('3');
176  IF b IN (4,0);

NOTE: Character values have been converted to numeric values at the places given by:
      (Line):(Column).
      174:10   175:4    176:4
NOTE: There were 1 observations read from the data set WORK.S.
NOTE: The data set WORK.T has 1 observations and 2 variables.

179  WHERE a MAX b;
ERROR: Where clause operator requires compatible variables.
180  WHERE a IN ('3');
ERROR: Where clause operator requires compatible variables.
181  WHERE b IN (4,0);
ERROR: Where clause operator requires compatible variables.
NOTE: The SAS System stopped processing this step because of errors.
```

- The following program shows that we can use character values for MAX and MIN operators for both an IF statement and a WHERE statement. After evaluation, SAS uses different converting rules to convert them to Boolean value:

```
DATA s;
INPUT a $ b $;
CARDS;
-5 0
. a
. .
0 a
14 6
;
DATA p;
SET s;
IF a MAX b;
p=a MAX b;
PROC PRINT;
DATA t;
```

```
SET s;
WHERE  a MAX b;
p=a MAX b;
PROC PRINT;
RUN;
```

```
NOTE: Character values have been converted to numeric values at the places given by:
      (Line):(Column).
      318:6
NOTE: Invalid numeric data, 'a' , at line 318 column 6.
a=  b=a p=  _ERROR_=1 _N_=2
NOTE: Invalid numeric data, 'a' , at line 318 column 6.
a=0 b=a p=  _ERROR_=1 _N_=4
NOTE: There were 5 observations read from the data set WORK.S.
NOTE: The data set WORK.P has 1 observations and 3 variables.
```

Obs	a	b	p
1	14	6	6

Obs	a	b	p
1	-5	0	0
2		a	a
3	0	a	a
4	14	6	6

- The following program shows that both WHERE and IF statements can use both types of values for the operators AND and OR, but the convertion rules are different (Boolean_w and Boolean_d):

```
DATA s;
INPUT a $ b;
CARDS;
. 4
2 4
a 4
-5 4
0 4
;
DATA t;
SET s;
IF a AND b;
DATA p;
SET s;
WHERE a AND b;
PROC PRINT DATA=t;RUN;
PROC PRINT DATA=p;RUN;
```

Obs	a	b
1	2	4
2	-5	4

Obs	a	b

```
1    2    4
2    a    4
3   -5    4
4    0    4
```

- A WHERE statement does not support the symbol >< and treats the symbol <> as NE. (It is very funny: If you write the statement "`WHERE 1 MAX 3;`", the log file will show "`WHERE 1<>3;`", but if you write the statement "`WHERE 1<>3;`", the log file will tell you: `The "<>" operator is interpreted as "not equals".` You can also try "WHERE 1 MIN 3;").

- The following program shows that in an IF statement, ** and MAX, MIN have the same precedence, but in a WHERE statement, ** has higher precedence than MAX and MIN:

```
DATA s;
a =3 ** 2 MAX 5;
b=2 MAX 1 **2;
PROC PRINT;
DATA t;
a=1;
DATA p1;
SET t;
WHERE 9=3**2 MAX 5;
DATA p2;
SET t;
WHERE 2=2 MAX 1 ** 2;
RUN;
```

```
Obs     a     b

 1     243    2
```

```
191  WHERE 9=3**2 MAX 5;
NOTE: There were 1 observations read from the data set WORK.T.
      WHERE 9=((3**2)<>5);

194  WHERE 2=2 MAX 1 ** 2;
NOTE: There were 1 observations read from the data set WORK.T.
      WHERE 2=(2<>(1**2));
```

- In an IF statement, the precedence of the negative prefix is lower than that of MAX and MIN, but in a WHERE statement, – has higher precedence. See the following example:

```
DATA t;
a=1;
DATA p1;
SET t;
WHERE 9=-1 MAX 9; *first - then MAX;
DATA p2;
SET t;
```

```
IF -9=-1 MAX 9;   *first MAX then -;
RUN;
```

Both data sets p1 and p2 have one observation. Notice that in a WHERE statement, you can give the exponentiation ** and the negative prefix the same precedence but keep their associativity from right to left.

- In an IF statement, the associativity of MAX and MIN is from right to left, but in a WHERE statement, it is from left to right.

```
DATA s;
INPUT a b c;
CARDS;
3 2 5
5 2 3
;
DATA s2;
SET s;
IF 3= a MAX b MIN c;
PROC PRINT;
DATA t2;
SET s;
WHERE 3=a MAX b MIN c;
PROC PRINT;
RUN;
```

```
                    Obs    a    b    c

                     1     3    2    5


                    Obs    a    b    c

                     1     3    2    5
                     2     5    2    3
```

- In a WHERE statement, there are operators with precedence 8L that cannot be used together with other operators with precedence 8 or 8L. All these operators, except IN and NOTIN, work only in a WHERE statement, not in an IF statement. In an IF statement, operators IN and NOTIN have higher precedence than other comparison operators, but in a WHERE statement they cannot be put together with other comparison operators. See the following example:

```
DATA s;
a=0;b=-1;
DATA t;
SET s;
IF a<b IN (-1);
DATA p;
SET s;
WHERE a<b IN (-1);
RUN;
```

```
228  IF a<b IN (-1);
NOTE: There were 1 observations read from the data set WORK.S.
NOTE: The data set WORK.T has 1 observations and 2 variables.

232  WHERE a<b IN (-1);
                 --
                 22
                 76
ERROR: Syntax error while parsing WHERE clause.
ERROR 22-322: Syntax error, expecting one of the following: !, !!, &, (, *, **, +, -, /,
<, <=, <>, =, >, >=, AND, EQ, GE, GT, LE, LT, NE, OR, ^=, |, ||, ~=.
ERROR 76-322: Syntax error, statement will be ignored.
```

In the above program, data set t uses an IF statement. According to Table 1, `a<b IN (-1)` is equivalent to `a<(b IN (-1))`, and the data set t is the same as data set s. But for the data set p, SAS just gives an error message and does not proceed because IN has precedence 8L, and it cannot be used together with < which has precedence 8. We have to rewrite the statement as `WHERE a<(b IN (-1));`.

The operands of truncated comparisons are Num/Char in an IF statement and Both in a WHERE statement. If two operands are character values, their effects are exactly the same for an IF statement and for a WHERE statement. Suppose that two values are numeric. As we have said, an IF statement treats it as a regular comparison. A WHERE statement gives a WARNING message, as follows:

```
WARNING: Truncated comparison ignored for numeric operands.
```

But here, *ignored* means to treat it as a regular comparison, so the results are the same.

Now we discuss operators that are used only for WHERE statements but not for IF statements.

A BETWEEN-AND operator is inclusive. The following two statements are equivalent:

```
WHERE var BETWEEN 50 AND 100;
WHERE 50 <= var <= 100;
```

Boundaries can also be expressions.

```
WHERE var BETWEEN salary*0.3 AND salary*0.5;
```

If we want to choose observations for the elderly (age>70) and children (<12), we can use the statement

```
WHERE age NOT BETWEEN 12 AND 70;
```

The operator CONTAINS works only for character values. It is the same as a question mark (?) operator. If the value of the variable STATE is 'North Dakota', then either of the following two statements returns true:

```
WHERE state ? 'North';
WHERE state CONTAINS 'North';
```

The operator LIKE is followed by a string within quotation marks. The string can be one or more sub-strings connected together with one or more underscores (_) and/or percent signs (%), where each underscore represents one character, and each percent sign represents a string.

Therefore, the statement "`WHERE lastname LIKE 'N%';`" (the same as "`WHERE lastname =: 'N';`") matches all LASTNAME values beginning with the letter N. "ab__cd" matches any LASTNAME value that begins with "ab", ends with "cd", and has a total of six characters. "ab%cd" matches any LASTNAME value that begins with "ab" and ends with "cd".

The phonetic match SOUNDS-LIKE operator =* is used for matches that "sound like" the given expression. See the following example:

WHERE lastname =*'Smith';

The above statement matches the names Smith, Smythe, and Smitt, etc.

Operators in PROC SQL

Now we will talk about operators in PROC SQL. Notice that there may be a WHERE= option (as well as KEEP=, DROP=, and RENAME=) following the table name, which uses rules from Table 2. We will first give a table of operators and their usage.

Table 4 Operators in PROC SQL
P: Precedence

Symbol	Mnemonic	Meaning	P.	Operands	Associativity
()		Parenthesis	0		
**		Exponentiation	1	Numeric_p	Right-to-left
+		Positive prefix	2	Either	
-		Negative prefix	2	Numeric_p	
	MAX	Maximum	3	Both	Left-to-right
	MIN	Minimum	3	Both	
*		Multiplication	4	Numeric_p	Left-to-right
/		Division	4	Numeric_p	
+		Addition	5	Numeric_p	Left-to-right
-		Subtraction	5	Numeric_p	
||		Concatenation	6	Character_p	
	IN	Belongs to	7L*	Both	
	NOTIN	Does not belong to	7L	Both	
	BETWEEN - AND		7L	Both	
?	CONTAINS		7L	Character_p	

	IS MISSING IS NULL		7L	Either	
	IS NOT MISSING IS NOT NULL		7L	Either	
	LIKE		7L	Character_p	
=*		Sounds-like	7L	Character_p	
	EXISTS		7L	Subquery	
=	EQ	Equal to	7	Both	Same time
^= ~= <>	NE	Not equal to	7		
>	GT	Greater than	7		
<	LT	Less than	7		
>=	GE	Greater than or equal	7		
<=	LE	Less than or equal	7		
	EQT	Truncated equal	7L	Character_p	
	NET	Truncated not equal	7L		
	GET	Truncated great than or equal	7L		
	GTT	Truncated great than	7L		
	LET	Truncated less than or equal	7L		
	LTT	Truncated less than	7L		
^,~,¬	NOT	Logical not	8	Boolean_p	
&	AND	Logical and	9	Boolean_p	
|	OR	Logical or	10	Boolean_p	

Operators with precedence 7L cannot be used together with any operator with precedence 7L or 7. In other words, there must be an & or an | between an operator with precedence 7L and any operator with precedence 7L or 7, if no parenthesis.

The operators for SQL are almost the same as those in Table 2, but there are still some differences, as we show in the following:

- Differences for truncated operators.
    - Symbols are different. In a DATA step and in a WHERE statement, truncated operators are regular comparison symbols followed by a colon sign. In PROC SQL, they are regular comparison symbols followed by the character 't'.
    - Operands are different. In a DATA step, it is Num/Char. In a WHERE statement, it is Both, i.e., no mixed cases. In PROC SQL, it is Character_p, i.e., no numeric values are allowed. See the following example:

```
DATA s;
a1=3;a2=2.56;
DATA t;
SET s;
WHERE a1>=:a2;
RUN;
PROC SQL;
SELECT * FROM s WHERE a1 GTT a2;
QUIT;
```

```
200  WHERE a1>=:a2;
WARNING: Truncated comparison ignored for numeric operands.
201  RUN;

NOTE: There were 1 observations read from the data set WORK.S.
      WHERE a1>=a2;

203  SELECT * FROM s WHERE a1 GTT a2;
ERROR: Arguments for truncated compares must be strings.
```

- In a WHERE statement, they can be used together with other comparison operators, but in WHERE clause, they cannot be used together with other comparison operators. In the following program, the WHERE statement is OK, the first two WHERE clauses are OK, but the last one has problem.

```
DATA s;
a='a';b='b';c='c';
DATA t;
SET s;
WHERE a LE: b LE c;
PROC SQL;
SELECT * FROM s WHERE a LE b LE c;
SELECT * FROM s WHERE a LET b;
SELECT * FROM s WHERE a LET b LE c;
```

- In PROC SQL, operators BETWEEN, CONTINS, and LIKE work not only for a WHERE clause but also for a HAVING clause and a SELECT clause. The following program gives an example. Notice that when using these operators, the value is 0 or 1 depending on whether the condition is false or true, the same as other comparison operators:

```
DATA S;
INPUT a b;
CARDS;
3 5
0 2
1 0
;
PROC SQL;
SELECT a IN (1,3) AS class,SUM(a IN (1,3)) AS total FROM s;
```

class	total
1	2
0	2
1	2

- Three tables (1, 2, and 4) give different precedence for the operator NOT (^). In Table 1 and Table 2, it is before multiplication, but in Table 4, it is after comparisons. The following program proves our claim. In a WHERE clause, ^a<b

is equivalent to ^(a<b), but in a WHERE statement and in DATA step, that is equivalent to (^a)<b.

```
DATA s;
INPUT a b;
CARDS;
3 5
0 2
1 0
;
PROC SQL;
SELECT * FROM s WHERE ^a*b;
SELECT * FROM s(WHERE =(^a*b));
SELECT * FROM s WHERE ^a IN (1 4);
SELECT * FROM s(WHERE =(^a IN (1 4)));
QUIT;
DATA t;
SET s;
WHERE ^a*b;
PROC PRINT;RUN;
```

a	b
0	2
1	0

a	b
0	2

a	b
3	5
0	2

a	b
0	2

Obs	a	b
1	0	2

Some books even put NOT after AND and OR. That is not correct. Let's see the following example:

```
SELECT * FROM s WHERE NOT a OR 1;
```

a	b
3	5
0	2
1	0

- In PROC SQL, there is one more operator: EXISTS or NOT EXISTS. Their right operand is a subquery. The result of an EXISTS condition is true if the subquery resolves to at least one row. The result of a NOT EXISTS condition is true if the subquery evaluates to zero rows. Usually the subquery contains columns in the outer query (correlated subquery). It is OK for syntax if the subquery does not contain any columns in the outer query. But in this case, the outer query either selects all rows or selects no rows, and it is meaningless. The following example shows you how to use them:

```
DATA student_record;
INPUT name $ sex $ grade;
DATALINES;
amanda F 4
bob M 5
cathy F 3
david M 5
emery F 2
RUN;
DATA ymca_sporter;
INPUT name $ sport $;
DATALINES;
amanda basketball
cathy soccer
george swimming
harry runner
;
RUN;
PROC SQL;
SELECT * FROM ymca_sporter AS y WHERE EXISTS
(SELECT * FROM student_record WHERE name =y.name);
QUIT;
```

output

name	sport
amanda	basketba
cathy	soccer

Operators in Macro

In Macro, all values are text. The statement %LET a=3+4; assigns the text string "3+4", not the text 7, to macro variable a. The character "+" here is just a character, not an operator. We cannot directly use operators. The only exception is period (.). When it follows a reference, it can be seen as a concatnation operator. The following program shows that a period can be directly used as well as being used in function %EVAL.

```
%MACRO s;
%LET a=ab;
%IF &a.ab=abab %THEN %PUT abc;
%LET b=&a.efg;
%PUT &b;
```

```
%MEND;
%s
```

```
abc
abefg
```

Operators are used only in functions %EVAL and %SYSEVALF. In the SAS macro facility, some places need numeric or Boolean values; then %EVAL will be implicitly called there. Expression in the following statements or function calls will automatically call %EVAL. Notice that these places all need integers:

%SCAN(text, expression, delimiters) (%QSCAN)
%SUBSTR(text, expression, expression) (%QSUBSTR)
%IF expression %THEN action
%DO index=expression %TO expression %BY expression
%DO %UNTIL (expression)
%DO %WHILE(expression)

Therefore, %IF &a=3+4 means %IF &a=7. %DO I=3+4 %TO 10; is equivalent to %DO I=7 %TO 10.

The function %SYSEVALF must be explicitly called.

Operators in %EVAL

Notice that function %EVAL does arithmetic operation and logic operation only on integers, but it can do comparison operation on both integer values or text values. Table 5 gives the operators and their rules in function %EVAL.

Table 5. Operators in function %EVAL (sym.=symbol, mne.=mnemonic, p.=precedence)

Sym.	Mne.	Meaning	P.	Operands	Return value	Associativity
()		Parenthesis	0			
**		Exponentiation	1	Integers	Integer	Right-to-left
+		Positive prefix	2	Integer	Integer	
-		Negative prefix	2	Integer		
^,~	NOT	Logical not	2	Boolean	Boolean	
*		Multiplication	3	Integers	Integer	Left-to-right
/		Division	3			
+		Addition	4	Integers	Integer	Left-to-right
-		Subtraction	4			
=	EQ	Equal to	5	Integer/Text	Boolean	Left-to-right
^= ~=	NE	Not equal to	5			
>	GT	Greater than	5			
<	LT	Less than	5			
>=	GE	Greater than or equal	5			
<=	LE	Less than or equal	5			
&	AND	Logical AND	6	Boolean_i	Boolean	Left-to-right
		OR	Logical OR	7	Boolean_i	Boolean	Left-to-right

Notice differences between Table 5 and three other tables:

- For arithmetic operators, you have to use integers as operands with no decimal number and no missing value (period). Otherwise, the function does not work. Unlike in a DATA step, 1/0 returns missing value. In macro, 1/0 will stop the execution of macro. For division, it is similar to the function INT in a DATA step. See the following example:

```
DATA s;
a1=%EVAL(4/5);
a2=INT(4/5);
a3=%EVAL((-7)/4);
a4=INT((-7)/4);
a5=%EVAL(4/5+4/5);   *not INT(4/5+4/5);
a6=INT(4/5)+INT(4/5);
PROC PRINT;RUN;
```

Obs	a1	a2	a3	a4	a5	a6
1	0	0	-1	-1	0	0

- For comparison, you can use any values as operands. If both operands are integers, the SAS macro processor does numeric comparison but otherwise text comparison. So %EVAL(6<10) returns true, and %EVAL(6.5<10) returns false because the latter is text comparison.

The following message shows that the operands of the logic operators AND and OR are Boolean_i:

```
146  %MACRO s;
147  %IF 2.1 & 1 %THEN %PUT abc;
148  %MEND;
149  %s
ERROR: A character operand was found in the %EVAL function or %IF condition where a
numeric operand is required. The condition was: 2.1 & 1
ERROR: The macro S will stop executing.
```

- %EVAL will be called automatically in a %IF statement and a %DO statement and in some macro functions mentioned above but not in other statements, such as %LET, %PUT, or other macro functions. But you can explicitly call the function. See the following example:

```
DATA s;
a=3<5;
PUT 'data set variable ' a=;
RUN;
%LET a=3<5;
%LET b=%EVAL(3<5);
%PUT macro variable a= &a;
%PUT macro eval b= &b;
%PUT macro eval %EVAL(3<5);
```

You will see the following output in the log file:

```
data set variable a=1
macro variable a= 3<5
macro eval b= 1
macro eval 1
```

- We don't put an assignment sign = in Table 5 because in an assignment statement (%LET statement), there are no other operators, no arithmetic operator, no comparison operator, no logic operator. All of them are just texts, and only a period may be understood as an operator. The macro function %EVAL only works on expressions, and there is no assignment. Therefore, you cannot compare precedence of assignment (=) with other operators.
- Since the function %EVAL recognizes only integers, statement %DO I=2+3 %TO 3+4 %BY 2; works, but %DO I=1.4 %TO 2 %BY 0.2 does not work. As we said previously, %DO I=1,2,3 %TO 5; does not work because the macro facility calls %EVAL by default, and %EVAL(1,2,3) does not work. Notice that the statement %DO I=1.4 %TO 4; does not work, but %DO I=7/4 %TO 4 works.

The following statements illustrate the usage of %EVAL:

```
Statements                   value of c      reason
%LET a=4+5; %LET b=7;
%LET c=%EVAL(&a);              9
%LET c=%EVAL(&a/&b);           4             4+5/7
%LET c=%EVAL(&a&b+5);          66            4+57+5
%LET c=%EVAL(3<&a);            1             3<9
%LET c=%EVAL(3<&a & 2<&b);     1             3<9 & 2<7
%LET c=%EVAL(aa<bb);           1             text comparison
%LET c=%EVAL(6.5<10);          0             text comparison
```

- There are no operators || and MAX, MIN.

- The big difference between Table 5 and other tables is the associativity for comparison operations. In other tables it is "same time," so the expression a<b<c is equivalent to the expression a<b AND b<c. But here the associativity is left-to-right. So the expression &a<&b<&c is equivalent to the expression (&a<&b)<&c; Therefore, although neither 4<3 nor 3<1 is true, 4<3<1 is evaluated as true because 4<3 is 0 (false), and 0<1 is true. For the same reason, 0=1 is false, but 0=1=0 is true.

- The statement %LET a=b=3; treats the first equal sign as an operator and the second one as text. However, in the function %EVAL, all operators are treated as operators. See the following example. If you want to treat an operator as part of a value, you have to use a quoting function:

```
%MACRO s;
%LET a=2=2;
%LET b=2=2;
```

```
%LET c=3;
%IF &b=&a %THEN %LET c=5;
%PUT _USER_;
%MEND;
%s
```

In this example, the macro facility treats the expression &b=&a as 2=2=2=2, i.e., ((2=2)=2)=2. You know that the result is false.

- Empty text is treated as text, not as an integer in the functions %EVAL and %SYSEVALF. Therefore, for arithmetic operators and logic operators, empty text is not OK, but in comparison, empty text is OK. The following program shows how %EVAL works on empty text:

```
%LET a1=%EVAL(3 &);
%LET a2=%EVAL(& 3);
%LET a3=%EVAL(3 -);
%LET a4=%EVAL(- 3);
%LET a5=%EVAL(3 >);
%LET a6=%EVAL(> 3);
%LET a7=%EVAL(=);
%LET a8=%EVAL(>);
%PUT _USER_;
```

```
205  %LET a1=%EVAL(3 &);
ERROR: A character operand was found in the %EVAL function or %IF condition where a
numeric operand
       is required. The condition was: 3 &
206  %LET a2=%EVAL(& 3);
ERROR: A character operand was found in the %EVAL function or %IF condition where a
numeric operand
       is required. The condition was: & 3
207  %LET a3=%EVAL(3 -);
ERROR: A character operand was found in the %EVAL function or %IF condition where a
numeric operand
       is required. The condition was: 3 -
208  %LET a4=%EVAL(- 3);
209  %LET a5=%EVAL(3 >);
210  %LET a6=%EVAL(> 3);
211  %LET a7=%EVAL(=);
212  %LET a8=%EVAL(>);
213  %PUT _USER_;
GLOBAL SQLOBS 0
GLOBAL A6 0
GLOBAL SQLOOPS 0
GLOBAL A7 1
GLOBAL A8 0
GLOBAL SQLXOBS 0
GLOBAL SQLRC 8
GLOBAL A1
GLOBAL A2
GLOBAL A3
GLOBAL A4 -3
GLOBAL A5 1
```

- The following code is perfect (in syntax), and the condition is true. Do you know why? It is because the condition is equivalent to ((3 NE) GE) LE 3, which is OK for syntax.

```
%MACRO s;
%IF 3 NE GE LE 3 %THEN %PUT b;
%MEND;
%s
```

Let me talk about the ampersand symbol (&). As a keyword, it may have two possible meanings: logical AND or trigger. It has meaning as logical AND only if it is in functions %EVAL or %SYSEVALF. Now we will talk about the rules of %EVAL and %SYSEVALF to handle the ampersand.

1. If it is followed by a blank or an integer, then it is treated as logical AND.
2. If it is followed by a character or an underscore, SAS tries to treat it as a reference.
3. In case 2, if it cannot be resolved, SAS treats it as logical AND.

Let's see the following example:

```
%PUT p1=%EVAL(1 & 0);
%PUT p2=%EVAL(0 &1);
%LET a=3;
%PUT p3=%EVAL(&a =1);
%PUT p4=%EVAL(&b =1);
%PUT p5=%EVAL(1 &b =1);
```

Now check the printout in the log file.

```
160  %PUT p1=%EVAL(1 & 0);
p1=0
161  %PUT p2=%EVAL(0 &1);
p2=0
162  %LET a=3;
163  %PUT p3=%EVAL(&a =1);
p3=0
164  %PUT p4=%EVAL(&b =1);
WARNING: Apparent symbolic reference B not resolved.
WARNING: Apparent symbolic reference B not resolved.
ERROR: A character operand was found in the %EVAL function or %IF condition where a
numeric operand is required. The condition was: &b =1
p4=
165  %PUT p5=%EVAL(1 &b =1);
WARNING: Apparent symbolic reference B not resolved.
WARNING: Apparent symbolic reference B not resolved.
p5=0
```

You can find that for p1 and p2, the SAS macro processor treats & as logical AND. For p3, & is treated as a reference. For p4 and p5, the SAS macro processor tries to treat & as a reference, but fails. Therefore, in both cases, the SAS macro processor treats it as logical AND. For p4, it is equivalent to %EVAL(&(b=1)). (= has higher precedence than

&.) Here, the left operand is empty text and cannot be an operand of &. The SAS macro processor gives an ERROR message. For p5, we put 1 before the & sign. Now, it is OK.

Notice the following difference:

```
%PUT a1=%EVAL(>=);
%PUT a2=%EVAL(> =);
```

Here in the first statement, >= is one operator. SAS compares two empty texts, and the result is true. The second statement has two operators. SAS first compares two empty texts for operator >, and the result is false (0). Then SAS compares 0 with empty text for operator =, and the result is false. They are equivalent to the following two statements, respectively:

```
%PUT a1=%EVAL(GE);
%PUT a2=%EVAL(GT EQ);
```

Now let's run the following two macros:

```
%MACRO ge_macro(company);
%IF &company EQ GE %THEN %PUT The company is GE;
%MEND;
%ge_macro(GE)


%MACRO or_macro(state);
%IF &state EQ OR %THEN %PUT The state is Oregon;
%MEND;
%or_macro(OR)
```

For the first macro, we have the following printout:

```
The company is GE
```

For the second macro there is an ERROR message:

```
ERROR: A character operand was found in the %EVAL function or %IF condition where a
numeric operand is required. The condition was: &state EQ OR
ERROR: The macro OR_MACRO will stop executing.
```

You may wonder why one macro works OK, and the other does not. Actually in the first macro, the %IF statement will be resolved as

```
%IF GE EQ GE %THEN %PUT company is GE;
```

Here, GE, EQ, and EQ are all treated as operators. They have the same precedence, and the associativity is from left to right. Therefore, the statement is equivalent to the following:

```
%IF ((GE) EQ ) GE %THEN %PUT company is GE;
```

As we know, a missing operand means empty text. SAS first compares empty text with empty text. The result is true (1). Then SAS compares 1 with empty text, and the result is 0. Then SAS compares 0 to empty text, and the result is 1. Actually, you can put any parameter in the macro ge_macro, and the condition is true. It is the same as in the following program:

```
%MACRO ge_macro(company);
%IF &company = >= %THEN %PUT company is >=;
%MEND;
%ge_macro(>=)
```

Why is the first macro executed correctly as we understand? This is just by accident. For the second macro, the %IF statement is equivalent to the following because the operator EQ has higher precedence than OR. However, the problem is that the operator OR recognizes only integers as its operands. Here operator OR has empty text as operand, and this causes problem.

```
%IF OR ( EQ ) OR %THEN %PUT State is Oregon;
%IF OR OR %THEN %PUT State is Oregon;
%IF (OR ) OR %THEN %PUT State is Oregon;
```

Therefore, in order to correctly use the %EVAL function, you have to use the quoting function as in the following:

```
%IF %STR(&company) EQ %STR(GE) %THEN %PUT company is GE;
%IF %STR(&state) EQ %STR(OR) %THEN %PUT State is Oregon;
```

Operators in %SYSEVALF

If we want to do arithmetic operation on decimal numbers, we have to use the function %SYSEVALF. It is a common understanding that %SYSEVALF is an generalization of %EVAL because it does operations on both integers and decimal numbers. That is right. But we also have to know the difference between these two functions. %SYSEVALF has the following characteristics:

- It allows decimal operands for arithmetic operations and returns a decimal number. Therefore, %EVAL(1/3 ge 2/3) returns true, but %SYSEVALF(1/3 ge 2/3) returns false.
- It recognizes missing value. In the following program, although SAS gives a NOTE to indicate the problem, it still treats 1/0 as a missing value:

```
%MACRO pp;
%IF %SYSEVALF(1/0<1) %THEN %PUT abc;
%PUT a=%SYSEVALF(1/0);
%MEND;
%pp
```

```
NOTE: Division by zero in %SYSEVALF is invalid.
abc
NOTE: Division by zero in %SYSEVALF is invalid.
a=.
```

- When doing comparison, if both operands are numeric, it uses numeric comparison. Otherwise, it uses text comparison. So %EVAL(6.5<10) returns false, but %SYSEVALF(6.5<10) returns true.
- Even if you explicitly call %SYSEVALF in the place that needs numeric or Boolean, the function %EVAL will still be implicitly invoked. Therefore, both statements in the following program do not work. The latter does not work because the return value is 0.9999999999, rather than 1, which cannot be an argument of %EVAL.

```
%MACRO s;
%IF %SYSEVALF(1.4+1) %THEN %PUT abc;
%MEND;
%MACRO t;
%IF %SYSEVALF(2/3+1/3) %THEN %PUT abcdd;
%MEND;
%s; %t
```

```
ERROR: A character operand was found in the %EVAL function or %IF condition where a
numeric operand is required. The condition was: %SYSEVALF(1.4+1)
ERROR: The macro S will stop executing.
ERROR: A character operand was found in the %EVAL function or %IF condition where a
numeric operand is required. The condition was: %SYSEVALF(2/3+1/3)
ERROR: The macro T will stop executing.
```

- Actually, the function %SYSEVALF allows two arguments, and usually the second argument is omitted. The second argument can be CEIL, FLOOR, INTEGER, and BOOLEAN, such as the following. The following statements show you how the function %SYSEVALF works:

Function call	Return value
%SYSEVALF(1.4,INTEGER)	1
%SYSEVALF(1.4,BOOLEAN)	1
%SYSEVALF(1.4,CEIL)	2
%SYSEVALF(1.4,FLOOR)	1
%SYSEVALF(-1.4,INTEGER)	-1
%SYSEVALF(-1.4,BOOLEAN)	1
%SYSEVALF(-1.4,CEIL)	-1
%SYSEVALF(-1.4,FLOOR)	-2

Positive prefix +

As we know, the sign + has two functionalities: a plus sign and a positive prefix. Let's talk about the positive prefix +. Different from Table 1, 2, and 4, the positive prefix in the macro facility only works for integers. Let's run the following program.

```
%ge_macro(+GE)
%ge_macro(+3)
```

We can find the following printouts in the log file:

```
627  %ge_macro(+GE)
ERROR: A character operand was found in the %EVAL function or %IF condition where a
numeric operand is required. The condition was: &company EQ GE
ERROR: The macro GE_MACRO will stop executing.
628  %ge_macro(+3)
The company is GE
```

Now we will talk the positive prefix in a DATA step, including in an IF statement and in a WHERE statement. Everyone knows about it, but I doubt if anyone has ever used it, so there is not much of a reason to talk about it because no one uses it. But it is helpful to learn about it in order to understand SAS.

The positive prefix + is a null operator, which means that it does nothing. Although usually we give its precedence the same as the negative prefix –, actually we can give it any precedence. It does not change anything.

A positive prefix is different from a negative prefix. A negative prefix has the operand numeric_c in Table 1 and numeric_p in Table 2 and Table 4. For a negative prefix, in an IF statement, if the operand is a string, SAS converts the operand to numeric, and in a WHERE statement, if the operand is a string, SAS stops processing. However, a positive prefix works on both numeric and character values for both IF and WHERE statements. In the following program, the data set t1 is the same as data set s because – works on numeric values, so both values have been converted to missing values. The DATA step for data set t2 does not work because negative prefix in WHERE statement needs a numeric value and no converting. The data set t3 has one observation, because SAS uses character comparison.

```
DATA s;
INPUT a $ b $;
CARDS;
a b
b a
;
DATA t1;
SET s;
IF a>=-b;
DATA t2;
SET s;
WHERE a>=-b;
DATA t3;
SET s;
WHERE a>=+b;
*IF a>=+b;
PROC PRINT;RUN;
```

```
39   DATA t1;
40   SET s;
41   IF a>=-b;

NOTE: Character values have been converted to numeric values at the places given by:
      (Line):(Column).
```

```
      41:4   41:8
NOTE: Invalid numeric data, b='b' , at line 41 column 8.
NOTE: Invalid numeric data, a='a' , at line 41 column 4.
a=a b=b _ERROR_=1 _N_=1
NOTE: Invalid numeric data, b='a' , at line 41 column 8.
NOTE: Invalid numeric data, a='b' , at line 41 column 4.
a=b b=a _ERROR_=1 _N_=2
NOTE: Missing values were generated as a result of performing an operation on missing
values.
      Each place is given by: (Number of times) at (Line):(Column).
      2 at 41:8
NOTE: There were 2 observations read from the data set WORK.S.
NOTE: The data set WORK.T1 has 2 observations and 2 variables.

42    DATA t2;
43    SET s;
44    where a>=-b;
ERROR: Where clause operator requires numeric variables.

NOTE: The SAS System stopped processing this step because of errors.
WARNING: The data set WORK.T2 may be incomplete.  When this step was stopped there were 0
         observations and 2 variables.
WARNING: Data set WORK.T2 was not replaced because this step was stopped.

45    DATA t3;
46    SET s;
47    where a>=+b;

NOTE: There were 1 observations read from the data set WORK.S.
      WHERE a>=b;
NOTE: The data set WORK.T3 has 1 observations and 2 variables.
```

The following statement is from SAS manual about prefix +:

The plus (+) sign can be either a prefix or arithmetic operator. A plus sign is a prefix operator only when it appears at the beginning of an expression or when it is immediately preceded by a left parenthesis or another operator.

However, this statement is not accurate. Notice that an expression can be used in the following clauses: IF, WHERE, UNTIL, WHILE, SELECT, WHEN, TO and BY (in DO statement). However, the expression in clauses UNTIL, WHILE, SELECT and WHEN must be surrounded with parenthesis, so prefix cannot be at beginning of the expression. The prefix + at the beginning of an expression is OK in BY and TO clauses, but cannot be in IF and WHERE clauses. Let's see the following example.

```
DATA s;
INPUT a b;
CARDS;
1 3
2 2
;
DATA t;
SET s;
```

```
WHERE +a=b;
*IF +a=b;
PROC PRINT;RUN;
```

Obs	a	b	WHERE
1	1	3	0
2	2	2	1

Here, WHERE +a=b; is a sum statement, and the word "WHERE" is treated as a variable name rather than as a keyword. It is different from the statement WHERE a=b;. Let's see one more examples.

```
85    DATA s;
86    a=+3;
87    *IF +a=3 THEN b=3;
88    IF +3=a THEN b=3;
              ---- -
              388  202
ERROR 388-185: Expecting an arithmetic operator.

ERROR 202-322: The option or parameter is not recognized and will be ignored.

NOTE: The SAS System stopped processing this step because of errors.
```

The above example shows that SAS treats + as a sum operator, and then SAS cannot recognize THEN clause.

The positive prefix + also has strange behavior in PROC SQL when it is used at the beginning of the expression. The expression can be in the following clauses: WHERE, HAVING, ORDER BY, and GROUP BY, but it cannot be in the SELECT clause. In the following PROC SQL, the first statement is not OK, but the second is OK:

```
DATA record;
name ='pp';
test=90;
PROC SQL;
SELECT +test FROM record;
SELECT name FROM record WHERE +test>80;
QUIT;
```

You will see the following message in the log file:

```
226  SELECT +test FROM record;
     ------
     180
ERROR 180-322: Statement is not valid or it is used out of proper order.
```

References

Burlew, Michele M. (2006) SAS Macro Programming Made Easy. 2nd ed. Cary, NC: SAS Institute Inc.

Carpenter, Arthur L.(2004) Carpenter's Complete Guide to the SAS Macro Language. Cary, NC: SAS Institute Inc.

SAS 9.1 Macro Language Reference, 2004 Cary, NC: SAS Institute Inc.
http://support.sas.com/documentation/onlinedoc/91pdf/sasdoc_91/base_macro_6997.pdf

"SAS Operators in Expressions" in *SAS Language Reference: Concepts* 2005. Cary, NC: SAS Institute Inc.
http://support.sas.com/documentation/onlinedoc/91pdf/sasdoc_913/base_lrconcept_9196.pdf

Variable List

Introduction

Variable lists are very useful. They can be used in many statements, such as DROP, KEEP, INPUT, LENGTH, RETAIN, FORMAT, RENAME, PUT, BY(DATA step and some PROCs), CLASS (TABULATE), TABLE (FREQ), VAR(MEANS, TABULATE, UNIVARIATE, TRANSPOSE), and COLUMN (REPORT), as well as in arguments of statistical functions.

Notice that among the above statements, the first eight statements are in DATA step. Among them, DROP, KEEP, and RENAME are non-definition statements, and others are definition statements. Refer to [III]. A BY statement can be in both DATA step and PROC step. In DATA step, a BY statement is responsible only for the previous SET (MERGE, MODIFY and UPDATE) statement, i.e., variables in a BY statement must be in the previous SET statement.

Definition

There are different ways to define a variable list.

Dash list (Numbered range list)

If we have several variables whose names are the same string followed by consecutive integers, for example, TEST1, TEST2, ...TEST10, or YEAR01, YEAR02, ...YEAR05, we can use a dash list. TEST1 – TEST10 represents ten variables: TEST1 to TEST10. A dash list is different from other lists (except an array list) in the following ways:

- It specifies variables explicitly. Therefore, it can be used to define variables.
- The order of variables in the list is according to numbers. In other lists, the order of variables is according to their positions.

The following is an example of how to use a dash list:

```
DATA s;
INPUT id test1-test3;
CARDS;
33 89 78 88
34 90 78 90
35 88 68 99
;
RUN;
```

Colon list (Name Prefix List)

For variables with the same prefix, we can use a colon list. TEST: means all variables that begin with a prefix TEST. See the following example, where _: is a colon list, which includes all variables that begin with underscore (_). As a style, many programmers use variables begin with _ to represent intermediate variables, so it is easy to delete them without confusion.

```
DATA s;
INPUT a1-a3;
_a=a1+a3;b=_a+5;
DROP _:;
CARDS;
1 2 3
2 3 1
;
RUN;
```

Double dash list (Name range list)

If we know the creation order of variables, say ID, NAME, ADDRESS, and HEIGHT, we can use a double dash list: ID -- ADDRESS represents the variables ID, NAME, and ADDRESS. Notice that when we run PROC CONTENTS, as default, SAS prints out variables according to the alphabetic order. We can use options VARNUM or POSITION in PROC CONTENTS statement to ask for ordering variables according to their creation order.

```
DATA s;
INPUT id name $ hometown $ age;
KEEP id--hometown;
CARDS;
33 Peter Middletown 45
;
RUN;
```

Type double dash list

From a double dash list we can get two list notations: z-NUMERIC-a and z-CHAR-a (z-CHARACTER-a). The former is for all numeric variables in the double dash list z--a, and the latter is for all character variables in z--a.

```
DATA s;
INPUT id $ name $ test1 test2 ;
avg=MEAN(OF id-numeric-test2);
CARDS;
33 Peter 98 45
34 Jimmy 87 57
;
RUN;
```

Special SAS name list

There are three SAS defined lists: _ALL_, _NUMERIC_, and _CHARACTER_ (_CHAR_). They represent all variables, all numeric variables, and all character variables, respectively. The following is an example to use them.

```
DATA s;
INPUT id $ name $ day1 day2 ;
INFORMAT _NUMERIC_ MMDDYY8.;
CARDS;
33 Peter 04/05/06 04/08/07
;
RUN;
```

Array list

An array is used to represent several variables. For example, the following statement defines an array, arr, with four elements representing the variables A, B, C, and D. Here arr(1) means variable A, etc.

```
ARRAY arr(4) a b c d;
```

The array list arr(*) means all four variables in order. It can only be used in PUT, INPUT, and statistical functions. Notice that array must be defined before it is used.

```
DATA s;
INPUT x1 x2 a;
ARRAY x(*) x1-x2;
PUT x(*);
CARDS;
1 2 3
;
```

Usage

Now we talk about the usage of these lists.

KEEP, DROP, and RENAME statements

- KEEP and DROP can use all lists, but RENAME can use only a dash list.

```
RENAME a1 - a2=c1 - c2;
```

- These statements cannot be used to define variables. The following program creates data set s with two variables:

```
DATA s;
a2=4;a3=5;
KEEP a1-a4;
RENAME a1-a3=c1-c3;
RUN;
```

```
WARNING: Not all variables in the list a1-a4 were found.
WARNING: Not all variable names in the RENAME list a1-a3 were used.
NOTE: The data set WORK.S has 1 observations and 2 variables.
```

- They are all declarative statements, and you can think that they are in effect at the end of a data step, so a list in any of these statements includes variables defined after the statement. The following program is OK:

```
DATA s;
a1=4;a3=5;
RENAME a1-a3=c1-c3;
a2=5;
RUN;
```

The following two pieces of code are equivalent:

```
KEEP a:;
INPUT a1 a2 b1 b2;

INPUT a1 a2 b1 b2;
KEEP a:;
```

FORMAT, INFORMAT, ARRAY, and RETAIN statements

- They can be used to define variables using dash list. The data set created in the following program has four variables:

```
DATA s;
a1=4; a3=5;
FORMAT a1-a4 MMDDYY8.;
RUN;
```

```
NOTE: Variable a2 is uninitialized.
NOTE: Variable a4 is uninitialized.
NOTE: The data set WORK.S has 1 observations and 4 variables.
```

- Any other list, other than dash list, only affects already defined variables. The following program shows that only variables a1 and a3 get format because they are defined before a FORMAT statement:

```
DATA s;
a1=3;a3=5;
KEEP a1 a2 a3;
FORMAT a: 3.1;
a2=4;
PROC PRINT;RUN;
```

```
Obs    a1    a3    a2

  1   3.0   5.0     4
```

If we replace a: with `_numeric_`, the results are the same. However, if we replace a: with a1-a3, the format will also apply to variable a2 because a dash list defines variables. In the following program, you cannot change the DO statement to DO i=1 to 3; because the array has only two variables:

```
DATA s;
a1=4;a3=5;
ARRAY a(*) a:;
DO i=1 TO 2;
a(i)=5;
END;
a2=5;
RUN;
```

PUT statement

- A PUT statement is an executable statement. Therefore, it uses only the variables with values assigned.

- It can be used to define variables. Therefore, it can use a dash list even if some variables are not defined before. In this case, their values are missing.

```
DATA s;
a1=4; a3=5;
PUT a1-a4;
RUN;
```

```
NOTE: Variable a2 is uninitialized.
NOTE: Variable a4 is uninitialized.
4 . 5 .
NOTE: The data set WORK.S has 1 observations and 4 variables.
```

- Notice its behaviors in a special SAS name list, as we talked in [III]. See the following:

```
PUT _ALL_;          put all variables.
PUT _NUMERIC_;      ERROR: Cannot use _numeric_ as a variable name.
PUT _CHAR_;         ERROR: Cannot use _char_ as a variable name.
PUT _CHARACTER_;    NOTE: Variable _character_ is uninitialized.
```

INPUT statement

- It can use a dash list or a double dash list, including type double dash list, and an array list. No others. For a double dash list, variables must appear before the INPUT statement. Notice that as in the PUT statement, INPUT treats _CHARACTER_ as a variable name. In the following example, data s has three variables: a1, a2, and _character_. Data set t has four variables: a, b, c, and _character_, and b gets missing value (uninitialized).

```
DATA s;
ARRAY a(*) a1-a2;
INPUT a(*) _character_;
CARDS;
1 3 4
;
RUN;

DATA t;
LENGTH a 5 b $5 c 5;
INPUT a-NUMERIC-c _character_;
CARDS;
1 3 4
;
RUN;
```

LENGTH statement

A LENGTH statement is used to define a variable. As indicated in [III], it is effective for a variable only if it defines variables, i.e., no other definition statement before it with the same variable. As we have seen, only a dash list can be used to define variables. We can get the conclusion: Only a dash list in a LENGTH statement will work. Therefore, neither of the following two pieces of code works although there is no ERROR message. The first piece does not work because the variable a1 represented by "a:" in the LENGTH statement is not its first appearance in this statement. The second piece does not work because a colon list works only for already defined variables.

```
INPUT a1 $8. b1 $7.;
LENGTH a: 5;

LENGTH a: $5;
INPUT a1 $8. b1 $7.;
```

BY statement (in DATA step or in PROC) and VAR statement (in PROC)

- A BY statement is different from other statements. It can only specify variables in input data set(s) in a SET, MERGE, MODIFY, or UPDATE statement. All other statements are for variables in PDV. BY variables can be empty lists, and this just means no BY statement, except in PROC SORT.

For a dash list and a double dash list, if SAS finds a missing variable, SAS gives an ERROR message and stops.

```
DATA s;
a1=3;a3=5;
DATA t;
SET s;
a2=5;
BY a1-a3;
RUN;
```

```
ERROR: BY variable a2 is not on input data set WORK.S.
NOTE: The SAS System stopped processing this step because of errors.
```

However, for a colon list or a SAS special name list, if it is empty, it is OK for a BY statement, except in PROC SORT. It just acts as though there is no BY statement. In PROC SORT, it is not OK for empty BY list.

```
DATA s;
a1=3;a3=5;
DATA p;
SET s;
BY _CHARACTER_;
RUN;
PROC MEANS;
BY b:;
PROC SORT DATA=p;
BY b:;
RUN;
```

```
DATA p;
SET s;
BY _CHARACTER_;
RUN;
```

```
NOTE: There were 1 observations read from the data set WORK.S.
NOTE: The data set WORK.P has 1 observations and 2 variables.

322  PROC MEANS;
323  BY b:;
WARNING: No variables found beginning with 'B' in data set WORK.P.

NOTE: There were 1 observations read from the data set WORK.P.
NOTE: PROCEDURE MEANS used (Total process time):

324  PROC SORT DATA=p;
325  BY b:;
WARNING: No variables found beginning with 'B' in data set WORK.P.
326  RUN;

ERROR: No BY statement used or no BY variables specified. A BY statement must be used
with variable names to sort on.
NOTE: The SAS System stopped processing this step because of errors.
```

- Variables in a dash list is ordered by the postfix number in the variable names, and that in all others are ordered according to their positions in the data set.

Let's see the data set, program, and output in the following example:

```
DATA s;
INPUT be $ b1 b3 b2 b7 $ b6;
CARDS;
a 2 3 4 b 7
b 5 3 2 d 6
c 7 7 8 g 5
e 7 7 5 t 8
i 7 4 8 r 7
;
PROC SORT;
BY _NUMERIC_;
PROC PRINT;RUN;
```

Obs	a	b1	b3	b2	b7	b6
1	a	2	3	4	b	7
2	b	5	3	2	d	6
3	i	7	4	8	r	7
4	e	7	7	5	t	8
5	c	7	7	8	g	5

For this particular data set, we have the following equivalent pairs of BY statements:

BY b:;	BY be b1 b3 b2 b7 b6;
BY b1-b3;	BY b1 b2 b3;
BY b1—b3;	BY b1 b3;
BY _numeric_;	BY b1 b3 b2 b6;

Although variables must be in an input data set, the order is according to that in PDV if they are defined before the SET statement. Therefore, in the following program, the BY statement is understood as BY a c;, not BY a b c; and there is a problem.

```
DATA s;
INPUT a b c d;
CARDS;
1 2 3 4
1 3 2 4
;
DATA t;
LENGTH a c b d 3;
SET s;
BY a--c;
RUN;
```

Arguments in statistical functions

SAS has the following statistical functions. Each function needs arguments that form an argument list.

COALESCE, CSS, CV, GEOMEAN, GEOMEANZ, HARMEAN, HARMEANZ, IQR, KURTOSIS, LARGEST, MAD, MAX, MEAN, MEDIAN, MIN, MISSING, MODZ, N, NMISS, ORDINAL, PCTL, RANGE, RMS, SKEQNESS, SMALLEST, STD, STDERR, SUM, USS, VAR.

There are some important rules for all statistical functions:

- For a WHERE statement, arguments must be numeric values (Numeric_p). This means that character values will stop processing. For other statements, arguments should be numeric values (Numeric_c). This means that character values will be converted to numeric values. See [XII] and the following example:

```
DATA s;
LENGTH a 5 b $5 c 5;
INPUT a -- c;
CARDS;
1 3 4
;
DATA t;SET s;
WHERE MEAN(a, b, c)>1;
DATA p; SET s;
IF MEAN(a,b,c)>1;
RUN;
```

```
333  DATA t;SET s;
334  WHERE MEAN(a, b, c)>1;
ERROR: Function MEAN requires a numeric expression as argument 2.

NOTE: The SAS System stopped processing this step because of errors.

335  DATA p; SET s;
336  IF MEAN(a,b,c)>1;
```

```
337  RUN;

NOTE: Character values have been converted to numeric values at the places given by:
      (Line):(Column).
      336:11
NOTE: There were 1 observations read from the data set WORK.S.
NOTE: The data set WORK.P has 1 observations and 3 variables.
```

- They have requirement for the number of arguments. See [XII].

- Any of these functions returns a missing value if the number of non-missing values is fewer than that required, except the function MAX. Otherwise, the corresponding statistic is calculated using the non-missing values. The function MAX needs at least two arguments, and returns a non-missing value is at least one is non missing.

Cody (2004) gives usages and examples of these statistical functions.

Now we talk about how to use arguments for these functions. We can use variable lists in an arg-list. The following rules show how to specify an arg-list:

- An arg-list consists of OF lists and expressions separated by commas. An OF list consists of the keyword OF followed by a variable list, including array lists, and single variables separated by a blank. A single variable can also be treated as an expression. The following examples are OK:

  ```
  a=MEAN(OF x1-x6 p,x1+x2,LOG(p), OF q y1-y5, OF z(*));
  a=MEAN(OF x1-x6 test: y--a);
  a=MEAN(OF _NUMERIC_);
  ```

  The following two statements are equivalent:

  ```
  a=MEAN(OF x1-x6 p, OF q y1-y5, OF z1 z2);
  b=MEAN(OF x1-x6 p q y1-y5 z1 z2);
  ```

  However, the following statements are not OK:

  ```
  a=MEAN(OF x1-x6 y1+y2);
  a=MEAN(x1 x2 x3);
  a=MEAN(OF x1-x5, y2 y3);
  a=MEAN(OF z(1) - z(3));
  ```

  For the first case, y1+y2 is an expression that cannot be in an OF list, so it must be separated from the OF list by a comma. For the second case, three variables are not in an OF list and must be separated by a comma. For the third case, either put a comma between y2 and y3 or remove the comma between x5 and y2. For the last case, there is no such list. The only array list is z(*).

- Notice that a dash list in an OF list can also be used to define variables.

```
DATA s;
INPUT a3 a2 a1;
a=SUM(OF a0-a1);
CARDS;
1 2 3
2 3 1
;
RUN;
```

```
NOTE: Variable a0 is uninitialized.
NOTE: The data set WORK.S has 2 observations and 5 variables.
```

Let's see an example:

```
DATA s;
ARRAY x(10);
ARRAY y(10);
DO i=1 TO 10;
x(i)=i;
y(i)=2*i;
END;
a=MEAN(OF x1-x6, y1-y5);
b=MEAN(OF x1-x6 y1-y5);
KEEP a b;
PROC PRINT;
RUN;
```

```
Obs        a          b

  1     1.85714    4.63636
```

For variable a, y1-y5 is not in an OF list, so it is understood as an expression. For variable b, y1-y5 is in an OF list, so it is understood as a variable list.

Summary

Summarizing the above discussion, we have Table1. In this table, the mark "x" means it can be used; if there is no "x", that means that either the syntax or the logic is wrong.

Table 1. Usage of variable lists

A. _ALL_
B. _CHAR_, _CHARACTER_
C. z-CHARACTER-a
D. _NUMERIC_
E. z-NUMERIC-a
F. colon list a:
G. double dash list z—a
H. dash list a1-a5
I. array list x(*)

	A	B	C	D	E	F	G	H	I
ARRAY		X	X	X	X	X[1]	X[1]	X[1]	
PUT	X		X		X	X	X	X	X
BY	X	X	X	X	X	X	X	X	
RENAME								X	

KEEP, DROP		X	X	X	X	X	X	X	
LENGTH								X[1]	
FORMAT		X	X	X	X	X[1]	X[1]	X[1]	
INFORMAT		X	X	X	X	X[1]	X[1]	X[1]	
INPUT			X		X		X	X	X
RETAIN	X	X	X	X	X	X	X	X	
SORT/BY	X	X	X	X	X	X	X	X	
PRINT/BY		X	X	X	X	X	X	X	
TRANSPOSE/BY, VAR		X	X	X	X	X	X	X	
FREQ/BY, TABLE	X	X	X	X	X	X	X	X	
MEANS/BY	X	X	X	X	X	X	X	X	
MEANS/VAR	X[2]			X	X	X[2]	X[2]	X[2]	
TABULATE/BY, CLASS	X	X	X	X	X	X	X	X	
TABULATE/VAR	X[2]			X	X	X[2]	X[2]	X[2]	
UNIVARIATE/BY	X	X	X	X	X	X	X	X	
UNIVARIATE/VAR	X[2]			X	X	X[2]	X[2]	X[2]	
UNIVARIATE/CLASS									
REPORT/COLUMN, BY	X	X	X	X	X	X	X	X	
OF list in statistical function	X	X	X	X	X	X	X	X	X

[1]: Needs the same type;
[2]: Needs numeric type.

Missing elements

Now we will consider cases in which some variables do not exist in the list. There are three cases.

- A dash list, in which some variables in the list are missing.
  - For definition statements, it is not a syntax error. Maybe we will get "uninitialized" message.
  - Also, it has no problem for KEEP, DROP, and RENAME if a missing variable is defined after the statement. It is not an error.
  - If a variable in the list is never defined, for KEEP, DROP, and RENAME, SAS give WARNING message, or ERROR message and stops processing, depending on setting.
- In a double dash list, we consider the situation in which an end variable is not defined.
  - In FORMAT, INFORMAT, ARRAY, and RETAIN statements, if it does not exist before the statement, SAS gives an ERROR message and stops processing.

```
DATA s;
INPUT a3 a2 a1;
FORMAT a1--a5 MMDDYY8.;
a5=3;
CARDS;
1 2 3
2 3 1
```

```
;
RUN;
```

```
36   FORMAT a1--a5 MMDDYY8.;
ERROR: a5 does not follow a1 on the list of previously defined variables.
```

- In DROP and KEEP statements, it is OK if the end variable is defined after the list. SAS treats the missing end variable after all defined variables. So if an ending variable is missing, then SAS picks all variables starting from the beginning variable. If the beginning variable is missing, no variable is picked. In both cases, SAS gives a WARNING message.

```
DATA s;
b=6;a=5;c=3;
KEEP a--b0;
RUN;
```

```
WARNING: Starting variable a of double-dash list exists, but ending variable b0 does not.
NOTE: The data set WORK.S has 1 observations and 2 variables.
```

- For statistical functions, it is not OK if one end is missing.

```
DATA s;
a1=3;a3=5;
a=SUM(OF a3--b);
RUN;
```

```
329   a=sum(of a3--b);
        ---
        71
ERROR: b does not follow a3 on the list of previously defined variables.
ERROR 71-185: The SUM function call does not have enough arguments.
```

- A special SAS name list does not exist or a colon list does not exist.
  - In a statistical function, it is treated as one missing value. In the following program, `SUM(OF _NUMERIC_)` is OK, `MIN(OF _NUMERIC_)` is not OK, and `MIN(a,OF _NUMERIC_)` is OK, because the function SUM needs one argument and the function MIN needs two arguments.

```
DATA s;
INPUT a $ b $ c $;
e=SUM(OF _NUMERIC_);
CARDS;
1 2 3 4
1 3 2 4
;
RUN;
```

```
NOTE: Missing values were generated as a result of performing an operation on missing
values.
      Each place is given by: (Number of times) at (Line):(Column).
      2 at 65:3
NOTE: The data set WORK.S has 2 observations and 4 variables.
```

- In the following program, the BY statement is ignored:

```
DATA s;
INPUT a3 a2 a1;
CARDS;
1 2 3
2 3 1
;
DATA t;
SET s;
BY _CHARACTER_;
RUN;
```

- KEEP and DROP statements give a WARNING message.

```
DATA s;
a=3;b=4;
KEEP _CHAR_;
RUN;
```

```
WARNING: The variable _CHARACTER_ in the DROP, KEEP, or RENAME list has never been
referenced.
NOTE: The data set WORK.S has 1 observations and 0 variables.
```

In the following I give a summary for variable lists.

Table 2. Missing variables in variable lists

	Define variables?	**Dash list missing some elements**	**Double dash list end variable missing**	**Empty list**
ARRAY	y	OK	n	OK
PUT	y	OK	n	OK
RENAME	n	OK		
KEEP, DROP	n	OK	See note	OK
LENGTH	y	OK	n	OK
FORMAT	y	OK	n	OK
INFORMAT	y	OK	n	OK
INPUT	y	OK	n	
RETAIN	y	OK	n	OK
BY	n	n	n	Not OK in PROC SORT, OK otherwise.
VAR	n	n	n	OK
OF list in statistical function	y	n	n	OK

References

Cody, Ron. (2004) SAS Functions by Example. Cary, NC: SAS Institute Inc.

"Referring to variables using SAS variable lists. "
http://www.pauldickman.com/teaching/sas/variable_lists.php

"SAS Variable Lists. " in *SAS Language Reference: Concepts*, 2005. Cary, NC: SAS Institute Inc.
http://support.sas.com/documentation/onlinedoc/91pdf/sasdoc_913/base_lrconcept_9196.pdf

Comparison Between a WHERE Statement and a Subsetting IF Statement

Mostly there are two ways to subset a data set: a WHERE statement and a subsetting IF statement. The syntax of a subsetting IF statement is as follows:

IF condition;

It tells SAS to process the observation only if the IF condition is true. The syntax of a WHERE statement is

WHERE condition;

It tells SAS to read in observations only if the WHERE condition is true.

The two statements are so similar that sometimes we can use them alternatively, but there are still differences between them. Almost every SAS programmer knows that they are different here or there, but we need a complete comparison. We already compared them in the following papers from some points of view:

End of a data set;
Statements, options, and their order;
Operators in the SAS language.

The purpose of this paper is to summarize comparisons and also to give some points that are not included in the above papers. We display comparisons in Table 1. In this paper, when we say SET statement, it means any one of SET, MERGE, UPDATE, or MODIFY statements.

Table 1. Comparison between a subsetting IF statement and a WHERE statement

Situation	IF statement	WHERE statement
Define variables	Definition statement, may be used to define variables.	Non-definition statement.
In program	Only in DATA step.	In DATA step and any procedures that read a data set.
In DATA step	Any DATA step.	Only for data step with a SET statement.
Position in DATA step	Anywhere in the DATA step.	After a SET statement.
More than one statement	Work on PDV independently.	Between two SET statements, only the last one is in effect.
Executing time	When reaching statement.	Immediately after a SET statement.
Executing in iteration	Executing once.	Executing until a true WHERE condition.
END= variable	Does not reset END= values.	Reset END= values.

Statement or option	Only independent statement.	Independent statement, also WHERE= option: In DATA step, in a SET statement, or in a DATA statement. In PROC step, suboption in DATA= or OUT= option. One word, anywhere a data set is specified.
With BY statement	Data set(s) must be sorted, executed after BY statement.	Executed before the BY statement.
MERGE statement	First merge and then filters.	First filters and then merge.
Variable requirement	Any variables in PDV, including user defined variables and system variables.	Only variables in data set(s) specified in previous SET statement.
Operator between different type	OK for any operation, auto converting.	Converts character value to Boolean for logical operators AND and OR, no other conversion.
Arguments in function call	Any type is OK, auto converting.	Must follow the requirement, no auto converting.
Converting rules	See Table 3 in [V].	See Table 3 in [V].
Array	Array ok.	No array reference.
Statistical functions	OF lists in arguments OK.	OF lists in arguments not OK.
_N_, FIRST.var LAST.var	Set before IF.	Set after WHERE.
Operators	>< means MIN; <> means MAX.	Associativity for MAX and MIN are different; >< not support; <> means not equal; More operators.

Below, we explain these differences and give some examples:

- The most important thing is that a WHERE statement is used to control reading data (and subsetting IF is used to control processing). Therefore, no matter where you put a WHERE statement, it is executed immediately after a SET statement even if you use it as an action of an IF-THEN statement, regardless of whether the IF condition is true or false. We already discussed this in [III].

Each IF statement works in PDV independently, but only the last WHERE statement between two SET statements is in effect.

- As we know, a WHERE statement replaces the previous WHERE statement. To keep valid the previous WHERE statement, you can use a WHERE ALSO or a WHERE SAME AND statement. Therefore, the following three lines of codes are equivalent:

```
WHERE a=3; WHERE ALSO b=4;
WHERE a=3; WHERE SAME AND b=4;
WHERE a=3 AND b=4;
```

For both statements you will see the following message in the log file:

```
NOTE: There were 1 observations read from the data set WORK.S.
WHERE (a=3) and (b=4);
```

These two choices are really redundant since any statements between a WHERE statement and a WHERE ALSO (or WHERE SAME AND statement) are executed after a WHERE ALSO statement.

- For function calls, a subsetting IF statement automatically converts a value if its type is not suitable, but a WHERE statement will stop processing if its type is not suitable.

```
DATA s;
a=14; b='23';
DATA t;
SET s;
IF SUM(a, b)=37;
IF LEFT(a)='14';
DATA p;
SET s;
WHERE SUM(a, b)=37;
WHERE LEFT(a)='14';
RUN;
```

```
554  DATA t;
555  SET s;
556  IF SUM(a, b)=37;
557  IF LEFT(a)='14';

NOTE: Character values have been converted to numeric values at the places given by:
      (Line):(Column).
      556:11
NOTE: Numeric values have been converted to character values at the places given by:
      (Line):(Column).
      557:9
NOTE: There were 1 observations read from the data set WORK.S.
NOTE: The data set WORK.T has 1 observations and 2 variables.

558  DATA p;
559  SET s;
560  WHERE SUM(a, b)=37;
ERROR: Function SUM requires a numeric expression as argument 2.
561  WHERE LEFT(a)='14';
ERROR: Function LEFT requires a character expression as argument 1.
562  RUN;

NOTE: The SAS System stopped processing this step because of errors.
```

- For statistical functions, OF lists are not allowed in a WHERE statement, but they are OK in an IF statement. Let's run the following program:

```
DATA s;
a1=1;a2=2;
DATA t;
```

```
SET s;
WHERE N(OF a1-a2)>0;
PROC PRINT;RUN;
```

```
52    WHERE N(OF a1-a2)>0;
                --
                22
                76
ERROR: Syntax error while parsing WHERE clause.

ERROR 22-322: Syntax error, expecting one of the following: !, !!, &, (, *, **, +, ',', -
, /, <, <=, <>, =, >, >=, ?, AND, BETWEEN, CONTAINS, EQ, GE, GT, LE, LIKE, LT, NE, OR,
^=, |, ||, ~=.

ERROR 76-322: Syntax error, statement will be ignored.

NOTE: The SAS System stopped processing this step because of errors.
```

- There is no array allowed in a WHERE statement, but an IF statement is OK. Try the following program:

```
DATA s;
INPUT a b;
CARDS;
1 2
1 3
5 3
8 5
;
DATA t;
SET s;
ARRAY aa(*) a--b;
WHERE aa(1)^=5;
PROC PRINT;RUN;
```

```
ERROR: Function/subroutine AA not found
NOTE: The SAS System stopped processing this step because of errors.
```

- Variable _N_ is not allowed in a WHERE statement. It is set after a WHERE statement. See the following program:

```
DATA s;
a=4;OUTPUT;
a=5;OUTPUT;
DATA t;
SET s;
WHERE a>4;
k=_N_;
PROC PRINT;
DATA p;
SET s;
IF a>4;
k=_N_;
PROC PRINT;
RUN;
```

```
Obs    a    k

 1     5    1


Obs    a    k

 1     5    2
```

- FIRST.var and LAST.var are set after reading data. Therefore,
  - FIRST.var and LAST.var are not allowed in a WHERE statement,
  - FIRST.var and LAST.var may be different because of the use of IF and WHERE statements. See the following example:

```
DATA s;
a=4;b=2;OUTPUT;
a=4;b=3;OUTPUT;
DATA t;
SET s;
BY a;
WHERE b>2;
k=FIRST.a;
PROC PRINT;
DATA p;
SET s;
BY a;
IF b>2;
k=FIRST.a;
PROC PRINT;
RUN;
```

```
Obs    a    b    k

 1     4    3    1

Obs    a    b    k

 1     4    3    0
```

- As we discussed in [III], a BY statement is executed after a WHERE statement. The following table shows whether a data set needs to be sorted under different situations.

Table 2. Relationship between subsetting and sorting with a BY statement

	Must be sorted?
OBS= and FIRSTOBS= options	Subset
WHERE statement	Subset
IF statement	Whole set

Let's see the following example:

```
DATA s;
```

```
INPUT a @@;
CARDS;
2 3 4 5 1 2
;
DATA t1;
SET s(OBS=4);
BY a;
RUN;
DATA t2;
SET s;
BY a;
WHERE a>2;
RUN;
DATA t3;
SET s;
BY a;
IF _N_<4;
RUN;
```

In this program, t1 and t2 work, but t3 does not work.

- The following program shows that for an IF statement, SAS first does the merge and then filters. However, for a WHERE statement, SAS first filters and then does the merge:

```
DATA s;
INPUT a b;
CARDS;
1 2
6 7
;
DATA t;
a=4;b=5;
DATA s1;
MERGE s t;
IF a+b>6;
DATA s2;
MERGE s t;
WHERE a+b>6;
RUN;
```

```
Obs    a    b

  1    4    5
  2    6    7

Obs    a    b

  1    4    5
```

For data set s1, SAS reads in observation (1 2) from s and then reads from t and overwrites. The PDV is (4 5). The IF condition is satisfied. Then SAS goes to a second iteration, so there are two observations. For data set s2, in the first iteration, SAS reads observation (1 2). The WHERE condition is not satisfied, so SAS continues to read another observation (6 7). The WHERE condition is satisfied. Then SAS reads in from data set t and overwrites, so there is only one observation.

- It is a common thought that a WHERE statement is more efficient than an IF statement because a WHERE statement selects observations before they enter the program data vector, and an IF statement selects observations after they enter the program data vector. Theoretically, this is true, but from my experience, there is no significant difference in practice. See the following example. These results do not mean that an IF statement uses less time than a WHERE statement. They show that only "sometimes" an IF statement uses less time than a WHERE statement. Notice that when you run the same program again, the amount of time spent may be different from the first time, but times are within the same range.

```
DATA s;
DO i=1 TO 123456789;
OUTPUT;
END;

NOTE: The data set WORK.S has 123456789 observations and 1 variables.
NOTE: DATA statement used (Total process time):
      real time           1:38.67
      cpu time            17.07 seconds


DATA t;
SET s;
WHERE MOD(i,3)=1;

NOTE: There were 41152263 observations read from the data set WORK.S.
      WHERE MOD(i, 3)=1;
NOTE: The data set WORK.T has 41152263 observations and 1 variables.
NOTE: DATA statement used (Total process time):
      real time           2:29.03
      cpu time            40.71 seconds


DATA p;
SET s;
IF MOD(i,3)=1;
RUN;

NOTE: There were 123456789 observations read from the data set WORK.S.
NOTE: The data set WORK.P has 41152263 observations and 1 variables.
NOTE: DATA statement used (Total process time):
      real time           2:24.90
      cpu time            22.43 seconds
```

Reference

"WHERE-Expression Processing", in *SAS Language Reference: Concepts*, 2005.Cary, NC: SAS Institute Inc.
http://support.sas.com/documentation/onlinedoc/91pdf/sasdoc_913/base_lrconcept_9196.pdf

Is .1+.2 equal to .3?

Introduction

Is .1+.2 equal to .3? Let us run the following program on a PC first:

```
DATA _NULL_;
IF .1+.2=.3 THEN PUT 'equal';
ELSE PUT 'not equal';
RUN;
```

We will see 'not equal' in the printout. Now let's run the following program:

```
DATA s;
DO i=.1 TO .9 BY .1;
a=i;
OUTPUT;
END;
DATA t;
DO i=.1 ,.2,.3,.4,.5,.6,.7,.8,.9;
b=i;
OUTPUT;
END;
DATA p;
MERGE s t;
BY i;
PROC PRINT;
RUN;
```

Obs	i	a	b
1	0.1	0.1	0.1
2	0.2	0.2	0.2
3	0.3	.	0.3
4	0.3	0.3	.
5	0.4	0.4	0.4
6	0.5	0.5	0.5
7	0.6	0.6	0.6
8	0.7	0.7	0.7
9	0.8	0.8	.
10	0.8	.	0.8
11	0.9	0.9	.
12	0.9	.	0.9

You can see that there are three more observations in data set p than those in s and in t. SAS treats .3 (in s) ^=.3 (in t), .8 (in s)^=.8 (in t), and .9 (in s)^=.9 (in t). Furthermore, you can see that .3 (in s)>.3 (in t), .8(in s)<.8(in t), and .9(in s) <.9(in t).

So what is wrong in this program? Nothing is wrong. You have to notice that SAS uses the format BEST. to print out values. Values in the printout are not those stored in the computer, not those that SAS uses to make a comparison. To see exact values stored in the computer that SAS uses to make a comparison, we have to use BINARY64. format. Now let's run the following program:

```
DATA s;
a=.3;
b=.1+.2;
PUT a= BINARY64.;
PUT b= BINARY64.;
RUN;
```

You can find the following printout in the log file:

```
a=0011111111010011001100110011001100110011001100110011001100110011
b=0011111111010011001100110011001100110011001100110011001100110100
```

Notice the difference in the last three digits.

Format BINARY64. is very helpful, but there are too many digits, that are easy to cause confusing. Usually, we can use format HEX16. There is a one-to-one correspondence between BINARY64 and HEX16. Four digits in BINARY64 correspond to one digit in HEX16, as the following table shows:

Table 1. Conversion between binary values and hex values

Binary value	Hex value
0000	0
0001	1
0010	2
0011	3
0100	4
0101	5
0110	6
0111	7
1000	8
1001	9
1010	A
1011	B
1100	C
1101	D
1110	E
1111	F

According to this table, you can find that the HEX16 expression for .3 is `3FD3333333333333` and that for .1+.2 is `3FD3333333333334`. Now let's run the following program:

```
DATA s;
DO i=.1 TO .9 BY .1;
a=i;a1=put(i,HEX16.);
OUTPUT;
END;
DATA t;
DO i=.1 ,.2,.3,.4,.5,.6,.7,.8,.9;
```

```
b=i;b1=put(i,HEX16.);
OUTPUT;
END;
DATA p;
MERGE s t;
BY i;
PROC PRINT;
VAR i a b a1 b1;
RUN;
```

Obs	i	a	b	a1	b1
1	0.1	0.1	0.1	3FB999999999999A	3FB999999999999A
2	0.2	0.2	0.2	3FC999999999999A	3FC999999999999A
3	0.3	.	0.3		3FD3333333333333
4	0.3	0.3	.	3FD3333333333334	
5	0.4	0.4	0.4	3FD999999999999A	3FD999999999999A
6	0.5	0.5	0.5	3FE0000000000000	3FE0000000000000
7	0.6	0.6	0.6	3FE3333333333333	3FE3333333333333
8	0.7	0.7	0.7	3FE6666666666666	3FE6666666666666
9	0.8	0.8	.	3FE9999999999999	
10	0.8	.	0.8		3FE999999999999A
11	0.9	0.9	.	3FECCCCCCCCCCCCC	
12	0.9	.	0.9		3FECCCCCCCCCCCCD

You can see that .3^=.3 because one is 3FD3333333333333, and the other is 3FD3333333333334. Even if their printouts are both .3 in decimal, they are not equal. In this paper we will talk about how SAS stores numeric values and does addition.

What is the difference between .1+.2 and .3? Let's run the following program:

```
DATA s;
a=.1+.2-.3;
b=2**(-54);
PUT a= HEX16. a= b=;
RUN;
```

We have the following output in the log file:

```
a=3C90000000000000 a=5.551115E-17 b=5.551115E-17
```

The exact difference is 2**(-54). Its decimal approximation is 5.55E-17, and its hex16 expression is 3C90000000000000.

How does SAS store numeric values?

You may wonder how to understand a BINARY64 printout or a HEX16 printout. Then we have to talk about how SAS stores numbers and how SAS does operations. Readers can also find detailed information for storing numbers in "Numeric Precision in SAS software", in *SAS Language Reference: Concepts* (2005).

As we know, usually we use a base 10 decimal to represent a number in our daily life.

There is a decimal point, digits preceding the decimal point represent digits with 10 powers, and digits after the decimal point represent digits with negative 10 powers. Therefore,

```
34.56=3*10**1+4*10**0+5*10**(-1)+6*10**(-2)
```

However, in SAS, numbers are expressed in base 2. Representing a number as a binary decimal is similar to the expression of the number as a decimal.

```
34.56=2**5+2**1+2**(-1)+2**(-5)+...    (decimal)
   =10**101+10**1+10**(-1)+10**(-101)+...    (binary)
```

Therefore, 34.56(base 10)=100010.10001....(base 2).

To find the binary expression for 34.56, we can also use the following way to handle its integer portion and fraction portion, and then put them together:

34/2= 17 r 0
17/2= 8 r 1
8/2=4 r 0
4/2=2 r 0
2/2=1 r 0
½=0 r 1

Taking the remainder from the bottom to the top, we get the integer 100010.

.56*2=1.12
.12*2=0.24
.24*2=0.48
.48*2=0.96
.96*2=1.92
.92*2=1.84

Taking the integer part from the top to the bottom, we get 100011. . . . Therefore, the whole number is 100010.100011. . . . These expressions (34.56 in base 10 or 100010.100011... in base 2) are called *fixed-point representation.*

However, SAS, the same as in most computer systems, does not use fixed-point representation for numeric values. Instead, SAS uses 64 bits Floating-Point representation (the IEEE 754 Standard, double precision) to store numeric values. Over the years, several different floating-point representations have been used in computers; however, for the last ten years, the most commonly encountered representation is that defined by the IEEE 754 Standard. The advantage of floating-point representation over fixed-point representation is that it can support a much wider range of values (magnitude), but it sacrifices some precision. Let's see how the IEEE 754 standard saves numeric values. For the number 34.56, we first normalize it as the following:

100010.1000111...=10**101*1.000101000111...

Here, 10 is base (2 in base 10), 101 is power (5 in base 10), and the remainder has an integer part 1 and a fraction portion which is called *mantissa*. Notice that a number can have a sign, and also the power can have a sign.

The IEEE 754 standard (double precision) uses 64 bits to save a numeric value. The first bit (bit 63, left most) is for the sign (0 for positive, and 1 for negative), and bit 62-52 (eleven bits) are for an exponent field. We omit the power sign by adding power with a constant, called *Bias*. The IEEE 754 Standard uses 1023 (in decimal, or 11 1111 1111, 10 bits, in binary) as Bias. Bit 51-0 (total 52 bits, or 6.5 bytes) are for mantissa. Notice that the integer portion of the remainder, 1, is not saved. It is called a *hidden bit*. Let us consider number 1.

1=10**0*1.0000000000+

Therefore, 1 in a floating-point representation is

```
0011 1111 1111 0000 0000 0000 0000 0000 0000 0000 0000 0000 0000 0000 0000 0000
```

The hexadecimal representation of this number is

3FF0000000000000

Let's run the following program to validate:

```
DATA _NULL_;
x=1;
PUT x= HEX16. '(hex)   ' x= '(decimal)';
PUT x= BINARY64.;
RUN;
```

You can see the following printout in the log file:

```
x=3FF0000000000000 (hex)  x=1 (decimal)
x=0011111111110000000000000000000000000000000000000000000000000000
```

You can guess the floating-point representation for -1 is `BFF0000000000000`.

Now we will discuss a fraction number, a number that is less than 1. As we can see, a number with terminating expansion in base 10 may become a recurring decimal in binary representation. Since a computer stores only a limited number of bits for a number, we have to consider how to handle the last digit, by rounding or by truncating. IEEE 754 uses rounding in a floating-point representation. For number 34.56, i.e., 10**101*1.000101000111 ... in binary, its power in normalization is 101.

```
101+11 1111 1111=100 0000 0100

Therefore it is saved as

0100 0000 0100 0001 0100 0111...
```

Or it is 404147AE147AE148 in hex value. Its true binary expression is recurring. The last digit is rounding. Next we see how 0.1 is saved. It is easy to see that the binary expression of .1 is

0.000110011001100....=10**(-100)*1.1001 1001 1001...

Therefore, its floating-point representation is

0011 1111 1011 1001 1001 1001 ...1010

Its hex value is

```
3FB999999999999A
```

How does SAS do addition?

Next, we will talk about operation. Actually, we will only talk about addition, and only for positive numbers. We imitate how SAS does or the IEEE 754 standard does additions for floating point expressions. If two numbers have the same exponent portion (bits 63-52), then it is easy. We only have to add up their mantissas. As they both have a hidden bit 1, the sum will be 10. So for normalization, we have to add 1 to the exponent portion. Also, we have to move the decimal point one bit to the left for the sum.

Suppose that two mantissas of two numbers are 1101 and 1011. They represent 1.1101 and 1.1011.

```
     1.1101
+    1.1011
-----------
    11.1000
```

11.1000=10**1*1.11000

Therefore, when doing addition, we can do as follows: add one to the exponent portion, add up two mantissas, move the resulting mantissa one bit to the right, and do rounding.

If two numbers have different exponent portions, we first have to adjust the decimal point.

Let us see our example .1+.2. First, we will show you how we do additions on fixed point expressions.

0.1(dec)= 0.000110011001100....
0.2(dec)= 0.00110011001100....

```
      0.000|110011001100
+     0.001|10011001100
---------------------------
=     0.010|0110011001100
=10**(-10)*1.001100110011...
```

As we know, its floating-point representation is 3FD3333333333333. We can see the relationship between the IEEE standard and real numbers.

.1 in IEEE `3FB999999999999A > .1 in real number 3FB99999999999999999999...`
.2 in IEEE `3FC999999999999A > .2 in real number 3FC99999999999999999999...`
.3 in IEEE `3FD3333333333333 < .3 in real number 3FD33333333333333333333...`

It appears that .1+.2>.3, but we still have to do real addition. Now let us see how to do addition for a floating-point representation. The following are floating point expressions for .2 and .1:

```
.2  0011 1111 1100|100110011001......1001 1010  3FC999999999999A
.1  0011 1111 1011|100110011001......1001 1010  3FB999999999999A
```

Since they have a different power field, in order to do addition, we first have to adjust the decimal point. Since .2>.1, we keep the representation of .2 not changed, but we change .1. We add one to the power of .1 and move the mantissa of .1 one bit to the right. At this time, we have to get back a hidden bit of .1, such as the following:

```
    .2  0011 1111 1100|1001 1001 1001 1001 1001 ... 1001 1001 1001 1001 1001 1010
+   .1  0011 1111 1100|1100 1100 1100 1100 1100 ... 1100 1100 1100 1100 1100 1101
-------------------------------------------------------------------------------------
                     1 0110 0110 0110 0110 0110 ... 0110 0110 0110 0110 0110 0111
```

Notice that for this expression, the hidden bit for .2 (the bigger number) is still 1, but that for .1 (the smaller number) is 0.

Now we add up their mantissas. In general, there are two possibilities: Either there is 1 at bit 53, or there is not. In our example, the bit 53 is 1. It must be added to the hidden bit, which becomes 10. For normalization, 1 becomes the new hidden bit, 0 goes to the mantissa (move the mantissa one bit to the right and add 0 at the beginning), and raise the exponent field by 1. Therefore, the sum becomes

```
0011 1111 1101|0011 0011 0011 0011 0011 0011 0011 0011 0011 0011 0011 0011 0011 0011|1
```

At this time we have to do rounding. Finally, the floating-point representation of .1+.2 will be 3FD3333333333334. Therefore, .1+.2^=.3. Furthermore, .1+.2>.3. Moreover, the difference between .1+.2 and .3 is 2**(-54), or approximately `5.551115E-17`.

Let's see the example .1+.7^=.8.

```
.7  3FE6666666666666   0011 1111 1110 0110 0110 ... 0110
.1  3FB999999999999A   0011 1111 1011 1001 1001 ... 1010
```

```
.8  3FE999999999999A   0011 1111 1110 1001 1001 ... 1010

   .7  0011 1111 1110| 0110 0110 ... 0110
+  .1  0011 1111 1110| 0011 0011 ... 0011| 010
                       1001 1001 ... 1001
```

Since no 1 goes to hidden bit, we don't have to do anything.
Therefore, .1+.7=`3FE9999999999999 and` .1+.7<.8.

How can we avoid problems?

When doing analysis, for example, calculating the mean or other statistic values, the floating-point expression has almost no effect. Compared to .1, 5.55E-17 is really a small number. But for categorical values, it really matters. Also for comparison, it really matters. The results of comparison take only two values: true or false, so a very small difference may change the results. As we showed in the above, SAS cannot even do MERGE.

Now we will talk about how to avoid problems. The main point is to avoid using fraction operations.

1. Use integers to be levels of a categorical variable, instead of fractions.
2. When using fractions, make sure that fractions are the same as they are stored in the computer. If you use a DO loop, use hard code fraction values rather than accumulate adding, as in the following code:

```
DATA  s;
DO i=.1 ,.2,.3,.4,.5,.6,.7,.8,.9;
OUTPUT;
END;
RUN;
```

3. Use integer division,

```
DATA  s;
DO j = 1 TO 9;
i=j/10; OUTPUT;
END;
RUN;
```

4. You can use accumulate adding, but use the function ROUND to adjust them.

```
DATA  s;
DO j = .1 TO .9 BY .1;
i=ROUND(j,.1);
 OUTPUT;
END;
```

In order to make sure that the above approaches works, you can use the following simple program to check:

```
DATA t;
SET s;
```

```
IF i in (.1 .2 .3 .4 .5 .6 .7 .8 .9);
PROC PRINT;
RUN;
```

You can also modify the comparison.

5. Use a round function in comparison. Use IF ROUND(a,.1)=.7; instead of IF a=.7;
6. For greater than or lesser than comparison, we can use the round function, too. We can also use the tail number method. Instead of IF a<.4;, write IF a<.4-.000001;. Instead of IF a<=.4;, write IF a<=.4+.000001;.
7. For equal comparison, we can also use the function ABS with a small tail value: Instead of IF a=b;, use IF a<.4+.000001 AND a>.4-.000001; or IF ABS(a-b)<.00001;.

Magnitude and precision

Now we will talk about magnitude and precision. Magnitude is the biggest number that SAS can store. Precision is the biggest number (integer) such that all integers less than it can be saved exactly. Theoretically, the biggest number that SAS can store is the following:

7fff ffff ffff ffff

or

(2-2**(-52))*2**2**10

For the IEEE 754 standard, it should be OK. But for the SAS system, in reality, the biggest number is a little smaller than this. If you run the following program, you will get an error (2**1024=2**2**10):

```
data s;
a=2**1024;
NOTE: Invalid argument(s) to the exponential operator "**".
put a hex16.;
run;
```

But if you run the following program, it is OK:

```
data t;
a=2**1023*(2-2**(-52));
put a= hex16. @20 a;
run;

a=7FEFFFFFFFFFFFFF 1.797693E308
```

From the above analysis we can see that the magnitude is `2**1023*(2-2**(-52))`, and the precision is 2**53. The following program shows that SAS treats 2**53-1 and 2**53-2 as two different numbers but 2**53 and 2**53+1 as the same number:

```
DATA s;
a0=2**53-2;
```

```
a1=2**53-1;
a2=2**53;
a3=2**53+1;
b=a1=a0;c=a3=a2;
PROC PRINT;
RUN;
```

Obs	a0	a1	a2	a3	b	c
1	9.0072E15	9.0072E15	9.0072E15	9.0072E15	0	1

Length attribute

The range of a LENGTH attribute of a numeric variable is 3-8, counted in bytes. So if you define the length of a numeric variable to be 2 or 9, SAS will complain. The default length attribute of a numeric variable is 8. It is not related to a definition statement [III]. The only way to set the length attribute for a numeric variable is to use a LENGTH or ATTRIB/LENGTH statement. By setting length smaller than 8, we can save computer resources. So what does the length mean? How do different length settings affect operations and results?

As we know, an IEEE 754 expression uses one bit for the sign, 11 bits for the exponent field, and 52 bits for the mantissa. A different length setting will not change bits for the sign and the exponent field, but it will reduce bits for the mantissa. Their correspondence is shown in the following:

Length setting	3	4	5	6	7	8
Space for mantissa (bits)	12	20	28	36	44	52

Different length attribute settings have a similar magnitude (the same number of bits for a power field) but different accuracy (a different number of bits for a mantissa). You can also use the function CONSTANT() to find the largest integer that SAS can save as exact integers for all integers less than it in an absolute value. For example, CONSTANT('exactint',3)=8192 (=2**13) tells us that when using length=3, all integers less than 8192 have an exact representation. But if the integer is more than 8192(=2**13), there will possibly be an accuracy problem. For example, SAS saves 8193 as 8192, 8195 as 8194, etc. Let us run the following program:

```
DATA s;
LENGTH a b 3;
a=8192; b=8193;
DATA t;
SET s;
PUT a= b=;
IF a=b THEN PUT "They are equal.";
RUN;
```

We can see the following printout in the log file:

```
a=8192 b=8192
They are equal.
```

Notice that the length setting for a numeric variable is in effect only for a saved data set, but not in the PDV (Program Data Vector) that SAS is working on. So if we put the PUT statement in the first DATA step, we will see different results.

Now we know that if an integer is big, a small length setting will affect the results. A different length setting will also affect the results on fraction operations. To see how different length settings affect the operation, let us first run the following program:

```
DATA s;
LENGTH a 3;
a=.1;
PUT a HEX16.;
DATA t;
SET s;
PUT a HEX16.;
RUN;
```

We see the following output in the log file:

```
3FB999999999999A

3FB9990000000000
```

This example tells us

- In PDV, SAS always uses 64 bits to handle numeric values, no matter what the length setting is. When writing to a data set, SAS truncates the value according to the length setting, rather than rounding.

The following program shows how the length setting affects results:

```
DATA s;
LENGTH i 3;
DO i=.1 TO 1.6 BY .1;
IF i IN (.1 .2 .3 .4 .5 .6 .7 .8 .9 1 1.1 1.2 1.3 1.4 1.5 1.6)
      THEN PUT 'in s   ' i=;
OUTPUT;
END;
DATA t;
SET s;
IF i IN (.1 .2 .3 .4 .5 .6 .7 .8 .9 1 1.1 1.2 1.3 1.4 1.5 1.6)
      THEN PUT 'in t   ' i=;
PROC PRINT;
RUN;
```

We can see the following output in the log file:

```
in s  i=0.1
in s  i=0.2
in s  i=0.4
in s  i=0.5
in s  i=0.6
```

```
in s  i=0.7
in s  i=1.2
in s  i=1.3

in t  i=0.5
in t  i=1.5
```

Here in the first data step, it is the same as we have discussed. However, in the second data step, it is totally different. If a number is recurring, then in its length=3 representation, bits 44-0 are all zero. But in length=8 representation, for a recurring number, usually they are not zero. Therefore, they are not equal. We only have to check terminating decimals .5 (3FE0000000000000),1 (3FF0000000000000), and 1.5 (3FE8000000000000). The following are corresponding values of i:

	Before saving	After saving (come back to PDV)
.5	3FE0000000000000	3FE0000000000000
1	3FEFFFFFFFFFFFFF	3FEFFF0000000000
1.5	3FF8000000000001	3FF8000000000000

Therefore, only two values are equal.

In this example, we compare values with length=3 with values with length=8. Next, we compare values with the same length, say length=3. See the following example:

```
DATA s;
LENGTH i a 3;
DO i=.1 TO 1 BY .1;
a=i;
OUTPUT;
END;
DATA t;
LENGTH i b 3;
DO i=.1 ,.2,.3,.4,.5,.6,.7,.8,.9,1;
b=i;
OUTPUT;
END;
DATA p;
MERGE s t;
BY i;
a1=PUT(a,HEX16.);
b1=PUT(b,HEX16.);
PROC PRINT;
VAR i a b a1 b1;
RUN;
```

Obs	i	a	b	a1	b1
1	0.09999	0.09999	0.09999	3FB9990000000000	3FB9990000000000
2	0.19998	0.19998	0.19998	3FC9990000000000	3FC9990000000000
3	0.29999	0.29999	0.29999	3FD3330000000000	3FD3330000000000
4	0.39996	0.39996	0.39996	3FD9990000000000	3FD9990000000000
5	0.50000	0.50000	0.50000	3FE0000000000000	3FE0000000000000

6	0.59998	0.59998	0.59998	3FE3330000000000	3FE3330000000000
7	0.69995	0.69995	0.69995	3FE6660000000000	3FE6660000000000
8	0.79993	0.79993	0.79993	3FE9990000000000	3FE9990000000000
9	0.89990	0.89990	0.89990	3FECCC0000000000	3FECCC0000000000
10	0.99988	0.99988	.	3FEFFF0000000000	.
11	1.00000	.	1.00000	.	3FF0000000000000

We can see that, the results are totally different from that with length 8.

The above discussion is based on a PC Windows. Since UNIX also uses the IEEE standard, the results are the same. Also, VAX/VMS uses different representation, different bit assignments for exponent, bias and mantissas, but it also uses rounding rather than truncating, and the results should not be affected. However, IBM uses a different method: truncating. The result is different from this paper. The following is the output from an IBM mainframe for the second program in this paper.

Obs	I	A	B	A1	B1
1	0.1	0.1	0.1	4019999999999999	4019999999999999
2	0.2	0.2	.	4033333333333332	
3	0.2	.	0.2		4033333333333333
4	0.3	0.3	.	404CCCCCCCCCCCCB	
5	0.3	.	0.3		404CCCCCCCCCCCCC
6	0.4	0.4	.	4066666666666664	
7	0.4	.	0.4		4066666666666666
8	0.5	0.5	.	407FFFFFFFFFFFFD	
9	0.5	.	0.5		4080000000000000
10	0.6	0.6	.	4099999999999996	
11	0.6	.	0.6		4099999999999999
12	0.7	0.7	.	40B333333333332F	
13	0.7	.	0.7		40B3333333333333
14	0.8	0.8	.	40CCCCCCCCCCCCC8	
15	0.8	.	0.8		40CCCCCCCCCCCCCC

Other softwares

There are many languages that use the IEEE 754 standard. Therefore, their behaviors are similar to SAS. I put C++, JAVA, and AWK programs and output in the following so that readers can compare:

C++

```
===========================
#include <stdio.h>
#include <stdio.h>
#include <stream.h>

main()

{
```

```
 double d[] = {0.1, 0.2, 0.3, 0.4, 0.5, 0.6, 0.7, 0.8, 0.9};
 double a = 0.1;
 for (int i = 0; i < 8; i++)
   {
    cout.precision(2);
    if ((a + d[i]) == d[i+1])
      cout << 0.1 << " + " << d[i]  << " = " << d[i+1] << endl;
    else
      {
       cout << 0.1 << " + " << d[i]  << " != " << d[i+1] << endl;
       double dif = (a + d[i]) - d[i+1];
       cout.precision(30);
       cout << "(" << 0.1 << " + " << d[i]  << ") - " << d[i+1] <<
         " = " << dif << endl;
      }
   }
}
==========================
0.1 + 0.1 = 0.2
0.1 + 0.2 != 0.3
(0.1000000000000000055511151231 26 + 0.200000000000000011102230246252) -
0.299999999999999988897769753748 = 5.55111512312578270211815834045e-17
0.1 + 0.3 = 0.4
0.1 + 0.4 = 0.5
0.1 + 0.5 = 0.6
0.1 + 0.6 = 0.7
0.1 + 0.7 !- 0.8
(0.100000000000000005551115123126 + 0.699999999999999955591079014994) -
0.800000000000000044408920985006 = -1.11022302462515654042363166809e-16
0.1 + 0.8 = 0.9
```

****

Jiva:

```
=======================================
public void test_double()
  {
   double d[] = {0.1, 0.2, 0.3, 0.4, 0.5, 0.6, 0.7, 0.8, 0.9};
   double a = 0.1;
   for (int i = 0; i < 8; i++)
     {
      if ((a + d[i]) == d[i+1])
        System.out.println("0.1   + " + d[i]  + " = " + d[i+1]);
      else
        {
         System.out.println("0.1   + " + d[i]  + " != " + d[i+1]);
         double dif = (a + d[i]) - d[i+1];
         System.out.println("(0.1   + " + d[i]  + ") - " + d[i+1] +
                  " = " + dif);
        }
     }

  }

==========================
```

```
0.1  + 0.1 = 0.2
0.1  + 0.2 != 0.3
(0.1  + 0.2) - 0.3 = 5.551115123125783E-17
0.1  + 0.3 = 0.4
0.1  + 0.4 = 0.5
0.1  + 0.5 = 0.6
0.1  + 0.6 = 0.7
0.1  + 0.7 != 0.8
(0.1  + 0.7) - 0.8 = -1.1102230246251565E-16
```

AWK

```
##############

BEGIN {

a[1]=b[1]=0.1
a[2]=b[2]=0.2
a[3]=b[3]=0.3
a[4]=b[4]=0.4
a[5]=b[5]=0.5
a[6]=b[6]=0.6
a[7]=b[7]=0.7
a[8]=b[8]=0.8
a[9]=b[9]=0.9

for (i=1; i<=8; i++ ) {
  if ( a[i] + 0.1 == b[i+1] ) {
    printf("%s%i%s%i\n", "0.1 + 0.", i, " = 0.", i+1)
  } else {
    printf("%s%i%s%i%s", "0.1 + 0.", i, " != 0.", i+1, "; difference=")
    print a[i] + 0.1 - b[i+1]
  }
}

}
########## end ########

0.1 + 0.1 = 0.2
0.1 + 0.2 != 0.3; difference=5.55112e-17
0.1 + 0.3 = 0.4
0.1 + 0.4 = 0.5
0.1 + 0.5 = 0.6
0.1 + 0.6 = 0.7
0.1 + 0.7 != 0.8; difference=-1.11022e-16
0.1 + 0.8 = 0.9
```

References

"Dealing with Numeric Representation Error in SAS Applications. "
http://support.sas.com/techsup/technote/ts230.html

"Floating point. "
http://en.wikipedia.org/wiki/Floating_point

"IEEE-754 Floating-Point Conversion. " http://babbage.cs.qc.edu/IEEE-754/Decimal.html

"Numeric Precision in SAS software. " in *SAS Language Reference: Concepts*, 2005.Cary, NC: SAS Institute Inc. http://support.sas.com/documentation/onlinedoc/91pdf/sasdoc_913/base_lrconcept_9196.pdf

"TS-DOC: TS-654 - Numeric Precision 101. " http://support.sas.com/techsup/technote/ts654.pdf

Binary Expression of Values and Related Formats and Informats

Introduction

In [VIII] we talked about how SAS stores numbers. First, we talked about how to convert a decimal number (base 10) to binary (base 2) and then how to convert it to a floating-point expression. We showed you how to do the converting manually.

We can also use SAS programming to do converting by using format or informat. Notice that for floating-point expression, if we remove some right most bits, it will cause precision problem, similar to length setting, but if we remove some left most bits, the value will be totally different. We will first consider the format BINARY.

BINARYw. format

Format BINARYw. can be used to convert a number from decimal expression to binary expression. It has the following characteristics:

- The range of width is 1-64. The default is 8.
- Width w=1-58 converts a decimal number to its binary expression. This only works on integers. For a fraction number, it picks the integer part. For a negative number a, the result is the same as in a binary expression of a positive integer a+2**w.
- Width w>=59 converts a decimal number to its floating-point expression. It works on fractions and negative numbers.
- No matter to convert a number to a binary expression (suppose it has x digits) or a floating-point expression (always 64 digits), picks only the last (rightmost) w digits if x>w or 64>w.

The following program shows different behaviors of different width settings. We give only partial printouts here:

```
%MACRO s;
DATA s;
a=.1;
%DO i=1 %TO 64;
PUT "i=&i" @6 a BINARY&i..;
%END;
RUN;
%MEND;
%s
```

```
i=55 0000000000000000000000000000000000000000000000000000000
i=56 00000000000000000000000000000000000000000000000000000000
i=57 000000000000000000000000000000000000000000000000000000000
i=58 0000000000000000000000000000000000000000000000000000000000
i=59 11110111001100110011001100110011001100110011001100110011010
i=60 111110111001100110011001100110011001100110011001100110011010
i=61 1111110111001100110011001100110011001100110011001100110011010
i=62 11111110111001100110011001100110011001100110011001100110011010
i=63 011111110111001100110011001100110011001100110011001100110011010
```

```
i=64 0011111110111001100110011001100110011001100110011001100110011010
```

Because integer part of .1 is 0, all w<59 printouts treat .1 as 0.

Now run the following program:

```
DATA s;
INPUT a;
PUT a BINARY.;
CARDS;
123.45
123
-123
133
;
RUN;
```

The following are printouts in the log file:

```
01111011
01111011
10000101
10000101
```

The first two outputs show that BINARY format ignores the fractional part of a number. The last two outputs are the same because 133+123=2**8, where 8 is the default width of the format BINARY.

Therefore, to use the format BINARYw., you have to notice the following:

- Don't use it for fractional numbers with w<59.
- Make sure w is big enough.
- Don't work on negative numbers for w<59 unless you understand them.
- Don't use widths of 59-63. They cause confusion.

BINARYw.d informat

A BINARY informat is used to convert a binary number or a floating-point expression (character type) to a decimal number. The range of its width is also 1-64, where 1-56 is for binary, 57-64 is for a floating-point, and the default is 8. We will talk first about informat BINARYw. (without optional d). Let's run the following program. In the program, variable a has 64 characters. For w from 1 to 56, SAS takes the leftmost w digits and treats them as a binary expression. In our example, for w>12, when w increases 1, the number will be double. (You can figure out what happens when w<12.) For w from 57 to 63, SAS takes the leftmost w characters (SAS drops some rightmost characters) and then fills in 0 on the left to make it 64 digits, treats it as a floating-point expression, and does converting. So the printout may seem strange. The value of a in the assignment is a floating-point expression of number 1. So when w=64, we get the number 1.

```
%MACRO s;
DATA s;
LENGTH j $64;
```

```
a='0011111111110000000000000000000000000000000000000000000000000000';
%DO i=1 %TO 64;
j=INPUT(a,BINARY&i..);
OUTPUT;
%END;
PROC PRINT;VAR j;
RUN;
%MEND;
%s
```

52	1124800395214848
53	2249600790429696
54	4499201580859392
55	8998403161718784
56	17996806323437568
57	2.8369691695966E-306
58	7.2341601287786E-304
59	4.7036486372562E-299
60	1.9881350131289E-289
61	3.5491565585003E-270
62	1.1272010346795E-231
63	1.11875110968E-154
64	1

For w<57, the result is always a positive integer. For w between 57 and 63, the result may include a fractional part, but it is always positive. W=64 converts binary to positive or negative depending on the first digit.

Notice how SAS does for the informat BINARYw.:

- Remove trailing blanks.
- Replace leading blanks by 0s.
- After the above two steps, if the number of digits of the value is less than w, fill in 0's on the left to make the number of digits equal to w, and if there are more digits than w, SAS takes the leftmost w digits.
- For w=1-56, SAS treats it as a binary number and converts it to an integer.
- For w from 57 to 64, SAS fills in 0 on the left to make it 64 characters, treats it as a floating-point expression, and converts it to a decimal number.

Now consider optional d. The informat BINARYw.d can be used to create a fraction using option d. BINARYw.d means first to convert the value to a decimal using the BINARYw. informat, and then to divide the resultant value by 10**d.

See the following program:

```
DATA s;
LENGTH a $16;
a='100100';OUTPUT;
a='  1001001   ';OUTPUT;
a='001001001001';OUTPUT;
DATA t;
```

```
SET s;
b=INPUT(a,BINARY.);
c=INPUT(a,BINARY8.2);
PROC PRINT;RUN;
```

Obs	a	b	c
1	100100	36	0.36
2	100100	36	0.36
3	001001001001	36	0.36

BINARYw.d can read negative values, but only if w=64, and the first character is 1. Notice that in SAS Language Reference: Dictionary (2006, p. 1054), the following statement is not true:

BINARYw.d cannot read negative values. It treats all input values as positive (unsigned).

Let's see the following example:

```
DATA s;
a='1011111111110000000000000000000000000000000000000000000000000000';
b=INPUT(a,BINARY64.3);
PUT b=;
RUN;
```

```
b=-0.001
```

HEXw. format

In [VIII] we talk about the conversion between hex values and binary values and relationship between BINARY64 and HEX16. For general width, we have the following conclusions: The format HEXw. is equivalent to BINARYx. where x=4*w, except w=15, because BINARY60 converts a number to a floating-point expression, and HEX15 converts a number to a hex expression, not a floating-point expression. See the following example. Here a1 and b1 show the same values (floating-point), a3 and b3 show the same value (binary), but a2 and b2 are different. Notice that b2 can be obtained from b1 by removing four leading bits, and a3 can be obtained from a2 by removing five leading bits:

```
DATA s;
a1=123;a2=123;a3=123;b1=123;b2=123;b3=123;
PUT a1= HEX16. @21 b1= BINARY64.;
PUT a2= HEX15. @21 b2= BINARY60.;
PUT a3= HEX10. @21 b3= BINARY40.;
RUN;
```

```
a1=405EC00000000000  b1=0100000001011110110000000000000000000000000000000000000000000000
a2=00000000000007B   b2=000001011110110000000000000000000000000000000000000000000000
a3=000000007B        b3=0000000000000000000000000000000001111011
```

HEXw. informat

Similar to a BINARY informat, a HEX informat can be used to read a hex value. w=16 treats the value as a floating-point expression in hex format and converts. W<16 treats the value as a hex expression integer and converts. Other rules are the same as for BINARY informat. See the following example:

```
DATA s;
LENGTH a $16;
a='241';OUTPUT;
a='  241  ';OUTPUT;
a='2413';OUTPUT;
DATA t;
SET s;
b=INPUT(a,HEX3.);
PROC PRINT;RUN;
```

```
Obs     a        b

  1    241      577
  2      241      2
  3    2413     577
```

As the example shows, the following statement in SAS Language Reference: Dictionary (2006, p. 1067) is not accurate:

The HEXw. informat ignores leading or trailing blanks.

Hexdecimal expression

We know that we can also directly assign a value to a variable using a hex expression. However, directly assigning works only for positive integers and always treats the number as a binary expression, not a floating-point, even if you have 16 digits of hex value. In the following program, b1 and c1 are read from instream input, where b1 uses HEX16 informat, and c1 uses a HEX15 informat. As we discussed before, SAS treats b1 as a floating-point expression. Therefore, the values read in and that printed out of b1 are the same. But that of b2, c1, and c2 are different. SAS treats them as binary values and converts them to a floating-point expression. Notice that SAS also does rounding when converting binary to a floating-point expression in our example. In the following we show how to calculate a binary value 7feffffffffffff (hex expression). Notice that the cases for c1 and c2 are similar to that of b2. Since we read in using a format HEX15 informat, save it as floating-point (rounding appears), and then print it out using HEX15, the printouts are slightly different from that input.

7feffffffffffff
=111 1111 1110 1111 1111 1111 1111 1111 1111 1111 1111 1111 1111 1111 1111 1111
=10**111110*1. 1111 1111 1100 0000 0000 0000 0000 0000 0000 0000 0000 0000 0000

```
DATA s;
INPUT b1 HEX16. +1 c1 HEX15.;
b2=7fefffffffffffffx;c2=7feffffffffffffx;
PUT b1= HEX16. c1= HEX16. c1= HEX15.;
PUT b2= HEX16. c2= HEX16. c2= HEX15.;
CARDS;
7fefffffffffffff 7feffffffffffff
;
```

```
RUN;
```

```
b1=7FEFFFFFFFFFFFFF c1=439FFC0000000000 c1=7FF000000000000
b2=43DFFC0000000000 c2=439FFC0000000000 c2=7FF000000000000
```

For a hexdecimal expression, you have to notice the following points:

- Begin with a digit and end with x with 0-9, a-f in the middle.
- Max length is 17 including ending x.
- Suppose you want to put a number in a hexdecimal expression beginning with a-f. If the length is less than 17, you can add 0 in the front. However, if the length is already 17, you cannot do this.
- Therefore, the biggest integer that a hexdecimal expression can express is `9FFFFFFFFFFFFFFFx`. However, if a number is greater than `10000000000000x`, it may have a precision problem, as we have discussed.

Characters and their hex values

Now we will talk about character values. As we know, computer also uses binary expression to store character values, but converting is totally different for numeric values.

SAS uses 8 bits or 1 byte to store one character. Therefore, in all there are 2**8=256 different characters. We can use the function BYTE to get these characters. Let us first see what they are.

```
PROC FORMAT;
VALUE a 10='a' 11='b' 12='c' 13='d' 14='e' 15='f';
DATA s;
LENGTH a0-a15 $1;
ARRAY a(0:15) $ a0-a15;
DO i=0 TO 15;
DO j=0 TO 15;
a(j)=BYTE(i*16+j);
END;
OUTPUT;
END;
LABEL i=' ' a0='0' a1='1' a2='2' a3='3' a4='4' a5='5' a6='6' a7='7'
   a8='8' a9='9' a10='a' a11='b' a12='c' a13='d' a14='e' a15='f';
   FORMAT i a.;
RUN;
OPTION NOCENTER;
PROC REPORT DATA=S SPACING=1 HEADSKIP NOWD;
COLUMN i a0-a15;
DEFINE a0 /DISPLAY SPACING=2 ;
RUN;
```

Table 1. Characters and their hex values (SAS monospace font)

i	0	1	2	3	4	5	6	7	8	9	a	b	c	d	e	f
0		□	□	□	□	□	□	□	□	□	□	□	□	□	□	□
1	□	□	□	□	□	□	□	□	□	□	□	□	□	□		□
2		!	"	#	$	%	&	'	(	)	*	+	,	-	.	/
3	0	1	2	3	4	5	6	7	8	9	:	;	<	=	>	?
4	@	A	B	C	D	E	F	G	H	I	J	K	L	M	N	O
5	P	Q	R	S	T	U	V	W	X	Y	Z	[	\	]	^	_
6	`	a	b	c	d	e	f	g	h	i	j	k	l	m	n	o
7	p	q	r	s	t	u	v	w	x	y	z	{	¦	}	~	□
8	€	□	│	─	┌	┬	┐	├	┼	┤	└	┴	┘	□	□	□
9	□	‘		║	═	╓	╥	╖	╟	╫	╢	╙	╨	□	□	╜
a		¡	¢	£	¤	¥	¦	§		©	ª	«	¬	-	®	¯
b	°	±	²	³	´	µ	¶		¸	¹	º	»	¼	½	¾	¿
c	À	Á	Â	Ã	Ä	Å	Æ	Ç	È	É	Ê	Ë	Ì	Í	Î	Ï
d	Ð	Ñ	Ò	Ó	Ô	Õ	Ö	×	Ø	Ù	Ú	Û	Ü	Ý	Þ	ß
e	à	á	â	ã	ä	å	æ	ç	è	é	ê	ë	ì	í	î	ï
f	ð	ñ	ò	ó	ô	õ	ö	÷	ø	ù	ú	û	ü	ý	þ	ÿ

The table gives 256 characters. Combining the left column and the head gives you the hex value of each character. We can divide them into three categories:

- Regular characters, characters corresponding to hex values 20-7e are regular characters, where 20 corresponds to a blank.
- Special characters, such as 82-8c.
- Unprintable characters, such as 00-1f, 7f, 8d, 8f, although some have a print out, but they are not stable, depending on platforms.

Notice that 09 corresponds to tab as we used in an INFILE statement. DLM='09'x means we are reading a tab delimited file. It is useful, but it is also an unprintable character. Other unprintable characters include line feed (0a) and page feed (0c).

Notice the following:

- They are related to fonts. However, for regular characters, most fonts are the same. Their difference is appearance.
- For special characters and unprintable characters, they may be totally different for different fonts.
- The SAS default font for output and log is the SAS monospace font. In the Edit window, it is Courier New.

To see the correspondence of hex values to different fonts, we can do this in a Word document file: Copy the SAS output to a Word document and change the font. Table 2 gives the Courier New font for corresponding hex values.

Table 2. Characters and their hex values (Courier New font)

i	0	1	2	3	4	5	6	7	8	9	a	b	c	d	e	f
0		_	_	_	_	_	_	_	_		_		_	_		
1	_	_	_	_	_	_	_	_	_	_	_	_	_	_	_	_

```
2     !  "  #  $  %  &  '  (  )  *  +  ,  -  .  /
3  0  1  2  3  4  5  6  7  8  9  :  ;  <  =  >  ?
4  @  A  B  C  D  E  F  G  H  I  J  K  L  M  N  O
5  P  Q  R  S  T  U  V  W  X  Y  Z  [  \  ]  ^  _
6  `  a  b  c  d  e  f  g  h  i  j  k  l  m  n  o
7  p  q  r  s  t  u  v  w  x  y  z  {  |  }  ~  ▯
8  €  ▯  ‚  ƒ  „  …  †  ‡  ˆ  ‰  Š  ‹  Œ  ▯  Ž  ▯
9  ▯  ‘  ’  “  ”  •  –  —  ˜  ™  š  ›  œ  ▯  ž  Ÿ
a     ¡  ¢  £  ¤  ¥  ¦  §  ¨  ©  ª  «  ¬  -  ®  ¯
b  °  ±  ²  ³  ´  µ  ¶  ·  ¸  ¹  º  »  ¼  ½  ¾  ¿
c  À  Á  Â  Ã  Ä  Å  Æ  Ç  È  É  Ê  Ë  Ì  Í  Î  Ï
d  Ð  Ñ  Ò  Ó  Ô  Õ  Ö  ×  Ø  Ù  Ú  Û  Ü  Ý  Þ  ß
e  à  á  â  ã  ä  å  æ  ç  è  é  ê  ë  ì  í  î  ï
f  ð  ñ  ò  ó  ô  õ  ö  ÷  ø  ù  ú  û  ü  ý  þ  ÿ
```

You can see that for some characters, the Courier New font is totally different from the SAS monospace font, such as 83-8c, 93-9c.

Why is it useful to know these correspondences?

First, it gives the order of characters and tells you how SAS makes the comparison.

Second, you can use special characters in your printout, such as characters with hex values b1, b2, b3.

Let us run the following program:

```
PROC OPTIONS OPTION=FORMCHAR;RUN;
```

You can find results in the log file.

```
FORMCHAR=|–┌┬┐├┼┤└┴┘+=|-/\<>*
```

You may wonder what these characters are. Now you know that the first 11 characters are special characters with hex values 82-8c.

Next, try the following program:

```
DATA s;
a=1;OUTPUT;
a=1;OUTPUT;
a=2;OUTPUT;
PROC FREQ;
TABLE a;
RUN;
```

The FREQ Procedure

a	Frequency	Percent	Cumulative Frequency	Cumulative Percent
1	2	66.67	2	66.67
2	1	33.33	3	100.00

We see a solid line in the printout. It comes from the FORMCHAR setting (the second character). We can change the option setting as follows, and run the program again:

```
OPTIONS FORMCHAR='|----|+|---+=|-/\<>*';
```

The following is output.

```
                                      Cumulative    Cumulative
a     Frequency       Percent        Frequency       Percent
------------------------------------------------------
1             2         66.67                2         66.67
2             1         33.33                3        100.00
```

Now suppose that we want to go back to the original setting. How can we do this? We can copy the following statement:

```
OPTIONS  FORMCHAR='|-┌┬┐├┼┤└┴┘+=|-/\<>*';
```

When pasting it to the Edit window, it becomes

```
OPTIONS FORMCHAR=‚ƒ„…†‡ˆ‰Š‹Œ+=|-/\<>*;
```

This is OK because these characters have the same hex values. The difference is font. As you can see, for some special characters, we can copy, but we cannot type them. However, we can use the Character Map (start ->All Programs -> Accessories -> System Tools -> Character Map). Then we can do copy and paste. See the following picture:

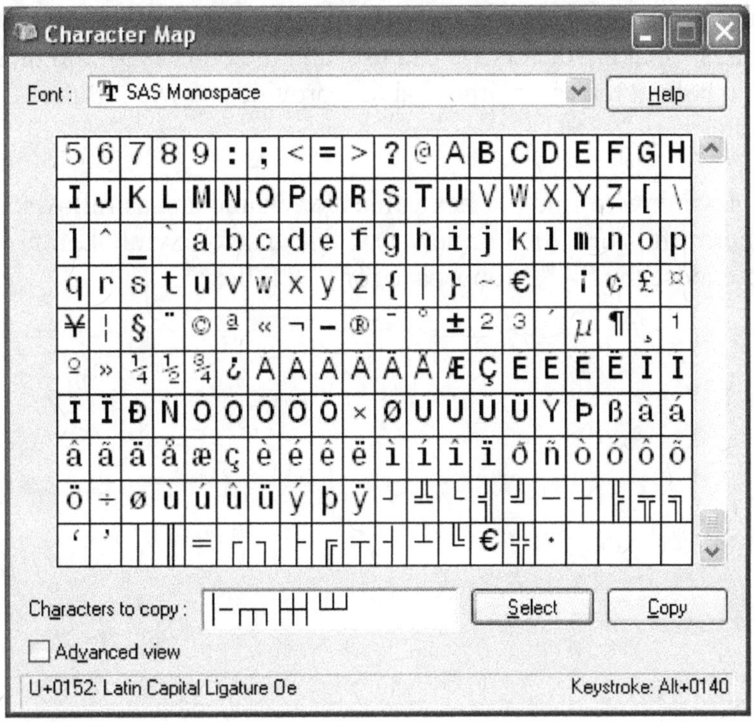

We can also use hex values and type the following statement. The results are the same:

```
OPTIONS FORMCHAR='82838485868788898a8b8c2b94052d2f5c3c3e2a'x;
```

Many people have had the following experience: When they copy the output of the above PROC FREQ (with a solid line) to a Word document and change the font to Courier New, they get a totally different display, as follows:

```
                                 Cumulative    Cumulative
a     Frequency      Percent      Frequency       Percent
ƒƒƒƒƒƒƒƒƒƒƒƒƒƒƒƒƒƒƒƒƒƒƒƒƒƒƒƒƒƒƒƒƒƒƒƒƒƒƒƒƒƒƒƒƒƒƒƒƒƒƒƒƒƒƒƒƒ
1             2        66.67              2         66.67
2             1        33.33              3        100.00
```

Why does this happen? The solid line comes from a character with a hex value of 83. When you change the font to Courier New, the hex value is still 83, but corresponding character is different. Checking Table 2, it is ƒ. Notice that it is not character f in italics. It is a special character called Florin. So if you want to change the output to Courier New at last, and you want to keep a solid line, you have to change the FORMCHAR setting as follows:

```
OPTIONS FORMCHAR='82978485868788898a8b8c2b94052d2f5c3c3e2a'x;
```

You will see, however, that the printout is strange, but when you change the font to Courier New, it will be OK. Would you like to change the font to Times New Roman? Notice that '96'x and '97'x are called an En dash and an Em dash in most fonts.

Now suppose we want to use special characters in our printout. We have to do two things. One is to know what special characters we can use, and the other is to find their hex values. Actually, we do both at the same time. Table 1 provides us with all the characters and their hex values.

We can use the Symbol window to find out hex values for characters, as follows: Open Microsoft Word (Microsoft Word 2003 or newer). Click Insert->Symbol. You will see a pop-up window, and choose the SAS Monospace font, as following.

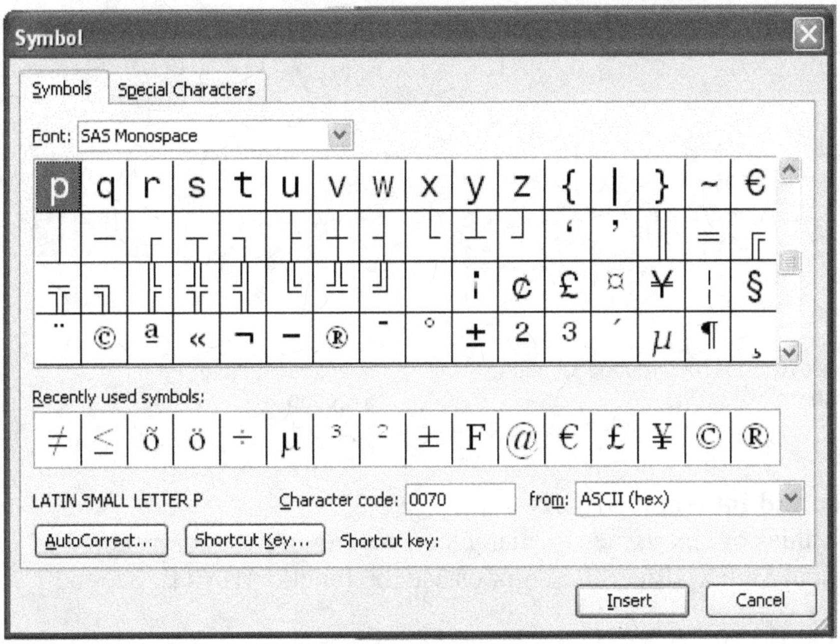

In the lower right corner of the window, there are choices ASCII (hex) and ASCII (decimal) in the "from" box. They correspond to hex value and decimal value that can be used for the character. Click on any character. You will see its hex value or byte value. For example, click on character 'p'. You will find that its ASCII (hex) value is 0070, and its ASCII (decimal) value is 112. Actually, 112=16*7. So BYTE (112) and '70'x are the same, and they are both character 'p'. Notice that the Character Map also shows U+0070 for character 'p'.

Converting characters to binary values or hex values

Now we will talk about conversion. There are two cases: to convert a character string to a binary value or hex value, and to convert a binary value or hex value to a character string.

To get the binary values or hex value for a character string, we can use the $BINARY format and the $HEX format.

The ranges of both the $BINARY format and the $HEX format are 1-32767. The default width is calculated based on the length of value (including leaning and trailing blanks). That is twice the length of the character string for $HEX or 8 times the length of the character string for $BINARY.

Suppose the width w is specified. You can think that SAS first converts the character value, including leading and trailing blanks, to binary or hex value, and then SAS shows the leftmost w digits if w<=8*length for the $BINARY format or if w<=2*length for the $HEX format. SAS pads blanks on the right if w>8*length for the $BINARY format or if w>2*length for the $HEX format.

Therefore, it is better not to specify width for these two formats. See the following program:

```
DATA s;
a='  ab  ';
PUT a= $BINARY. @60 a= $HEX.;
PUT a= $BINARY25. @60 a= $HEX5.;
c=PUT(a,$HEX15.)||'pp';
PUT c=;
RUN;
```

```
a=001000000010000001100001011000100010000000100000          a=202061622020
a=0010000000100000011000010                                  a=20206
c=202061622020   pp
```

Informat $BINARYw. and informat $HEXw.

To convert binary values or hex values to characters, we can use the informat $BINARY or the informat $HEX, directly assign, or use the function BYTE. See the following example:

```
DATA s;
a='abcd';
b='61626364'x;
c='61'x||'62'x||'63'x||'64'x;
d=BYTE(97)||BYTE(98)||BYTE(99)||BYTE(100);
e=INPUT('01100001011000100110001101100100',$BINARY32.);
f=INPUT('61626364',$HEX8.);
PROC PRINT;RUN;
```

Obs	a	b	c	d	e	f
1	abcd	abcd	abcd	abcd	abcd	abcd

Notice that for direct assignment, you have to put an even number of hex digits. Otherwise, SAS will complain. You cannot put blanks at the beginning or at the end.

The ranges of the width for the $HEX informat and the $BINARY format are also1-32767. The default is 8 for the $BINARY informat and 2 for the $HEX informat.

Suppose that ***w***< 8. $BINARY***w***. reads min{length(value), w} characters. If they are all blanks, SAS converts the value to a blank ('20'x). Otherwise, SAS removes leading blanks and pads trailing 0 so that the value has 8 characters and then converts. If w>=8, let z=MAX{x: x<=w, MOD(x,8)=0}. SAS reads in MIN{length, w} characters, removes leading blanks, and pads 0 on the right to make the number of characters is multiple of 8 and then takes the z characters from left and uses the informat $BIARYz to convert. If the $BINARY is used to determine the length attribute, then it is z/8 if w>=8, and is 1 if w<8.

Suppose that *w*=1. $HEX***1***. reads 1 character. If it is blank, SAS converts the value to a blank ('20'x). Otherwise, SAS pads one trailing 0 and then converts. If w>=2, let z =MAX{x: x<=w, MOD(x,2)=0}. SAS reads MIN{LENGTH(value), w} characters, removes leading blanks, and pads trailing 0 to make the number of character is multiple of 2, and then takes the z characters from left and uses the informat $HEXz to convert. If the $BINARY is used to determine the length attribute, then it is z/2 if w>=2 and is 1 if w=1. Let's see the following example.

```
DATA s;
a=INPUT('  6162',$HEX5.);a1=LENGTHC(a);a2=PUT(a,$HEX.);
b=INPUT('  616',$HEX8.);b1=LENGTHC(b);b2=PUT(b,$HEX.);
PROC PRINT;
RUN;
```

```
Obs    a    a1    a2      b    b1    b2          d

 1     a`    2    6160    a`    4    61602020    `
```

In the above example, for both variables a and b, SAS reads in five characters ' 616'. Then SAS removes leading blanks and pads a trialing 0 to make the value become '6160' and then converts. Notice that although in the printout a and b are the same, they have different length attributes. For variables a2 and b2, we use the format $HEX with the default width, which are 4 and 8, respectively.

Therefore, it is better to specify width w as an even number for a $HEX informat and as a multiple of 8 for a $BINARY informat.

Table 3 is a summary of informats and formats discussed in this paper. In the table, fp means a floating-point expression. Notice that fp has two expressions: binary and hex.

Table 3. Some informats and formats and their width

	Functionality	**Width range**	**Default width**	**Best use of width**
Informat BINARYw.d	Binary -> positive integer (w: 1-56) Fp -> numeric (w: 57-64)	1-64 (0-31 for d)	8	Don't use w: 57-63
Informat HEXw	Hex value -> positive integer (w: 1-15) Fp (hex) -> numeric (w=16)	1-16	8	
Format BINARYw	Integer -> binary (w: 1-58) Numeric -> fp (w: 59-64)	1-64	8	Don't use w: 59-63
Format HEXw	Positive Integer -> binary (w: 1-15) Numeric -> fp (hex) (w=16)	1-16	8	
Informat $BINARYw	Binary -> character	1-32767	8	Use multiple of 8
Informat $HEXw	Hex -> character	1-32767	2	Use even number
Format $BINARYw	Character -> binary	1-32767	calculated	Use default
Format $HEXw	Character -> hex	1-32767	calculated	Use default

Reference:

SAS Language Reference: Dictionary, 2006.Cary, NC: SAS Institute Inc.
http://support.sas.com/onlinedoc/913/getDoc/en/lrdict.hlp/a000245852.htm

Comparison among DATA Step, PROC SQL, and PROC REPORT

Introduction

Every SAS programmer uses DATA step very often and knows DATA step very well, but most of them do not use PROC SQL so often and do not know PROC SQL so well. Therefore, it is better to make a comparison between them so that people can take full advantage of PROC SQL and have more choices. In general, as you know, DATA step is more flexible and more powerful, but if you know PROC SQL well, sometimes you will feel that it is not a bad idea to use PROC SQL in some situations.

We all know that we can use DATA step or PROC SQL to create a data set from a data set. To create a data set using PROC SQL from a table, use the statement CREATE TABLE tbl_name AS statement. Actually, you can also use PROC REPORT to create a data set using the option OUT=data-set in the PROC REPORT statement. Mainly, they are doing the following tasks:

DATA step: creates a data set, assigns macro variables, or creates a raw data file.
PROC REPORT: creates a detailed report, a summary report, or assigns macro variables.
PROC SQL: creates a detailed report or a summary report, or assigns macro variables.

Create an empty data set

One difference between DATA step and PROC SQL is that PROC SQL always creates an empty table with columns defined, but DATA step usually does not do this. The following program shows that to create an empty data set using DATA step, we will get an "`uninitialized`" message, and you will get one observation with all missing values. DATA step does not like an empty data set.

```
DATA s;
LENGTH a $8;
RUN;

NOTE: Variable a is uninitialized.
NOTE: The data set WORK.S has 1 observations and 1 variables.
```

Maybe you will wonder: What is the purpose of creating an empty table? Actually, it is a common practice now. In clinical trials, we usually design data set structure first: variables and their attributes including names, formats, lengths, types, and labels. They form the standard of a data set. Then we use different methods and steps to get values for these variables. In order to make the data set standardized, we have several ways to proceed.

1. Whenever we get or create a variable, we define its attributes.
2. Manipulate data sets and define attributes for all variables for the final data set.
3. Create an initial (empty) table with standard attributes. Then, every time we get a partial data set, we append it to the initial table.

In practice, the first way is not good because it is easy to miss something. Now, many people use the second or third way (PROC SQL). The following is a sample code creating an initial table AE:

```
PROC SQL;
   CREATE TABLE adae
   (SUBID        CHAR(10)    LABEL='Subject Identifier',
    DOMAIN       CHAR(2)        LABEL='Domain Abbreviation',
    AETERM       CHAR(200)      LABEL='Reported Term for the Adverse
Event',
    AEDECOD      CHAR(200)      LABEL='Dictionary-Derived Term',
    AEBODSYS     CHAR(120)      LABEL='Body System or Organ Class',
    AESEV        CHAR(20)       LABEL='Severity/ Intensity',
    AESER        CHAR(1)        LABEL='Serious Event',
    AEAC         CHAR(50)       LABEL='Action Taken',
    AEREL        CHAR(1)        LABEL='Related to drug taken',
    AEOUT        CHAR(50)       LABEL='Outcome of Adverse Event',
    AESTDT       NUM(8)         LABEL='Start Date of Adverse Event'
FORMAT = YYMMDD10.,
    AEENDT       NUM(8)         LABEL='End Date of Adverse Event'
FORMAT = YYMMDD10.,
    AEDURN       NUM(8)         LABEL='Duration of Adverse Event in
Days',
    AESTDY       NUM(8)         LABEL='Study Day of Start of Adverse
Event',
    AEENDY       NUM(8)         LABEL='Study Day of End of Adverse
Event',
    AETRTEM      CHAR(1)        LABEL='Treatment Emergent AE
Classification',
  );
QUIT;
```

Change order of variables

As we know, variables in a data set have their order (positions), which are according to their definition order. The following program creates a data set s with four variables a, b, c, and d, in order. Double clicking the data set will show you the order. When using procedures such as PROC PRINT, PROC REPORT, or SELECT * in PROC SQL, the default order of variables in the printout is the order of variables in the data set. We can also use PROC CONTENTS with the option VARNUM or POSITION to find their order.

```
DATA s;
a=1;b=2;c=3;d=5;
RUN;
```

Now we want to change their order to b, c, a, d. We can use DATA step with a SET statement by defining variable b, c, and a before the SET statement to do this. Usually, we use a LENGTH statement to define variables. See the following example:

```
DATA s;
LENGTH b c a 8;
SET s;
RUN;
```

As we know, both a LENGTH statement and a SET statement are definition statements. Since variables b, c, and a are defined in the LENGTH statement, and variable d is defined in the SET statement, they form a new order in a new data set s. This means that it is not necessary to list all variables in the LENGTH statement. This method keeps all the attributes of variables except their position.

In a word, to change positions of variables and to keep their other attributes, we must define variables before the SET statement. To keep length attributes for character variables, we must find their length attributes in the original data set and put them in the LENGTH statement. We can use PROC CONTENTS to find their length attributes. However, if the original data set has many character variables with different length attributes, it is boring to find their length attributes and copy them to the code.

We can use PROC SQL to do this, so we don't have to care about the length of variables. See the following program:

```
PROC SQL;
CREATE TABLE t AS SELECT c,b,a,d FROM s;
QUIT;
```

We can also use PROC REPORT to do this. See the following example:

```
PROC REPORT OUT=t(DROP=_BREAK_);
COLUMN c b a d;
DEFINE a/DISPLAY;
RUN;
```

To use PROC REPORT, we have to make sure it is a detailed report rather than a summary report (either there is a display variable or define one). And the new data set has one more column _BREAK_ that needs to delete.

Create new variables

Using PROC SQL to create a data set, we can create new variables. If the calculations are simple, we can put them in the SELECT statement as the following example shows:

```
DATA s;
a=1;b=2;c=3;d=5;
PROC SQL;
CREATE TABLE t AS SELECT *,(a+b)/2 AS a1, MOD(d,3) AS b1 FROM s;
QUIT;
```

If the calculations are complicated, we may need a CASE clause, or sometimes this situation will be hard to handle.

PROC REPORT can handle both simple and complicated calculations, but even for simple ones, we have to use a COMPUTE block.

Remove duplicate rows

Although PROC SORT has the option NODUPLICATES|NODUPREC|NODUP, this option is used to remove adjacent duplicate observations. To remove duplicate observations, we can use PROC SORT, as the following:

```
PROC SORT NODUP; /*NODUPKEY is OK*/
BY _ALL_; RUN;
```

We can also use PROC SQL to remove duplicate observations, such as in the following program:

```
PROC SQL;
SELECT DISTINCT * FROM s;
QUIT;
```

Notice that PROC SORT sorts the data set, but PROC SQL only removes duplicates; it does not sort the table.

Sort tables

Usually, we use PROC SORT to sort a data set. However, the sorting variables must be in the data set. PROC SQL can sort a data set, too. Moreover, it can sort a data set according to a column that is not in the data set. The following program sorts rows according to the sum of three columns:

```
DATA record;
INPUT id math1 math2 reading;
CARDS;
11 86 99 87
12 89 97 95
13 99 78 88
;

PROC SQL;
SELECT *
FROM record
ORDER BY sum(math1, math2, reading) DESC;
QUIT;
```

Combine with summary results

One big advantage of PROC SQL is that it can do re-merge, i.e., you can merge summary results back to the original table. The following program gives you an example of re-merge with the ground total. In DATA step, we have to use PROC to get required statistics and merge back, but when using PROC SQL, we only need to add one more column in the SELECT statement. We consider the following data set:

```
DATA sales;
LENGTH name $20;
INPUT id dept $ location name & sales;
DATALINES;
1013 A 1 Martin, Virginia  3500
1014 A 1 Singleton, MaryAnn   2400
1015 A 2 Leighton, Maurice 2300
```

```
1016 B 3 Freuler, Carl  3750
1018 B 3 Cage, Merce  4370
1020 B 4 Gates, Alexis  3000
;
RUN;
```

The following program re-merges the total and the average.

```
PROC SQL;
SELECT dept,name,sales,SUM(sales) AS tot,sales/CALCULATED tot AS
   percent, AVG(sales) AS avg, sales-CALCULATED avg AS diff FROM sales;
```

dept	name	sales	tot	percent	avg	diff
A	Martin, Virginia	3500	19320	0.181159	3220	280
A	Singleton, MaryAnn	2400	19320	0.124224	3220	-820
A	Leighton, Maurice	2300	19320	0.119048	3220	-920
B	Freuler, Carl	3750	19320	0.194099	3220	530
B	Cage, Merce	4370	19320	0.22619	3220	1150
B	Gates, Alexis	3000	19320	0.15528	3220	-220

This program provides the ground total and the ground mean. We say that the percent is ind/total. However, we can also calculate group total and ind/group percent by using a GROUP BY clause. See the following program:

```
SELECT dept,name,sales,SUM(sales) AS tot,sales/CALCULATED tot AS
   percent, AVG(sales) AS avg, sales-CALCULATED avg AS diff
FROM sales GROUP BY dept;
```

dept	name	sales	tot	percent	avg	diff
A	Martin, Virginia	3500	8200	0.426829	2733.333	766.6667
A	Leighton, Maurice	2300	8200	0.280488	2733.333	-433.333
A	Singleton, MaryAnn	2400	8200	0.292683	2733.333	-333.333
B	Gates, Alexis	3000	11120	0.269784	3706.667	-706.667
B	Cage, Merce	4370	11120	0.392986	3706.667	663.3333
B	Freuler, Carl	3750	11120	0.33723	3706.667	43.33333

PROC REPORT and PCTSUM

There is no re-merge in PROC REPORT. However, it has two statistics: PCTSUM and PCTN, which are similar to re-merge. Let's run the following program:

```
PROC REPORT DATA=sales NOWD HEADLINE;
COLUMN id dept name sales sales,PCTSUM;
RUN;
```

id	dept	name	sales	sales PCTSUM
1013	A	Martin, Virginia	3500	0.1811594
1014	A	Singleton, MaryAnn	2400	0.1242236
1015	A	Leighton, Maurice	2300	0.1190476
1016	B	Freuler, Carl	3750	0.1940994
1018	B	Cage, Merce	4370	0.2261905

```
1020  B         Gates, Alexis              3000  0.1552795
```

You can see that we get ind/total percent, thc same as in PROC SQL. We can find ind/group percent, but we have to use a BY group.

```
PROC REPORT DATA=sales NOWD;
COLUMN id dept name sales sales,PCTSUM;
RUN;
```

```
------------------------------ dept=A -------------------------------

                                                             sales
  id  dept      name                            sales      PCTSUM
1013  A         Martin, Virginia                 3500   0.4268293
1014  A         Singleton, MaryAnn               2400   0.2926829
1015  A         Leighton, Maurice                2300   0.2804878
------------------------------ dept=B -------------------------------

                                                             sales
  id  dept      name                            sales      PCTSUM
1016  B         Freuler, Carl                    3750   0.3372302
1018  B         Cage, Merce                      4370   0.3929856
1020  B         Gates, Alexis                    3000   0.2697842
```

However, it is easy to find group/total percent. Try the following program:

```
PROC REPORT DATA=sales NOWD HEADLINE;
COLUMN  dept  sales sales,PCTSUM;
DEFINE dept/GROUP;
RUN;
```

```
                            sales
dept          sales        PCTSUM
-----------------------------------
A              8200     0.4244306
B             11120     0.5755694
```

Comparing PROC REPORT and PROC SQL, PROC SQL can put a total (ground total or group total) together with individual values and calculate percentage. PROC REPORT can provide individual values and PCNSUM with a ground total, but it cannot provide a ground total and a group total at the same time. However, with a little trick, we can get both totals from PROC REPORT, as the following program shows:

```
PROC REPORT NOWD HEADLINE;
COLUMN id dept sales group ground;
DEFINE id/DISPLAY;
DEFINE dept/GROUP;
DEFINE group/COMPUTED "group total";
DEFINE ground/COMPUTED "ground total";
COMPUTE BEFORE;
g1=sales.SUM;
ENDCOMP;
COMPUTE ground;
ground=g1;
```

```
ENDCOMP;
COMPUTE BEFORE dept;
g2=sales.SUM;
ENDCOMP;
COMPUTE group;
group=g2;
ENDCOMP;
RUN;
```

id	dept	sales	group total	ground total
1013	A	3500	8200	19320
1014		2400	8200	19320
1015		2300	8200	19320
1016	B	3750	11120	19320
1018		4370	11120	19320
1020		3000	11120	19320

In PROC SQL, to find group/total or group/group in the same report, we have to use a subquery that will be discussed in [XI].

The situation for PCTN and PETSUM is the same.

Macro variable assignment

In DATA step, we use a CALL SYMPUT routing to assign values to macro variables, and in PROC SQL, we use an INTO cause to assign values to macro variables. The rule for DATA step is that the last comer occupies, and that for PROC SQL is that the first comer occupies. See the following example:

```
DATA sales2;
INPUT dept $ sales;
DATALINES;
A 5400
B 3600
B 3450
C 4500
;
PROC SQL;
SELECT dept, sales
   INTO :dept, :sales
   FROM sales2;
QUIT;
%PUT SQL output &dept &sales;
DATA _NULL_;
SET sales2;
CALL SYMPUT('dept',dept);
CALL SYMPUT('sales',sales);
RUN;
%PUT DATA output &dept &sales;
```

In the log file, we can see the following:

```
SQL output A            5400
DATA output C           4500
```

If we want to assign value in each observation to a macro variable, in DATA step, we can use recursive variable names.

```
DATA _NULL_;
SET sales2;
CALL SYMPUT('dept'||LEFT(_N_),dept);
RUN;
```

But in PROC SQL, we have to give a list.

```
PROC SQL;
SELECT dept, sales
   INTO :dept1 - :dept4, :sales1 - :sales4
   FROM sales2;
QUIT;
%PUT &dept1 &sales1 &dept2 &sales2 &dept3 &sales3 &dept4 &sales4;
```

The following is output:

```
A 5400 B 3600 B 3450 C 4500
```

In many cases, we want to put categorical variables into macro variables. We can compare DATA step and PROC SQL, as in the following program:

```
DATA _NULL_;
SET sales2 END=end;
BY dept;
IF FIRST.dept THEN DO;ord+1;
CALL SYMPUT('dept'||LEFT(ord),dept);
END;
IF end THEN CALL SYMPUT('tot',ord);
RUN;
PROC SQL;
SELECT DISTINCT(dept),COUNT(DISTINCT(dept))
INTO :deptt1-:deptt5,:tott FROM sales2;
%PUT _USER_;
```

```
GLOBAL TOTT         3
GLOBAL TOT             3
GLOBAL DEPTT1 A
GLOBAL DEPT1 A
GLOBAL DEPT2 B
GLOBAL DEPTT3 C
GLOBAL DEPT3 C
GLOBAL DEPTT2 B
```

The example shows that if we are not sure how many depts there are, we can just use a big number. This is useful for macro programming.

However, if you have many different values, and we don't want to create too many macro variables, we can put all the depts into one macro variable, separated by a comma, for example, and we can do the same with sales.

```
PROC SQL;
SELECT DISTINCT(dept),SUM(sales)
   INTO :dept SEPARATED BY ',', :sales SEPARATED BY ','
   FROM sales2 GROUP BY dept;
QUIT;
%PUT &dept &sales;
```

output

```
A,B,C 5400,7050,4500
```

Examples of PROC SQL programming

For a clinical study, a lot of work for SAS programmers is to create tables, listings, and graphs (TLG). Statisticians first provide a table shell, and then programmers produce tables according to table shells. There are many different ways to create these tables, mostly using DATA steps, together with PROC SORT, PROC FREQ, PROC MEANS, and PROC TRANSPOSE. But I am sure that very few programmers use PROC SQL to create them. In the following, I try to use PROC SQL to create tables. Readers can compare these programs with DATA step programs. First, suppose we have the following table shell:

Table x. Summary of patients with concomitant medications
Randomized patients

Anatomic class Therapeutic class [n (%)]	Placebo (N=xx)	10mg (N=xx)	20mg (N=xx)	All (N=xx)
Any concomitant medications	xx (xx.x)	xx (xx.x)	xx (xx.x)	xx (xx.x)
Anatomic class 1	xx (xx.x)	xx (xx.x)	xx (xx.x)	xx (xx.x)
Therapeutic class 1	xx (xx.x)	xx (xx.x)	xx (xx.x)	xx (xx.x)
Therapeutic class 2	xx (xx.x)	xx (xx.x)	xx (xx.x)	xx (xx.x)
...				
Anatomic class 2	xx (xx.x)	xx (xx.x)	xx (xx.x)	xx (xx.x)
Therapeutic class 1	xx (xx.x)	xx (xx.x)	xx (xx.x)	xx (xx.x)
Therapeutic class 2	xx (xx.x)	xx (xx.x)	xx (xx.x)	xx (xx.x)
...				
...				
Not coded	xx (xx.x)	xx (xx.x)	xx (xx.x)	xx (xx.x)
Not coded	xx (xx.x)	xx (xx.x)	xx (xx.x)	xx (xx.x)

From the table shell, we can see that there are two levels in the leftmost column, except for the first row. They correspond to variables cmcl1 and cmcl2. Each cell consists of number count and percentage, where the denominator is the total number of patients in the group. We use two data sets, cm (concomitant medications) and dm (demographics). In the table we also have to provide the last column, All. In the table, we order rows first according to cmcl1 (alphabetic), and within each cmcl1, we order rows according to the descending count of the last column (numbers). We need to use "Any concomitant medications" as the first row and "Not coded" as the last row, where "Not coded" means a missing value.

Now we have the following data set:

```
DATA dm;
INPUT patid $ random $ trtgrp age height weight;
CARDS;
1001        Y 20   45   177 78
1002        Y 0    36   169 73
1003        Y 10   43   160 65
1004        Y 20   55   174 72
1005        N .    55   170 77
1006        Y 10   46   165 74
1007        Y 0    60   160 70
1008        Y 0    54   157 73
1009        Y 10   37   164 68
1010        N .    61   158 64
;
DATA cm;
INFILE cards MISSOVER;
INPUT trtgrp 1-2 random $5 patid $9-12 cmcl1 $15-36 cmcl2 $39-71;
CARDS;
20  Y   1001
20  Y   1001  CARDIOVASCULAR SYSTEM   CARDIAC THERAPY
20  Y   1001  CARDIOVASCULAR SYSTEM   BETA BLOCKING AGENTS
20  Y   1001  CARDIOVASCULAR SYSTEM   CARDIAC THERAPY
20  Y   1001  CARDIOVASCULAR SYSTEM   SERUM LIPID REDUCING AGENTS
 0  Y   1002
 0  Y   1002  ALIMENTARY TRACT        DRUGS USED IN DIABETES
 0  Y   1002  CARDIOVASCULAR SYSTEM   CALCIUM CHANNEL BLOCKERS
 0  Y   1002  CARDIOVASCULAR SYSTEM   CARDIAC THERAPY
 0  Y   1002  CARDIOVASCULAR SYSTEM   CALCIUM CHANNEL BLOCKERS
 0  Y   1002  CARDIOVASCULAR SYSTEM   BETA BLOCKING AGENTS
 0  Y   1002  CARDIOVASCULAR SYSTEM   CALCIUM CHANNEL BLOCKERS
10  Y   1003
10  Y   1003
10  Y   1003  ALIMENTARY TRACT        DRUGS USED IN DIABETES
10  Y   1003  CARDIOVASCULAR SYSTEM   CARDIAC THERAPY
10  Y   1003  CARDIOVASCULAR SYSTEM   BETA BLOCKING AGENTS
10  Y   1003  CARDIOVASCULAR SYSTEM   BETA BLOCKING AGENTS
10  Y   1003  CARDIOVASCULAR SYSTEM   DIURETICS
10  Y   1003  CARDIOVASCULAR SYSTEM   SERUM LIPID REDUCING AGENTS
 .  N   1005  CARDIOVASCULAR SYSTEM   CALCIUM CHANNEL BLOCKERS
10  Y   1006  ALIMENTARY TRACT        DRUGS FOR ACID RELATED DISORDERS
 0  Y   1008  ALIMENTARY TRACT        DRUGS FOR ACID RELATED DISORDERS
 0  Y   1008  CARDIOVASCULAR SYSTEM   CARDIAC THERAPY
10  Y   1009  CARDIOVASCULAR SYSTEM   CALCIUM CHANNEL BLOCKERS
10  Y   1009  CARDIOVASCULAR SYSTEM   BETA BLOCKING AGENTS
 .  N   1010  CARDIOVASCULAR SYSTEM   CARDIAC THERAPY
 .  N   1010  CARDIOVASCULAR SYSTEM   CALCIUM CHANNEL BLOCKERS
 .  N   1010  CARDIOVASCULAR SYSTEM   DIURETICS
 .  N   1010  CARDIOVASCULAR SYSTEM   SERUM LIPID REDUCING AGENTS
;
```

```
RUN;
PROC PRINT;RUN;
```

The following is a program using PROC SQL.

```
PROC FORMAT;
VALUE $cm ' '='Not coded';

PROC SQL;
CREATE TABLE dm0 AS SELECT 50 AS trtgrp,* FROM dm; ❶
*CREATE TABLE dm0 AS SELECT 50 AS trtgrp,patid,random FROM dm;  ❷
CREATE TABLE dm1(WHERE=(random='Y')) AS SELECT * FROM dm OUTER UNION
   CORR SELECT * FROM dm0; ❸
CREATE TABLE a0 AS SELECT COUNT(patid) AS tot,trtgrp FROM dm1
    GROUP BY trtgrp; ❹
SELECT COUNT(patid) INTO :a0-:a3 FROM dm1 GROUP BY trtgrp; ❺
CREATE TABLE cm0 AS SELECT trtgrp1, random, patid, PUT(cmcl1,$cm30.)
   AS cmcl1, PUT(cmcl2,$cm30.) AS cmcl2 FROM cm (WHERE=(random='Y'))  ;
CREATE TABLE cm1(DROP=trtgrp1) AS SELECT *,trtgrp1 as trtgrp FROM cm0
   UNION SELECT *,50 as trtgrp FROM cm0;
CREATE TABLE c0 AS SELECT 'Any concomitant medications' AS cmcl1,''
   AS cmcl2,'Any concomitant medications           ' AS cat,0 AS   cat1,
   trtgrp,COUNT(DISTINCT(patid)) AS coun FROM cm1  GROUP BY trtgrp; ❻
CREATE TABLE c1 AS SELECT cmcl1,'' AS cmcl2,cmcl1 AS cat,
   CASE cmcl1 WHEN 'Not coded' THEN 3 ELSE 1 END AS cat1,trtgrp,
   COUNT(DISTINCT(patid)) AS coun FROM cm1 GROUP BY cmcl1,trtgrp; ❼
CREATE TABLE c2 AS SELECT cmcl1,cmcl2,'  '||cmcl2 AS cat,CASE cmcl1
   WHEN 'Not coded' THEN 3 ELSE 1 end AS cat1,trtgrp, COUNT(DISTINCT
   (patid)) AS coun FROM cm1 GROUP BY cmcl1,cmcl2,trtgrp; ❽
CREATE TABLE c3 AS SELECT * FROM c0 UNION SELECT *
   FROM c1 UNION SELECT * FROM c2; ❾
CREATE TABLE c4 AS SELECT cmcl1,cmcl2,cat,cat1, c3.trtgrp,
   PUT(coun,5.)||' '||PUT(-coun/tot,PERCENT7.1) AS cell
   FROM c3,a0 WHERE c3.trtgrp=a0.trtgrp; ❿
QUIT;
```

Following is an explanation for the above program:

❶ is for the last column. It will have a WARNING because I want to use a wildcard (*) to save typing. (Sometimes you may need many variables.) It is OK. If you don't like the WARNING, you can use ❷ instead of ❶.

❸ combines the two tables. We can combine ❶ and ❸. Notice that the following statement does not work:

```
CREATE TABLE dm1(WHERE=(random='Y')) AS SELECT * FROM dm UNION CORR
   (SELECT 50 AS trtgrp,* FROM dm);
```

But the following statement works:

```
CREATE TABLE dm1(WHERE=(random='Y')) AS SELECT * FROM dm  UNION CORR
      ( SELECT 50 AS trtgrp,random,patid FROM dm);
```

❹ gets denominators for percentage

❺ gets counts in each group, will be used in column headers
❻ gets counts in the first row
❼ gets counts for the first level
❽ gets counts for the second level
❾ combines the above tables
❿ calculates percentage.

```
PROC TRANSPOSE DATA=c4 OUT=fin(DROP=_NAME_ );
   BY cmcl1 cmcl2 cat cat1;
   ID trtgrp;
   VAR cell;
RUN;
OPTION NOCENTER NODATE NONUMBER;
TITLE "Table x.   Summary of patients with concomitant medications";
TITLE2 "         Randomized patients";
FOOTNOTE "Note:   N = Number of patients in dose group, randomized
patients";
FOOTNOTE2 "        % = n divided by number of patients in dose group,
randomized patients";

PROC SQL;
CREATE TABLE fin1 AS SELECT cmcl1, cmcl2, cat, cat1,
   CASE _0 WHEN '' THEN '0' ELSE _0 END AS p0, CASE _10 WHEN '' THEN
   '0' ELSE _10 END AS p10, CASE _20 WHEN '' THEN '0' ELSE _20 END AS
   p20, CASE _50 WHEN '' THEN '0' ELSE _50 END AS p50 FROM fin; ❶
CREATE TABLE fin2 AS SELECT cmcl1 AS cmcl0,'' AS cmcl1,'' AS cmcl2,
   '' AS cat,cat1,'' AS p0,'' AS p10,'' AS p20,'' AS p50 FROM c1 UNION
   SELECT cmcl1 AS cmcl0,* FROM fin1; ❷
CREATE TABLE fin3 AS SELECT * FROM fin2 ORDER BY cat1, cmcl0,cmcl1,
   INPUT(SCAN(p50,1),5.) DESC,cmcl2; ❸
SELECT cat FORMAT=$35. LABEL="Anatomic class           Therapeutic
   class [n %]",LEFT(p0) FORMAT=$11. LABEL="Placebo (N=&a0)",
   LEFT(p10) FORMAT=$11. LABEL="10mg     (N=&a1)",LEFT(p20) FORMAT=$11.
   LABEL="20mg     (N=&a2)",LEFT(p50) FORMAT=$11. LABEL="All (N=&a3)"
   FROM fin3; ❹
QUIT;
```

In the following I give some explanation for the second part of the code:

❶ for missing value cells, fills in '0'
❷ creates blank rows between two cmcl1 values
❸ sorts table by cmcl1 and numbers in the last column
❹ creates the final printout.

The following is the table created:

Table x. Summary of patients with concomitant medications
Randomized patients

Anatomic class Therapeuticclass [n %]	Placebo (N=3)	10mg (N=3)	20mg (N=2)	All (N=8)
Any concomitant medications	2 (66.7%)	3 (100%)	1 (50.0%)	6 (75.0%)
ALIMENTARY TRACT	2 (66.7%)	2 (66.7%)	0	4 (50.0%)
DRUGS FOR ACID RELATED DISORDERS	1 (33.3%)	1 (33.3%)	0	2 (25.0%)
DRUGS USED IN DIABETES	1 (33.3%)	1 (33.3%)	0	2 (25.0%)
CARDIOVASCULAR SYSTEM	2 (66.7%)	2 (66.7%)	1 (50.0%)	5 (62.5%)
BETA BLOCKING AGENTS	1 (33.3%)	2 (66.7%)	1 (50.0%)	4 (50.0%)
CARDIAC THERAPY	2 (66.7%)	1 (33.3%)	1 (50.0%)	4 (50.0%)
CALCIUM CHANNEL BLOCKERS	1 (33.3%)	1 (33.3%)	0	2 (25.0%)
SERUM LIPID REDUCING AGENTS	0	1 (33.3%)	1 (50.0%)	2 (25.0%)
DIURETICS	0	1 (33.3%)	0	1 (12.5%)
Not coded	1 (33.3%)	1 (33.3%)	1 (50.0%)	3 (37.5%)
Not coded	1 (33.3%)	1 (33.3%)	1 (50.0%)	3 (37.5%)

You can see that the program is pretty straightforward. You can combine many steps, but I don't encourage you to do this. Creating separate tables makes steps clear and easy to debug. Notice that we only use one DATA step here. It can also be done using PROC SQL, but it needs more code. There is one PROC TRANSPOSE. With a little trick, we can even use PROC SQL to replace it. The only difference between the output and the table shell is the header of the first column. However, if we want to use PROC REPORT to create ODS RTF output, then it is perfect. Comparing PROC SQL and DATA steps, PROC SQL is more logical.

Next we consider the following table:

Table y. Summary of demographics and baseline characteristics
Randomized patients

	Placebo (N=xx)	10mg (N=xx)	20mg (N=xx)	All (N=xx)
Age (years)				
Number	xx	xx	xx	xx
Mean (SD)	xx.x (xx.x)	xx.x (xx.x)	xx.x (xx.x)	xx.x (xx.x))
Median	xx.x	xx.x	xx.x	xx.x
Min:Max	xx:xx	xx:xx	xx:xx	xx:xx
Height (cm)				
Number	xx	xx	xx xx	
Mean (SD)	xx.x (xx.x)	xx.x (xx.x)	xx.x (xx.x)	xx.x (xx.x))
Median	xx.x	xx.x	xx.x	xx.x
Min:Max	xx:xx	xx:xx	xx:xx	xx:xx
Weight (kg)				
Number	xx	xx	xx	xx
Mean (SD)	xx.x (xx.x)	xx.x (xx.x)	xx.x (xx.x)	xx.x (xx.x))
Median	xx.x	xx.x	xx.x	xx.x
Min:Max	xx:xx	xx:xx	xx:xx	xx:xx

The following is a program:

```
PROC SORT DATA= dm(WHERE=(random='Y'));
   BY trtgrp;
PROC MEANS DATA= dm;
   VAR age height weight;
   OUTPUT OUT=b3 MEDIAN=;
   BY trtgrp;
RUN;
PROC SQL;
SELECT COUNT(patid) INTO :a0-:a2 FROM dm GROUP BY trtgrp; ❶
CREATE TABLE b1 AS SELECT 1 AS catn,'  Number' AS cat,trtgrp,
   PUT(N(age),5.) AS age1, PUT(N(height),5.) AS height1,
   PUT(N(weight),5.) AS weight1 FROM dm GROUP BY trtgrp; ❷
CREATE TABLE b2 AS SELECT 2 AS catn,'  Mean (SD)' AS cat, trtgrp,
   PUT(MEAN(age),6.2)||'('||PUT(STD(age),6.2)||')' AS age1,
   PUT(MEAN(height),6.2)||'('||PUT(STD(height),6.2)||')' AS height1,
   PUT(MEAN(weight),6.2)||'('||PUT(STD(weight),6.2)||')' AS weight1
   FROM dm GROUP BY trtgrp; ❸
CREATE TABLE b3 AS SELECT 3 AS catn,'  Median' AS cat,trtgrp,
   PUT(age,5.1) AS age1,PUT(height,5.1) AS height1,PUT(weight,5.1) AS
   weight1 FROM b3; ❹
CREATE TABLE b4 AS SELECT 4 AS catn,'  Min:Max' AS cat,trtgrp,
   COMPRESS(PUT(MIN(age),5.1)||':'||PUT(MAX(age),5.1)) AS age1,
  COMPRESS(PUT(MIN(height),5.1)||':'||PUT(MAX(height),5.1))  AS  height1,
   COMPRESS(PUT(MIN(weight),5.1)||':'||PUT(MAX(WEIGHT),5.1)) AS weight1
   FROM dm GROUP BY trtgrp; ❺
CREATE TABLE b0 AS SELECT * FROM b1 UNION SELECT * FROM b2 UNION CORR
   SELECT * FROM b3 UNION SELECT * FROM b4; ❻
QUIT;
```

❶ for numbers in column headers
❷ for Number row
❸ for Mean (SD) row
❹ for Median row
❺ for Min: Max row
❻ combines the above tables.

```
PROC TRANSPOSE DATA=b0 OUT=fin0;
   BY catn cat;
   ID trtgrp;
   VAR age1 height1 weight1;
TITLE 'Table y.  Summary of demographics and baseline characteristics';
TITLE2 '         Randomized patients';
OPTION NODATE NONUMBER NOCENTER;
PROC SQL;
CREATE TABLE fin1 AS SELECT CASE _name_ WHEN 'age1' THEN 'Age (years)'
   WHEN 'height1' THEN 'Height (cm)' WHEN 'weight1' THEN 'Weight (kg)'
   END AS name,catn,cat,_0,_10,_20 FROM fin0 ORDER BY name,catn; ❶
CREATE TABLE fin02 AS SELECT name AS name0,name AS name1,name,. as
   catn,name AS cat,'' AS _0,'' AS _10, '' AS _20 FROM fin1; ❷
CREATE TABLE fin01 AS SELECT name AS name0, '' AS name1,name,. AS
   catn,'' AS cat,'' AS _0,'' AS _10, '' AS _20 FROM fin1; ❸
```

```
CREATE TABLE fin AS SELECT name AS name0,name AS name1,* FROM fin1
   UNION SELECT * FROM fin01 UNION SELECT * FROM fin02; ❹
SELECT cat||'',_0 LABEL="Placebo (N=&a0)",_10 LABEL="10mg (N=&a1)",_20
   LABEL="20mg (N=&a2)" FROM fin; ❺
QUIT;
```

An explanation for the second part of the code follows:

❶ creates row variable headers
❷ creates variable rows
❸ create blank rows
❹ combines the above tables
❺ produces the final printout.

The following is the printout:

```
Table y.  Summary of demographics and baseline characteristics
         Randomized patients

             Placebo (N=3)   10mg (N=3)      20mg (N=2)
___________________________________________________________


Age (years)
  Number        3               3               2
  Mean (SD)   50.00( 12.49)   42.00(  4.58)   50.00(  7.07)
  Median     54              43              50
  Min:Max    36.0:60.0       37.0:46.0       45.0:55.0

Height (cm)
  Number        3               3               2
  Mean (SD)  162.00(  6.24)  163.00(  2.65)  175.50(  2.12)
  Median     160             164             175.5
  Min:Max    157.0:169.0     160.0:165.0     174.0:177.0

Weight (kg)
  Number        3               3               2
  Mean (SD)   72.00(  1.73)   69.00(  4.58)   75.00(  4.24)
  Median     73              68              75
  Min:Max    70.0:73.0       65.0:74.0       72.0:78.0
```

Here we use one DATA step because as we said in [XI], there is no summary function MEDIAN. It is a statistical function in v9 that does not exist in v8.

Reference

Hu, Weiming. (2004) "Top Ten Reasons to Use PROC SQL." *Proceedings of the Twenty-ninth Annual SAS Users Group International Conference*, Paper 042-29, Cary, NC: SAS Institute Inc.
http://www2.sas.com/proceedings/sugi29/042-29.pdf

Table Operations in PROC SQL

Introduction

In DATA step, we use SET and MERGE to do set operations. In a MERGE statement, we also use an IN= variable to control processing observations, such as statement IF in1 OR in2; IF in1; IF in2; IF in1 AND in2; where in1 and in2 are IN= variables. The default is IF in1 OR in2;. There are four kinds of table operations in PROC SQL: match SELECT, JOIN, UNION, INSERT INTO, and subquery. In this paper we will discuss these four operations, compare them to DATA step set operations, discuss the equivalence of statements, and give examples.

Match SELECT

In a SELECT statement, the table name is specified in a FROM clause. If there is more than one table in a FROM clause, PROC SQL returns the *Cartesian product* of these tables. In a Cartesian product, each row in the first table is combined with each row in the second table. Therefore, suppose that table tbl1 has c1 columns and r1 rows, and table tbl2 has c2 columns and r2 rows. The following program creates an output with c1+c2 columns and r1*r2 rows. You can put more than two tables in a FROM clause, and the rules are the same. Suppose that we have two groups of chess players, group1 and group2. In each group there are several chess players with their levels and scores as the following table shows:

Group1			Group2		
Level	Name	Score	Level	Name	Score
1	Joe	9	1	Kim	8
2	Sam	7	2	Amanda	7
2	Ed	6	2	Tom	5
3	Barbara	6	4	Mary	6

Now there is a match between two groups. Each player in group1 will play with each player in group2. We can create the following table:

```
DATA group1;
INPUT level name $ score;
CARDS;
1      Joe         9
2      Sam         7
2      Ed          6
3      Barbara     6
;
DATA group2;
INPUT level name $ score;
CARDS;
1      Joe         9
2      Amanda      7
2      Tom         5
4      Mary        6
;
PROC SQL;
SELECT * FROM group1, group2;
QUIT;
```

level	name	score	level	name	score
1	Joe	9	1	Joe	9
1	Joe	9	2	Amanda	7
1	Joe	9	2	Tom	5
1	Joe	9	4	Mary	6
2	Sam	7	1	Joe	9
2	Sam	7	2	Amanda	7
2	Sam	7	2	Tom	5
2	Sam	7	4	Mary	6
2	Ed	6	1	Joe	9
2	Ed	6	2	Amanda	7
2	Ed	6	2	Tom	5
2	Ed	6	4	Mary	6
3	Barbara	6	1	Joe	9
3	Barbara	6	2	Amanda	7
3	Barbara	6	2	Tom	5
3	Barbara	6	4	Mary	6

There are a total of 16 games. Note that the names of the columns of the two tables are the same, and they all appear in the output. However, if we use this query to create a table, the last three columns will be dropped since they have the same names as the first three columns.

More often used cases are match SELECT. In the above example we want to change the rule to the following: Each player in group1 will play with every player in group2 if they have the same level. Then we add a clause WHERE group1.level=group2.level in a SELECT statement. In this case, SAS creates a Cartesian product for each matching pair. See the following example:

```
SELECT * FROM group1, group2
WHERE group1.level=group2.level;
```

level	name	score	level	name	score
1	Joe	9	1	Joe	9
2	Sam	7	2	Amanda	7
2	Sam	7	2	Tom	5
2	Ed	6	2	Amanda	7
2	Ed	6	2	Tom	5

Although we use an equal sign here, we can also use other comparison symbols. NE means that each player will play with whoever is at a different level. GT means that each player in group1 will play with the player in group2 who has the lowest level.

Now we will make a comparison between match SELECT in PROC SQL and MERGE/BY in DATA step.

- In PROC SQL for each match group, SAS creates a Cartesian product, and for the same BY values in MERGE, SAS retains values. So suppose that for a match group, there are m1 and n1 rows in two tables respectively. Match SELECT creates m1*n1 rows, but MERGE/BY creates max(m1,n1) observations. If one of m1, n1 is 1, then two methods create the same number of observations. See the following example:

```
DATA s;
INPUT a b;
CARDS;
1 2
1 3
2 4
;
DATA t;
INPUT a c;
CARDS;
1 5
2 6
2 8
;
DATA p;
MERGE s t;
BY a;
PROC PRINT;RUN;
PROC SQL;
SELECT * FROM s,t WHERE s.a=t.a;
RUN;
```

Obs	a	b	c
1	1	2	5
2	1	3	5
3	2	4	6
4	2	4	8

a	b	a	c
1	2	1	5
1	3	1	5
2	4	2	6
2	4	2	8

As we know, usually we don't do MERGE/BY for m1>1 and n1>1. There will be a note in the log file when this happens.

```
NOTE: MERGE statement has more than one data set with repeats of BY values.
```

- In a MERGE statement we can use an IN= variable to control observations. In MERGE, the default is IF in1 OR in2, but SQL only takes match groups, so it is equivalent to IF in1 AND in2. Here in1 and in2 are two IN= variables.
- If there are variables with the same name, MERGE will overwrite and keep values that are in the last data set. However, PROC SQL will keep both for printout (as the first example shows) and keep values that are in the first table when creating table. See the following program:

```
DATA s;
a=3;b=4;
DATA t;
a=3;b=5;
DATA p;
MERGE s t;
BY a;
PUT "in MERGE " a= b=;
PROC SQL;
CREATE TABLE x AS SELECT * FROM s,t WHERE s.a=t.a;
QUIT;
DATA _NULL_;
SET x;
PUT "in SQL " a= b=;
RUN;
```

```
in MERGE a=3 b=5
in SQL a=3 b=4
```

So when will match SELECT and MERGE/BY create the same data set?

- There are no columns in two tables that have the same names except match columns. (We can change names using RENAME= option or AS clause in PROC SQL.)
- In each match group, one table has only one row.
- In MERGE/BY, we use condition IF in1 AND in2.

With the above conditions satisfied, what are the benefits of using PROC SQL?

- PROC SQL does not need tables to be sorted.
- PROC SQL can join tables on different variable names.
- PROC SQL can join more than two tables by different variables.

See the following example:

```
SELECT * FROM demog, deposit, sitecd WHERE demog.id=deposit.patid AND
demod.site=sitecd.site;
```

Join operations

There are four kinds of joins. One is INNER JOIN, and three are outer joins: They are LEFT JOIN, RIGHT JOIN, and FULL JOIN.

The INNER JOIN is exactly the same as the above match SELECT although they have different syntax. In the following program, we use INNER JOIN:

```
PROC SQL;
SELECT * FROM group1 INNER JOIN group2
ON group1.level=group2.level;
QUIT;
```

The INNER JOIN removes all players that have no opponent. However, it is possible that the coach of group1 also wants to see his players in the table even if they have no opponents, and in this case, the coach puts missing values as their counterparts. We just need to change 'INNER JOIN' to 'LEFT JOIN'. If the coach of group2 has the same request, we change it to 'RIGHT JOIN'. They are similar to the statement IF in1; or IF in2; in MERGE/BY.

If we want the table to contain all players, change it to 'FULL JOIN'. See the following code and output:

```
PROC SQL;
SELECT * FROM group1 FULL JOIN group2
ON group1.level=group2.level ;
QUIT;
```

level	name	score	level	name	score
1	Joe	9	1	Joe	9
2	Ed	6	2	Tom	5
2	Ed	6	2	Amanda	7
2	Sam	7	2	Tom	5
2	Sam	7	2	Amanda	7
3	Barbara	6	.		.
.		.	4	Mary	6

Notice that in the ON clause in the above example, we have only one column, but we can put more columns using AND or OR. For example, there is one more rule: female players play with female players, male players play with male players, then you can change the ON clause in the following way:

```
ON group1.level=group2.level AND group1.gender=group2.gender;
```

If you don't want to specify an ON clause but want name match to be done by SAS itself, you can use NATURAL JOIN. For NATURAL JOIN, SAS finds the same names of columns in both tables and matches them. If a column has the same name but different type, SAS shows an error message and stops. Otherwise, for each matching value, SAS creates a Cartesian product. In many cases, a programmer is familiar with the structure of data sets. He/she knows what common variables are. In this case, NATURAL JOIN can save some typing. The following four statements are equivalent. (The data set dm has one row for each patid. If there is no column random in the data set ae, the last statement does not show column random, but others show.):

```
SELECT * FROM ae NATURAL JOIN dm(KEEP=patid random WHERE=(random='Y'));
SELECT * FROM ae JOIN dm(KEEP=patid random WHERE=(random='Y'))
   ON ae.patid=dm.patid;
SELECT * FROM ae,dm(KEEP=patid random WHERE=(random='Y'))
   WHERE ae.patid=dm.patid;
SELECT ae.* FROM ae,dm(WHERE=(random='Y')) WHERE ae.patid=dm.patid;
```

There is also CROSS JOIN operation. Like NATURAL JOIN, it does not specify an ON keyword, but it creates a Cartesian product without any match. The following two statements are equivalent:

```
SELECT * FROM a,b;
SELECT * FROM a CROSS JOIN b;
```

UNION JOIN is similar to OUTER UNION as in the following section.

Union operations

We can also do union operations in a SELECT statement. There are four clauses: UNION, OUTER UNION, INTERSECT, and EXCEPT. The following is the syntax of these clauses:

INTERSECT <CORRESPONDING| CORR > <ALL>
OUTER UNION <CORRESPONDING| CORR
UNION <CORRESPONDING| CORR > <ALL>
EXCEPT <CORRESPONDING| CORR > <ALL>

The CORRESPONDING| CORR option is for name match. It works for columns. The ALL option works for rows. We use this option to keep duplicate rows. If no ALL option is used, SAS will remove duplicate rows. Suppose we have two tables tbl1 and tbl2 with column sets C1 and C2 respectively. Notice that in join operations, we put a keyword between two table names. But in union operations, we put a keyword between two SELECT clauses, such as the following:

```
SELECT * FROM tbl1 INTERSECT select * from tbl2;
```

UNION

If the option CORR is used, SAS uses a name match, and it takes only columns with the same names in both tables. The resultant table has a column set $C1 \cap C2$. If the option CORR is not specified, SAS uses a position match, and the resultant table has $\max(|C1|, |C2|)$ columns. It takes first $|C1|$ column names from C1, and if $|C2|>|C1|$, it takes another $|C2|-|C1|$ names from C2. You have to make sure that the corresponding columns have the same type. Otherwise, it will not work. Then SAS fills in missing values.

A UNION concatenates two tables vertically if the option ALL is used. The resultant table will be sorted, and duplicate rows will be removed if the option ALL is not used.

Let's see the following program:

```
DATA s;
INPUT a b;
CARDS;
1 3
1 2
1 3
;
DATA t;
INPUT a c d;
CARDS;
3 1 .
3 1 4
```

```
5 6 5
;
PROC SQL;
SELECT b,a FROM s UNION SELECT * FROM t;
```

b	a	d
2	1	.
3	1	.
3	1	4
5	6	5

You can imagine that the following program produces two identical outputs:

```
DATA rep_group;
INPUT level name $ score;
CARDS;
1    Joe       9
2    Sam       7
2    Ed        6
3    Barbara   6
1    Joe       9
;
PROC SQL;
SELECT * FROM rep_group UNION SELECT * FROM rep_group;
SELECT DISTINCT * FROM rep_group ORDER BY level, name, score;
```

OUTER UNION

Compared to the UNION that creates max(|C1|, |C2|) columns, OUTER UNION creates |C1|+|C2| columns. It creates a 2X2 table (R1,R2)X(C1,C2), where R1XC1 is table1 and R2XC2 is table2, and two others are filled with a missing value. See the following example:

```
PROC SQL;
    SELECT * FROM group1 OUTER UNION SELECT * FROM group2;
QUIT;
```

output

level	name	score	level	name	score
1	Joe	9	.		.
2	Sam	7	.		.
2	Ed	6	.		.
3	Barbara	6	.		.
.		.	1	Joe	9
.		.	2	Amanda	7
.		.	2	Tom	5
.		.	4	Mary	6

If you use the CORRESPONDING|CORR option, SAS will combine columns with the same name, and the resultant table will have column set $C1 \cup C2$.

EXCEPT

For columns, SAS works the same as UNION: If there is no CORR option, the resulting table has max(|C1|, |C2|) columns. Otherwise, the column set will be C1∩C2. For rows if there is no ALL option, SAS removes rows from table1 that appear in table2. The ALL option works slightly differently. Suppose that there is a row which appears m times in table1 and n times in table2. Then SAS keeps max(0, m-n) the same rows. See the following example:

```
PROC SQL;
SELECT * FROM group1 EXCEPT ALL SELECT * FROM group2;
```

output

level	name	score
2	Ed	6
2	Sam	7
3	Barbara	6

INTERSECT

INTERSECT works the same as UNION for columns. For rows, it takes rows that appear in both tables. For duplicate rows, SAS keeps only one row if there is no ALL option, and SAS keeps min(m,n) rows if there is an ALL option, where m and n are defined as in the above. See the following example:

```
PROC SQL;
SELECT * FROM group1 INTERSECT CORR  SELECT * FROM group2;
```

level	name	score
1	Joe	9

In Table 1, I summarize the usage of the keywords ALL and CORR inUNION operations. "Both" means using both options, and "Neither" means using neither of them. A and B are row sets, and C1 and C2 are column sets of tables T1 and T2, respectively. The top left corner shows you how to read cells.

Table 1. Comparison of options in union operations

Column set Row operation # of rows Match output	ALL	CORR	Both	Neither
UNION	C1∪(C2\C1) A+B m+n Position match Not ordered	C1∩C2 A∪B\dup ∑(mi>0)|(ni=0) Name match Ordered (no duplicate)	C1∩C2 A+B m+n Name match Not ordered	C1∪(C2\C1) A∪B\dup ∑(mi>0)|(ni=0) Position match Ordered (no duplicate)
OUTER UNION		C1∪C2 A+B		C1+C2 A+B

		m+n Name match Not ordered		m+n No match Not ordered
EXCEPT	C1∪(C2\C1) A\B ∑max(0,mi-ni) Position match Ordered (keep duplicate)	C1∩C2 A\B ∑(mi>0)&(ni=0) Name match Ordered (no duplicate)	C1∩C2 A\B ∑max(0,mi-ni) Name match Ordered (keep duplicate)	C1∪(C2\C1) A\B ∑(mi>0)&(ni=0) Position match Ordered (no duplicate)
INTERSECT	C1∪(C2\C1) A∩B ∑Min(mi,ni) Position match Ordered (keep duplicate)	C1∩C2 A∩B ∑(mi>0)&(ni>0) Name match Ordered (no duplicate)	C1∩C2 A∩B ∑Min(mi,ni) Name match Ordered (keep duplicate)	C1∪(C2\C1) A∩B ∑(mi>0)&(ni>0) Position match Ordered (no duplicate)

Row operation is based on all columns.
m is the number of rows in the first table, and n is that in the second table. mi and ni are numbers of rows in the first table and the second table of matching group i.
Order is based on all columns.

In the above table, the notations C1∩C2 (for name match) and C1∪C2 and C1+C2 (OUTER UNION) are easy to understand. Their meanings are as usual. The notation C1∪(C2\C1) is different from usual. It is only for position match and has total max(|C1|,|C2|) columns, consisting of the first |C1| columns of C1 and the last max(0, |C2|-|C1|) columns of C2. If C1={a,b}, C2={c,d,e}, then C1∪(C2\C1)={a,b,e}. So in this case, if |C1|≠|C2|, SAS expands one table by adding columns, fills in missing values, and then does operations.

The operations between A and B are based on columns, either column set C1∩C2 if name match or column set C1∪(C2\C1) if position match with missing values filled, except OUTER UNION.

From Table 1, we can see the following points:

- Using the option CORR, we get name match with columns C1∩C2.
- We can use position match (no option CORR) by specifying column names (change order of columns), so the operation is name match and keep columns set C1∪(C2\C1).
- Only OUTER UNION can have columns C1∪C2 if C1\C2≠∅ and C2\C1 ≠∅.
- Without option ALL, SAS will do no-duplicate sort, except for OUTER UNION.

The following program gives you some examples for UNION operators:

```
DATA s;
INPUT a b c;
CARDS;
1 2 5
1 3 4
1 2 3
1 2 .
2 2 4
```

```
;
DATA t;
INPUT a d;
CARDS;
1 5
1 2
2 3
;
PROC SQL;
SELECT * FROM s EXCEPT ALL SELECT * FROM t;
SELECT * FROM s INTERSECT SELECT * FROM t;
```

a	b	c
1	2	3
1	2	5
1	3	4
2	2	4

a	b	c
1	2	.

Like arithmetic or comparison operators, we can do these operations on more than two tables, such as A UNION B INTERSECT C. SAS handles this in the same way as arithmetic operators, i.e., from left to right and according to precedence. The precedence is that INTERSECT has high precedence (do first) than others, and all the other three operators have the same precedence.

INSERT INTO operation

INSERT INTO statement can use SET clause, VALUES clause, and SELECT clause, where SELECT can be viewed as table operation. INSERT INTO operation is similar to UNION operator with ALL option. The differences are the following:

- UNION operator is for display. If we want to create a table, we have to use CREATE TABLE clause and specify the table name, but INSERT INTO statement is to modify a table. The table name is the same as that specified in INSERT INTO clause.
- UNION operator will create column set $C1\cup(C2\setminus C1)$. When $C2\subseteq C1$, they are the same.

Comparisons among table operations

The following table gives a rough comparison among table operations, except subquery:

Table 2. Comparisons among table operations
(Compared to DATA step MERGE, in1 and in2 are two IN= variables.)

	Row operation equivalence	Column operation	Note
Match SELECT	IF in1 AND in2;	$C1\cup C2$	Cartesian product
Join	IF a1 AND a2 (INNER JOIN)	$C1\cup C2$	Cartesian product (for ON

	IF a1 (LEFT JOIN) IF a2 (RIGHT JOIN) IF a1 OR a2 (FULL JOIN)		columns)
Union	IF a1 OR a2 (UNION) IF a1 AND a2 (INTERSECT) IF a1 AND NOT a2 (EXCEPT)	$C1 \cap C2$ or $C1 \cup (C2 \setminus C1)$	Ordered for most cases Remove duplicate if CORR used

- Match SELECT and join create a Cartesian product. If it is not many-to-many match (For each match group, one table has only one row.), we don't have to think of a Cartesian product.

Union operation can order the resultant table and remove duplicate rows. We can think that this is an advantage of union operation. Sometimes we may want to use this, and sometimes we may not want to use it. Although both join and union can do IF in1 OR in2, union can do noduplicate sort, so it is similar to interleaving merge. As we know, IF in1 AND NOT in2 is also very often used in programming. We can use an EXCEPT operator to do this. However, the option CORR is too strict, so we will lose much information because the final column set is $C1 \cap C2$. Without the CORR option, it is a position match. A position match may not be suitable in some situations. Then we can specify column names in the SELECT clause. Since this is a position match, it is better for the case $C2 \subseteq C1$. If $C1 \setminus C2 \neq \emptyset$ and $C2 \setminus C1 \neq \emptyset$, then there are columns that we don't want to match, but they do match in the operation, and of course this is not good. If $C1 \subseteq C2$, then the resultant table will have missing values in all columns in $C2 \setminus C1$, and this is not very meaningful. Even for the case $C2 \subseteq C1$, this is also not very good because SAS first fills in missing values for columns $C1 \setminus C2$ in tbl2 and then works on all columns. This means that only rows in tbl1 with missing values in $C1 \setminus C2$ may be removed. I don't think programmers will like this. This restricts the use of the EXCEPT operation mostly to be used only for C1=C2. In the above example, there are two operators, EXCEPT and INTERSECT. Both operators work on rows (1 2 .), rather than on (1 2). In the following example, the first SELECT statement returns all observations and the second SELECT statement returns no observations.

```
DATA student_record;
INPUT name $ sex $ grade;
DATALINES;
Amanda F 4
Bob M 5
Cathy F 3
David M 5
Emery F 2
RUN;
DATA ymca_sporter;
LENGTH name $8 sport $10;
INPUT name $ sport $;
DATALINES;
Amanda basketball
Cathy  soccer
George smimming
Harry  runner
;
```

```
RUN;
PROC SQL;
SELECT * FROM ymca_sporter EXCEPT ALL SELECT * FROM
student_record(keep=name);
SELECT * FROM ymca_sporter INTERSECT SELECT * FROM
student_record(keep=name);
QUIT;
```

A subquery can do IF a1 AND NOT a2 operations as in the following statements. (Suppose $C2 \subseteq C1$, where C1 and C2 are column sets of the data sets record and contest respectively.):

```
SELECT * FROM record WHERE x NOTIN (SELECT a FROM contest);
SELECT * FROM record WHERE NOT EXISTS(SELECT a
   FROM contest WHERE record.x=a);
```

Subquery

We already see that we can use a query in another query as UNION operations and INSERT INTO clause show. In these cases, query is a requirement and works as a table. For the syntax, don't put parenthesis for the query. On the other hand, for FROM and JOIN clause we need a table, but we can also use a query. For the syntax, we have to put a parenthesis for the query. It is hard to say there are any big differences between these two kinds of queries. Roughly, I will call the latter subqueries.

A query can return a table, a set of values, or a single value. We can use a query (subquery or inner query) in another query (outer query) as a value, a value set, or a table. Notice that a value is also a value set, and a value set is also a table. A subquery can be used in WHERE, HAVING, SELECT, FROM, JOIN, and SET clauses, where

FROM, JOIN: needs a table;
SELECT, SET: needs a single value;
A WHERE clause and a HAVING clause use the following comparison operators:

EQ, NE, GE, LE, GT, LT, EQT, NET, GET, LET, GTT, LTT, CONTAINS, BETWEEN-AND: need a single value;
IN, NOTIN: need a value set.

Notice that whether a subquery works or not depends not only on its syntax but also on results of the subquery, especially when the query needs a single value from the subquery. If the subquery returns one value, it is OK, but otherwise, it is not OK. We will see an example soon.

The following example show usages of a subquery in FROM, JOIN, SELECT, and SET clauses:

```
DATA s;
INPUT a b;
CARDS;
1 2
```

```
1 3
;
DATA t;
INPUT a c;
CARDS;
1 4
2 5
;
PROC SQL;
SELECT * FROM s,(SELECT * FROM t);
SELECT * FROM s JOIN (SELECT * FROM t) AS p ON s.a=p.a;
SELECT *,(SELECT AVG(c) FROM t WHERE s.a=t.a) FROM s;
INSERT INTO s SET b=(SELECT AVG(c) FROM t) ;
INSERT INTO s SELECT * FROM t;
```

However, the most commonly used subqueries are in a WHERE clause and in a HAVING clause. They have the following characteristics:

- If there is no GROUP BY clause, then a HAVING clause is equivalent to a WHERE clause.
- A HAVING clause can have a summary function, but a WHERE clause cannot.
- For the alias of new column, a WHERE clause must use the keyword CALCULATED. The keyword can be omitted in clauses other than SELECT and WHERE clauses.

Let's look at the following program:

```
DATA class1;
INPUT fname $ lname $ test ;
CARDS;
Peter Gets 88 1 2
James Martin 99 1 3
Julie Cage 87 2 4
;
DATA class2;
INPUT fname $ lname $ test;
CARDS;
Peter Brain 93
James Martin 90
James Ting  88
;
PROC SQL;
SELECT class1.* FROM class1,class2 WHERE class1.test>AVG(class2.test);
   *not work; ❶
SELECT class1.* FROM class1,class2 HAVING
   class1.test>AVG(class2.test);*Cartesian product; ❷
SELECT class1.* FROM class1 HAVING
   class1.test>AVG(class2.test); ❸
SELECT DISTINCT(class1.*) FROM class1,class2 HAVING
   class1.test>AVG(class2.test); ❹
SELECT * FROM class1 WHERE test>(SELECT AVG(test) FROM class2); ❺
SELECT * FROM class1 WHERE test>(SELECT test FROM class2
   WHERE lname='Ting'); ❻
SELECT * FROM class1 WHERE test IN (SELECT test FROM class2
```

```
   WHERE fname='James'); ❼
SELECT * FROM class1 WHERE test>(SELECT test FROM class2
   WHERE fname='James'); *not work; ❽
```

Here ❶ does not work because a WHERE clause cannot have a summary function, and ❷ works. Both ❷ and ❸ create the same columns, but ❷ has three repeated rows and ❸ only creates one row. ❽ has exact expression as ❻, but ❻ returns one value and is OK. ❽ returns more than one value and is not OK.

As we see, comparison operators, except IN and NOTIN, need one value as an operand. When a subquery returns a value set, we can add the keywords ANY, SOME, or ALL between a comparison operator and a subquery. Also, notice that we cannot use a subquery as a parameter of a summary function, such as MAX, MIN, MEAN, but we can use summary functions in a subquery. In the following there are four groups of statements. Statements in the same group are equivalent:

```
SELECT firstname FROM student_table WHERE
   height>ALL(SELECT height FROM teacher_table);
SELECT firstname FROM student_table WHERE
   height> (SELECT MAX(height) FROM teacher_table);

SELECT firstname FROM student_table WHERE
   height>ANY(select height FROM teacher_table);
SELECT firstname FROM student_table WHERE
   height>(SELECT MIN(height) FROM teacher_table);

SELECT * FROM record WHERE x NE ALL(SELECT a FROM contest);
SELECT * FROM record WHERE x NOTIN (SELECT a FROM contest);
SELECT * FROM record WHERE NOT EXISTS(SELECT a
   FROM contest WHERE record.x=a); ❶

SELECT record.* FROM record,contest WHERE x=a;
SELECT * FROM record WHERE x EQ ANY(SELECT a FROM contest);
SELECT * FROM record WHERE x IN (SELECT a FROM contest);
SELECT * FROM record WHERE EXISTS(SELECT a
   FROM contest WHERE record.x=a); ❷
```

In the above statements, subqueries other than in ❶ and ❷, are independent from outer query. Notice that when we say independent, this does not mean that the outer query table must be different from that in the subquery. It means that columns in the outer query do not appear in the subquery. If the subquery and the outer query are not independent, such as ❶ and ❷, then we say the subquery is a *correlated subquery*. Suppose we have a table about students' information. Also, we have a table about students' scores. We want to find students' information, for example, who got at least one perfect score on their tests. We have the following program, which is a correlated subquery:

```
DATA info;
INPUT name $ sex $ age;
CARDS;
James m 15
```

```
Amenda f 14
Peter m 15
;
DATA record;
INPUT name $ score @@;
CARDS;
James 87 James 96 Peter 100 Peter 88 Amenda 97 Amenda 100
;
PROC SQL;
SELECT * FROM info WHERE 100 IN (SELECT score FROM record
   WHERE name=info.name);
QUIT;
```

Output

name	sex	age
Amenda	f	14
Peter	m	15

Notice that this is equivalent to the following match SELECT:

```
SELECT info.* FROM info,record WHERE info.name=record.name
   AND score=100;
```

As we know, for a query, SAS checks each row to see if the WHERE condition is satisfied. If so, SAS selects the row, and if not, SAS does not select the row. The correlated subquery works in the following way: For each row of the table in the outer query, SAS puts the needed value into the subquery and executes the subquery. Then it checks the WHERE condition in the outer query to determine if the row should be selected. In the above program, for each row of table info, SAS puts this information into the subquery, executes the subquery, and gets a set of scores back; then it checks to see if 100 is in the return set.

As we see from the above example, in PROC SQL, there is an operator: EXISTS (NOT EXISTS). Its right operand is a subquery. The result of an EXISTS condition is true if the subquery resolves to at least one row. The result of a NOT EXISTS condition is true if the subquery evaluates to zero rows. When using the operator EXISTS, usually it is a correlated subquery. It is OK for syntax if it is not a subquery, but in this case, the outer query selects either all rows or no rows, and it is meaningless.

Using one table to filter another table is a common doing. In data step, in order to filter, we use IF in1 AND in2; or IF in1 AND NOT in2; where in1 and in2 are both IN= variables. In PROC SQL, people usually use EXISTS or NOT EXISTS to do the same thing. See the following example:

```
DATA student_record;
INPUT name $ sex $ grade;
DATALINES;
Amanda F 4
Bob M 5
```

```
Cathy F 3
David M 5
Emery F 2
RUN;
DATA ymca_sporter;
LENGTH name $8 sport $10;
INPUT name $ sport $;
DATALINES;
Amanda basketball
Cathy  soccer
George smimming
Harry  runner
;
RUN;
PROC SQL;
SELECT * FROM ymca_sporter AS y WHERE EXISTS
(SELECT * FROM student_record WHERE name =y.name);
QUIT;
```

Output

name	sport
Amanda	basketball
Cathy	soccer

In the above example, as we have already indicated, for the EXISTS filter, we can use an IN operator or match SELECT. Notice that if there is more than one column in a WHERE clause in a subquery, we cannot use an IN operator, and if it is NOT EXISTS operator, we cannot use match SELECT.

Examples of subqueries

Now let's see some examples. First we want to count how many unique rows are in a table. We know we cannot use the following statement ([XII]):

```
SELECT COUNT(DISTINCT(*)) FROM s;
```

But we can use the following subquery to do this:

```
SELECT COUNT(*) FROM (SELECT DISTINCT *  FROM s);
```

Although in most cases ALL, ANY can be replaced by other operators, not all cases work. The following program gives the id who has the most rows:

```
DATA s;
INPUT dept $ id;
CARDS;
A 1002
A 1003
B 1006
B 1006
B 1007
```

```
;
SELECT DISTINCT * FROM s GROUP BY id having COUNT(*) >=
   ALL(SELECT COUNT(*) FROM s GROUP BY id );
```

The following program gives id who has the most rows for each dept:

```
PROC SQL;
SELECT DISTINCT * FROM s;
SELECT DISTINCT * FROM s AS a GROUP BY dept,id
   HAVING COUNT(*) >=ALL(SELECT COUNT(*) FROM s
   WHERE a.dept=dept GROUP BY dept, id);
```

In [X], we talked that in PROC SQL, we can find a ground total and a group total and also find percentages for an ind/total and an ind/group by using the following program:

```
SELECT id, dept, sales, SUM(sales) AS total, sales/SUM(sales)
   AS percent FROM sales;
SELECT id, dept, sales, SUM(sales) AS total, sales/SUM(sales)
   AS percent FROM sales GROUP BY dept;
```

But we cannot find a group total and a ground total at the same time. To find them at the same time, we can use a subquery.

```
DATA sales;
LENGTH name $20;
INPUT id dept $ name & sales;
DATALINES;
1013 A Martin, Virginia     3500
1014 A Singleton, MaryAnn    2400
1015 A Leighton, Maurice    2300
1016 B Freuler, Carl        3750
1018 B Cage, Merce          4370
1020 B Gates, Alexis         3000
;
RUN;

PROC SQL;
SELECT id, dept, (SELECT SUM(sales) FROM sales AS b WHERE a.dept=b.dept
   GROUP BY dept) AS total1, SUM(sales) AS total2, CALCULATED
   total1/SUM(sales) AS percent FROM sales AS a;
```

id	dept	total1	total2	percent
1013	A	8200	19320	0.424431
1014	A	8200	19320	0.424431
1015	A	8200	19320	0.424431
1016	B	11120	19320	0.575569
1018	B	11120	19320	0.575569
1020	B	11120	19320	0.575569

The following program creates two tables, t2 and t4, where t2 contains names of people who have the three highest sales, and t4 contains at least three names of people who have the highest sales in case there is a tie. Notice that in a subquery we cannot use an ORDER BY statement. Also, in this program, we use the function MONOTONIC, which returns the order number of a row in a table.

```
PROC SQL;
CREATE TABLE t1 AS SELECT DISTINCT sales FROM sales
   ORDER BY sales DESC;
CREATE TABLE t2 AS SELECT name,sales FROM sales
   WHERE sales IN (SELECT sales FROM t1 WHERE MONOTONIC()<=3) ;
CREATE TABLE t3 AS SELECT name,sales FROM t2 ORDER BY sales DESC;
CREATE TABLE t4 AS SELECT name,sales FROM sales
   WHERE sales >= (SELECT sales FROM t3 WHERE MONOTONIC()=3);
```

Reference

Granor, Tamar E. with Della Martin. (2005) Working with Subqueries, in Taming Visual FoxPro's SQL Real World Data Solutions For VFP. Hentzenwerke Publishing. http://www.hentzenwerke.com/samplechapters/sctamvfpsql_5.pdf

Zhang, Lei and Danbo Yi. "WORKING WITH SUBQUERY IN THE SQL PROCEDURE." *Proceedings of the NorthEast SAS Users Group Conference (NESUG 1998)*, Paper P005, Cary, NC: SAS Institute Inc. http://www.nesug.org/Proceedings/nesug98/dbas/p005.pdf

Middela, Sreekanth and Suhas R. Sanjee. (2007) "The SQL Procedure: Tricks and Techniques for Efficiency and Simplicity." *Proceedings of the NorthEast SAS Users Group Conference (NESUG 2007)*, Paper BB11, Cary, NC: SAS Institute Inc. http://www.nesug.org/Proceedings/nesug07/bb/bb11.pdf

Summary Report or Detail Report? -- PROC REPORT and PROC SQL

Introduction

As we know, PROC REPORT and PROC SQL can produce summary reports as well as detail reports. Our question is, when will they create a summary report, and when will they create a detail report? This question is closely related to statistics in PROC REPORT or statistical functions in PROC SQL. Therefore, this paper not only answers about the above question but also discusses statistical functions in great detail.

PROC REPORT

In PROC REPORT, there are three kinds of variables: group variables, display variables, and summary variables. For a detail report, group variables group observations together, order variable order observations, and each observation will have a row output. For a summary report, group variables are used to group values for the calculation of statistics for analysis variables, and each group will have a row output. PROC REPORT can calculate the following statistics:

Table 1. Statistics in PROC REPORT

Descriptive statistic keywords

CSS	MEAN	RANGE	SUM
CV	MIN	STD	USS
MAX	PCTSUM	STDERR	VAR
N	NMISS	PCTN	SUMWGT

Quantile statistic keywords

MEDIAN|P50	P10	P90	QRANGE
P1	Q1|P25	P95	
P5	Q3|P75	P99	

Hypothesis testing keyword

PRT	T

Let's first talk about COLUMN statement.

- In a COLUMN statement, you can specify variable names and statistics.
- The default is all variables if the statement is omitted.
- The default statistic for a numeric variable is SUM.
- N is the only statistic that can be an independent statistic without specifying a variable.
- If N is an independent report item, then N is counted as the number of observations.

- Statistics N, NMISS, PCTN, and SUMWGT can also be together with a character variable. Other statistics work only with numeric variables.
- If you specify a character variable together with a statistic other than N, NMISS, PCTN and SUMWGT, SAS will not give you an ERROR message. Instead, SAS just returns a missing value.
- N, if it is together with a variable, and PCTN are calculated based on non-missing values.
- In a DEFINE statement, we cannot specify N, NMISS, PCTN, and SUMWGT statistics for a character variable, but we can specify them for a numeric variable. In other words, a DEFINE/ANALYSIS statement works only for numeric variables.

In the following example, there are three items in a COLUMN statement. The first one, N, counts the number of observations. The second one is a variable together with statistic N, and it counts the number of non-missing values of variable a. The third one is variable b, and since it is a numeric column, it is an analysis column, and the default statistic is SUM. It is the same as b,SUM.

```
DATA s;
INPUT a $ b;
CARDS;
1 2
2 4
. 3
. .
;
PROC REPORT NOWD;
COLUMN N a,N b;
RUN;
```

```
            a
   n        n        b
   4        2        9
```

PROC REPORT has the following statements that affect report type:

DEFINE/GROUP
DEFINE/ACROSS
DEFINE/ORDER
DEFINE/DISPLAY
DEFINE/ANALYSIS

What kind of report will be created for a PROC REPORT depends on if there is a display variable. If there is no display column, then it is a summary report; otherwise, it is a detail report. DISPLAY and ORDER statements are for a detail report. The difference between DISPLAY and ORDER is that for an ORDER statement, the output is sorted by ORDER variables and only prints out the first value in the group. Another difference is that SAS will print out rows with missing DISPLAY values, but it will not print out rows with missing ORDER values. See the following example:

```
DATA s;
INPUT a b;
CARDS;
1 4
1 3
2 3
. 4
;
PROC REPORT NOWD HEADLINE;
DEFINE a/DISPLAY;
PROC REPORT NOWD HEADLINE;
DEFINE a/ORDER;
RUN;
```

```
          a         b
  -------------------
          1         4
          1         3
          2         3
          .         4

          a         b
  -------------------
          1         4
                    3
          2         3
```

A character variable is default to a display variable. However, we can define it as a group variable or an analysis variable. If it is defined as an analysis variable, the only statistics are N, NMISS, PCTN and SUMWGT.

Now we can describe the conditions for a detail report. In the following three cases, SAS prints out the detail report; otherwise, it prints out a summary report:

- A variable is defined as a DISPLAY variable.
- A variable is defined as an ORDER variable.
- There is a character variable in a COLUMN statement that is not defined as a GROUP variable or an ACROSS variable, and which is a single item with no statistic specified. By default, it is a DISPLAY variable.

The following example shows that we can define statistics N and PCTN for character variable(s), so they are not display variables anymore:

```
DATA s;
INPUT a $ b;
CARDS;
1 2
1 3
2 4
3 3
;
PROC REPORT NOWD;
```

```
COLUMN a,N a,PCTN b;
RUN;
```

```
          a          a
          n       pctn          b
          4          1         12
```

The following program shows that we can define character variable(s) as group variables:

```
DATA s;
INPUT a $ b $ c;
CARDS;
a c 3
a d 5
a d 10
b c 1
b c 2
b d 3
;
PROC REPORT NOWD;
DEFINE a/GROUP;
DEFINE b/ACROSS;
RUN;
```

```
                        b
  a           c           d           c
  a           1           2          18
  b           2           1           6
```

Summary functions in PROC SQL

When talking about PROC SQL, we have to talk about statistical functions seriously. In DATA step, we use statistical functions whose arguments are expressions of values in one row. They may have requirement for number of arguments. For example, MEAN needs at least one argument, MAX needs at least two arguments, and KURTOSIS needs at least four arguments. The following table shows statistical functions that are used in DATA step. For arguments, terminologies refer to [V].

Table 2. Statistical functions in DATA step

*: New in v9.
1 or 2: number of arguments needed
#: summary function if in PROC SQL and with one argument

*COALESCE 1	*HARMEANZ 1	MEAN 1 #	NMISS 1 #	*SMALLEST 2
CSS 1 (v9) 2 (v8) #	*IQR 1	*MEDIAN 1	ORDINAL 2	STD 2 #
CV 2 #	KURTOSIS 4	MIN 2 #	*PCTL 2	STDERR 2 #
*GEOMEAN 1	*LARGEST 2	MISSING 1	RANGE 1 #	SUM 1 #
*GEOMEANZ 1	*MAD 1	*MODZ 1	*RMS 1	USS 1 (v9) 2 (v8) #
*HARMEAN 1	MAX 2 #	N 1 #	SKEWNESS 3	VAR 2 #

In PROC REPORT, we already learned that we can use statistics in Table 1 for a summary report. We can also use statistical functions in Table 2 in COMPUTE blocks. See the following examples:

```
DATA s;
INPUT a $ b;
CARDS;
1 2
2 4
. 3
. .
;
PROC REPORT NOWD HEADLINE;
COLUMN N a,N b c;
COMPUTE c;
c=MEAN(b.SUM,10);
ENDCOMP;
RUN;
```

```
                a
      N         N         b         c
  ---------------------------------------
      4         2         9       9.5
```

```
DATA s;
a=1;b=2;c=3;d=4;f=KURTOSIS(a,b,c,d);
PROC PRINT;RUN;
PROC REPORT NOWD HEADLINE;
COLUMN a b c d e;
COMPUTE e;
e=KURTOSIS(a.SUM,b.SUM,c.SUM,d.SUM);
ENDCOMP;
RUN;
```

```
          Obs    a    b    c    d      f

            1    1    2    3    4   -1.2

         a         b         c         d         e
  ---------------------------------------------------
         1         2         3         4      -1.2
```

Notice the following points for statistical functions:

- Statistical functions have a minimum argument requirement, as we specified in the table.
- Functions MAX and MIN are slightly different from operators MAX and MIN. As operators, operands of MIN and MAX are Num/Char in DATA step, Both in a WHERE statement, and Both in PROC SQL, but as functions, arguments of MIN and MAX are Numeric_c in DATA step, Numeric_p in a WHERE statement, and Numeric_p in PROC SQL. See the following example:

```
DATA s;
```

```
a='13';b='4';
DATA t;
SET s;
WHERE a MAX b='4';
c=MAX(a,b);d=a MAX b;
PROC PRINT;RUN;
DATA t;
SET s;
WHERE MAX(a,b)='4';
RUN;
```

Obs	a	b	c	d
1	13	4	13	4

```
87   WHERE MAX(a,b)='4';
ERROR: Function MAX requires a numeric expression as argument 1.
```

- The function COALESCE needs argument type Numeric_c in DATA step, argument Numeric_p in a WHERE statement, and Both in PROC SQL. See the following example:

```
DATA s;
a='a';b='4';c='3';
DATA t;
SET s;
IF COALESCE(a,b,c)='4';
DATA t;
SET s;
WHERE COALESCE(a,b,c)='4';
RUN;
```

```
363  IF COALESCE(a,b,c)='4';

NOTE: Character values have been converted to numeric values at the places given by:
      (Line):(Column).
      363:13   363:15   363:17   363:20
NOTE: Invalid numeric data, a='a' , at line 363 column 13.
a=a b=4 c=3 _ERROR_=1 _N_=1
NOTE: There were 1 observations read from the data set WORK.S.
NOTE: The data set WORK.T has 1 observations and 3 variables.

364  DATA t;
365  SET s;
366  WHERE COALESCE(a,b,c)='4';
ERROR: Function COALESCE requires a numeric expression as argument 1.
```

```
PROC SQL;
SELECT COALESCE(a,b,c) FROM s;
SELECT * FROM s WHERE COALESCE(a,b,c)='a';
```

a	b	c	
a	4	3	a

a b c

```
______
a 4 3
```

- Besides functions MAX, MIN, and COALESCE, all other functions in Table 2 need argument type Numeric_c in DATA step, and Numeric_p in a WHERE statement and PROC SQL. See the following example:

```
DATA t;
SET s;
a2=MEAN(a,b,c);
a3=N(a,b,c);
a4=STD(a,b,c);
PROC PRINT;RUN;
```

```
Obs    a    b    c     a2    a3       a4

  1    a    4    3    3.5     2    0.70711
```

Table 3 gives a comparison of Operands of MAX and MIN and arguments of some functions in different places.

Table 3. Operands of MAX and MIN and arguments of some functions

	DATA step	WHERE statement	PROC SQL (statistical function)	PROC SQL (summary function)
MAX, MIN (operators)	Num/Char	Both	Both	
MAX, MIN (functions)	Numeric_c	Numeric_p	Numeric_p	Either
N, NMISS	Numeric_c	Numeric_p	Numeric_p	Either
COALESCE	Numeric_c	Numeric_p	Both	
All others	Numeric_c	Numeric_p	Numeric_p	Numeric_p

In PROC SQL, we have to differentiate *summary function* and *statistical function.*

- *A summary function* (scalar function in SQL) has only one argument. It returns a value based on the whole column. It can only be used in a SELECT, HAVING, and WHEN clause, not in WHERE and ORDER BY clauses.
- *A statistical function* (aggregate functions in SQL) can have more than one argument. It returns a statistic based on an argument list for each row. It can be used in a SELECT, HAVING, and WHEN clause as well as a WHERE and ORDER BY clause.
- Summary functions and statistical functions can have the same names, as indicated in Table 2. When this happens, a statistical function or a summary function depends on the number of arguments.
- As statistical functions, N, NMISS, MIN, and MAX all need numeric argument(s), but as summary functions, their argument can be either numeric or character.
- A summary function has only one argument, but a function having one argument is not necessary to be a summary function. Statistical functions new in v9 are especially not summary functions even if they have one argument such as

MEDIAN, IQR (returns the interquartile range[distance between the 25th percentile and the 75th percentile]) and COALESCE (returns the first non-missing valuc). See the following example. The example also shows that SUM and MEAN can be both summary functions and statistical functions:

```
DATA s;
INPUT a b c x $ y $;
CARDS;
. 4 6 ababa aba
2 3 4 ababa ab
6 7 4 ababa a
;
PROC SQL;
SELECT COALESCE(a),IQR(a),MEDIAN(a),MEAN(a),SUM(a),coalesce(a,b,c),
   IQR(a,b,c),MEDIAN(a,b,c),MEAN(a,b,c),SUM(a,b,c) FROM s;
```

.	.	.	4	8	4	2	5	5	10
2	0	2	4	8	2	2	3	3	9
6	0	6	4	8	6	3	6	5.666667	17

- COUNT is a very often used summary function in PROC SQL. It has one argument. In v9, there is a new character function, COUNT, which counts the number of letters or substrings in a string and takes two or three arguments. All arguments must be character type. Therefore it should be categorized as a character function, not a statistical function. So if you use numeric arguments, you will see a message as follows:

```
SELECT *,COUNT(a,b),N(x,y) FROM s ;
SELECT COUNT(x,y) AS count,N(a,b) AS n_ab, N(x) AS n_x FROM s;
```

The first SELECT statement gives the following message:

```
ERROR: Function COUNT requires a character expression as argument 1.
ERROR: Function COUNT requires a character expression as argument 2.
ERROR: Function N requires a numeric expression as argument 1.
ERROR: Function N requires a numeric expression as argument 2.
```

The second statement gives the following output:

count	n_ab	n_x
0	1	3
0	2	3
0	2	3

Notice that in SAS, these functions are called *function* or *summary function* as the following example shows. PCTL is a statistical function, and MEAN is a summary function:

```
DATA s;
    a='2'; b=3;c=4;
    PROC SQL;
    SELECT MEAN(a) FROM s;
    SELECT PCTL(b,c) FROM s;
    SELECT MEAN(b,c) FROM s;
    SELECT PCTL(b) FROM s;
    QUIT;
```

```
377  PROC SQL;
378  SELECT MEAN(a) FROM s;
ERROR: The MEAN summary function requires a numeric argument.
379  SELECT PCTL(b,c) FROM s;
380  SELECT MEAN(b,c) FROM s;
381  SELECT PCTL(b) FROM s;
ERROR: Function PCTL requires at least 2 argument(s).
382  QUIT;
NOTE: The SAS System stopped processing this step because of errors.
```

The following table gives summary functions in PROC SQL and makes a comparison to when they are used as statistical functions and are used in a DATA step.

Table 4. Summary functions in PROC SQL

Name in DATA step	Name in PROC SQL	Return value if one arg in DATA step	Return value if one arg in PROC SQL	More than one arg in DATA step or PROC SQL
CSS	CSS	Same as arg	Column statistic	Statistic for listed args, No AVG, COUNT, FREQ
CV	CV	NOT		
MAX	MAX	NOT		
MIN	MIN	NOT		
MEAN	AVG|MEAN	Same as arg		
N	COUNT|FREQ |N	1 if arg^=missing, 0 otherwise		
NMISS	NMISS	0 if arg=missing, 1 otherwise		
RANGE	RANGE	0		
STD	STD	NOT		
STDERR	STDERR	NOT		
SUM	SUM	Same as arg		
USS	USS	Square of arg		
VAR	VAR	NOT		
	T	NOT		NOT
	PRT	NOT		NOT
	SUMWGT	NOT		NOT

- N can be both a statistical function as well as a summary function. FREQ and COUNT are summary functions only. For summary functions, they are the same. COUNT also takes an asterisk as a parameter to calculate the number of rows (for groups or for the whole data set). COUNT(*) is the same as COUNT(1), SUM(1), FREQ(1), and N(1). They are the only summary functions that can have a character variable as an argument.

- MEAN can be both a statistical function and a summary function, but AVG is only a summary function. They are the same if MEAN is a summary function.

Now we will talk about the keyword DISTINCT. DISTINCT can be used like a summary function (with one argument), DISTINCT(var), but it is not a summary function. Many people have used this keyword. It has the following characteristics:

- If it specifies one column, for example, var, you can use either DISTINCT(var) or DISTINCT var.
- In the above case, both expressions can be used as an argument of a summary function.
- If there is more than one argument, for example, var1 and var2, or you use a wildcard (*), then you can use only DISTINCT * or DISTINCT var1,var2, but not DISTINCT(*) or DISTINCT(var1,var2).
- If there is more than one column, you cannot use it as an argument of COUNT.

See the following example:

```
DATA s;
INPUT a b;
CARDS;
1 1
1 2
1 2
2 3
2 2
;
RUN;
PROC SQL;
SELECT DISTINCT a FROM s;SELECT DISTINCT(a) FROM s;*They are the same;
SELECT COUNT(DISTINCT a) FROM s;SELECT COUNT(DISTINCT(a)) FROM s;*They
are the same;
SELECT DISTINCT a,b FROM s;SELECT DISTINCT * FROM s;*both work;
SELECT DISTINCT(a,b) FROM s;SELECT DISTINCT(*) FROM s;*neither work;
SELECT COUNT(*) FROM s; *OK;
SELECT COUNT(DISTINCT a,b) FROM s;SELECT COUNT(DISTINCT *) FROM s;*not
work;
SELECT COUNT(DISTINCT(a,b)) FROM s;SELECT COUNT(DISTINCT(*)) FROM
s;*not work;
```

The following statements are equivalent:

```
SELECT DISTINCT a,b FROM s;
SELECT DISTINCT(a),b FROM s;
```

The following statements do not work:

```
SELECT DISTINCT(a,b) FROM s;
SELECT a,DISTINCT(b) FROM s;
```

But the following statement is OK:

```
SELECT a,COUNT(DISTINCT(b)) FROM s GROUP BY a;* ok;
```

Summary report in PROC SQL

After we have discussed summary functions, we can give a sufficient and necessary condition for a SELECT statement to create a summary report. A summary report is created if the following two conditions are both satisfied:

- There is a summary function in a SELECT clause or in a HAVING clause.
- If any column in a SELECT clause, a HAVING clause, or an ORDER BY clause is not an argument of a summary function, then it is a GROUP BY column.

Suppose we have the following data set:

```
DATA s;
INPUT a b;
CARDS;
1 5
2 4
1 5
2 4
;
```

The following SELECT clauses create a summary report:

```
SELECT COUNT(*) FROM s;
SELECT SUM(a) FROM s;
SELECT SUM(a+b) FROM s ;
SELECT a+b FROM s GROUP BY a,b HAVING AVG(b)>0;
SELECT a+b,sum(b) FROM s GROUP BY a,b ;
SELECT a FROM s GROUP BY a,b HAVING AVG(b)>0;
SELECT a FROM s GROUP BY a HAVING AVG(b)>0;
SELECT *,SUM(a) FROM s GROUP BY a,b;
SELECT SUM(a),b FROM s GROUP BY b;
SELECT a,MEAN(b) FROM s GROUP BY a,b;
SELECT SUM(a),b FROM s GROUP BY b ORDER BY b DESCENDING ;
SELECT *,SUM(a) FROM s GROUP BY a,b;
SELECT *,SUM(a+b) FROM s GROUP BY a,b;
SELECT a+SUM(b) FROM s GROUP BY a,b;
SELECT 5+SUM(a/5) FROM s GROUP BY a,b;
SELECT SUM(a,b),SUM(b) FROM s GROUP BY a,b ;
SELECT SUM(a),b FROM s GROUP BY a,b ORDER BY a+b;
```

And the following SELECT clauses create a detail report:

```
SELECT SUM(a),SUM(a,b) FROM s;
SELECT SUM(a,b) FROM s GROUP BY a,b;
SELECT a+b FROM s GROUP BY a,b ;
SELECT a,b FROM s GROUP BY a HAVING AVG(b)>0;
SELECT SUM(a),b FROM s GROUP BY b ORDER BY a;
SELECT a FROM s GROUP BY a HAVING MEAN(b)>=b;
SELECT MOD(a,3) FROM s GROUP BY a,b;
```

Reference:
Fun with PROC SQL Summary Functions,
www.sascommunity.org/wiki/Fun_with_PROC_SQL_Summary_Functions

Statistical Procedures and Formats

Introduction

We always use statistical procedures to analyze a data set. There are six procedures that can be used to calculate descriptive statistics: PROC MEANS, PROC UNIVARIATE, PROC TABULATE, PROC FREQ, PROC REPORT, and PROC SQL. In addition, PROC REPORT and PROC SQL can create detail reports, similar to PROC PRINT. When using these procedures, you may have format requirement for the printout. In this paper we will discuss what formats SAS uses for the printout and how to modify them. We will discuss the following five procedures here: PROC MEANS, PROC TABULATE, PROC FREQ, PROC REPORT, and PROC SQL.

A format can be defined either in a data set as an attribute or in PROC using a FORMAT statement (but not in PROC SQL). Formats defined in PROC will overwrite those in a data step, but only for the PROC. Formats in the above two cases are called *classic formats*. In this paper, we will discuss how classic formats affect the output of statistical procedures, where else we can define formats (non-classic formats), and how these formats affect output.

General discussion

PROC FREQ is used to calculate one-way or n-way frequency. In n-way tables, variables are equivalent, and we can say that they are all class variables. For other procedures, there are two kinds of variables: class variables and analysis variables. Class variables are used for grouping. Variables defined in a BY statement, a CLASS statement, or a DEFINE/GROUP, a DEFINE/ACROSS statement in PROC REPORT are class variables. There is no big difference for analysis to define class variables in different ways. A BY statement needs a data set to be sorted, but others don't, and they have different appearances. On the other hand, statements VAR and DEFINE/ANALYSIS define analysis variables. For PROC SQL, columns to display are specified in a SELECT clause. A single column in a SELECT clause is a display column even if it is also a class column or an analysis column. A class variable is specified in a GROUP BY clause. Different from other procedures, we can put an expression in a GROUP BY clause. To analyze a column, specify a summary function.

Let's talk about the relationship between variable types and their functionalities in procedures. Usually, character variables are class variables, and numeric variables are analysis variables. PROC MEANS treats all numeric variables as analysis variables by default. In PROC REPORT, the default for character variables is DISPLAY and for numeric variables is ANALYSIS. However, a numeric variable cal also be treated as a class variable. For example, grade is a numeric variable, but usually it is a class variable. Also, many times we treat numeric variables as class variables by dividing their values into several groups using format. For example, age is a numeric variable, but we can divide its values into adult, old, and young. Income is a numeric variable, but we can divide its values into several classes.

For the outputs of these procedures, there are three parts: display values (a detail report in PROC REPORT and PROC SQL), header values (values of class variables in PROC FREQ, PROC MEANS, PROC TABULATE, and PROC REPORT, but not for PROC SQL), and cell values that are statistical results for analysis variables (frequency count in PROC FREQ).

From the syntax of statistical procedures, there are differences between class variables and analysis variables, as Table 1 shows.

Table 1. Specify class variables and analysis variables

	Class variables	Analysis variables
PROC MEANS	In BY statement or CLASS statement	In VAR statement, default is all numeric variables except that specified as class variables
PROC TABULATE	Either in BY statement or in CLASS + TABLE statements	In VAR + TABLE statements
PROC UNIVARIATE	In BY statement or CLASS statement	In VAR statement, default is all numeric variables except that specified as class variables
PROC REPORT	In BY, DEFINE/GROUP, DEFINE/ACROSS statements	In DEFINE/ANALYSIS statement
PROC SQL	In GROUP BY clause, can be expressions	Argument in a summary function in SELECT clause.

First, we will talk how a classic format affects procedures.

- It affects class variables in the following ways:
  - SAS groups observations according to unformatted values for PROC SQL and according to formatted values for other procedures.
  - SAS displays formatted values.
- It does not affect analysis, i.e., SAS uses original values to do analysis.
- It may affect the display of analysis results as follows:

  - No effect for PROC MEANS. The default is BEST7 format. You can use a MAXDEC= option in PROC MEANS to adjust.
  - No effect for PROC UNIVARIATE.
  - No effect for PROC TABULATE. The default format is 12.2. To show formatted values, you have to use a FORMAT=|F= option in the PROC TABULATE statement for the whole table or use a FORMAT=|F= modifier in a TABLE statement to specify column, row, or page.
  - Shows formatted results for PROC REPORT, no matter whether it is a detail report or a summary report. We can use an f= modifier in a DEFINE statement to overwrite it.
  - PROC SQL shows a formatted value for columns selected and has no effects on summary values.

In a summary, classic formats for analysis variables are useless in PROC MEANS, PROC TABULATE, and PROC SQL, but they are used for display in PROC REPORT.

On the other hand, we can define formats in these procedures. The following table gives an overview of non-classic formats.

Table 2. Non-classic formats in descriptive procedures

PROC	Where to define	How to affect output
FREQ	TABLE statement	Affect frequency in crosstabulation table
REPORT	DEFINE statement	Same as classic format, affect the corresponding column, group and display, may affect several columns.
TABULATE	PROC statement and TABLE statement	Affect the cell values, for the whole table, or whole row or whole column
SQL	SELECT clause	Same as classic format, affect the corresponding column for display, no matter it is display column or summary column.

The following table gives the relationship between formats and statistical values in descriptive procedures.

Table 3. Relationships between format and statistical values

	Display formatted value?	Default format	How to change format?
PROC MEANS	N	BEST12.	Define FW= and MAXDEC =, options same as w.d
PROC TABULATE	N	12.2	Define FORMAT= in PROC TABULATE statement or in TABLES statement.
PROC REPORT	Y	BEST9. for numeric analysis variables. 9. for N and PCTN of character variables.	Define F= in DEFINE/ANALYSIS statement or define CALL DEFINE in COMPUTE block.
PROC SQL	N		Define FORMAT= in SELECT clause
PROC FREQ		BEST6 or BEST7	Define FORMAT= in TABLE statement.

For numeric values, there are two kinds of formats, numeric format, such as 5.1, or user-defined formats. For example, we can define missing value as 'Missing'. SAS treats two kinds of formats in the same way. Two kinds of formats are similar. For example, the following program produces two outputs that are the same except that the symbols for the values of class variables are different. In this paper we are not discussing specified formats, but we will concentrate on how formats affect the output.

```
PROC FORMAT ;
VALUE scorex 1.5-<2.5=D 2.5-<3.5=C 3.5-<4.5=B 4.5-HIGH=A;
DATA s;
INPUT score sat;
CARDS;
2.5 780
3.5 760
4 770
4.5 790
;
PROC MEANS fw=7;
CLASS score;
FORMAT score scorex.;
```

```
PROC MEANS fw=7;
CLASS score;
FORMAT score 5.;
RUN;
```

score	N Obs	N	Mean	Std Dev	Minimum	Maximum
C	1	1	780.0	.	780.0	780.0
B	2	2	765.0	7.071	760.0	770.0
A	1	1	790.0	.	790.0	790.0

PROC FREQ

PROC FREQ is used to calculate frequency counts. There are two kinds of outputs for PROC FREQ: list tables or crosstabulation tables. If it is a one-way table, then it is a list table. If it is an n-way table, the default is a crosstabulation table, but we can specify an option LIST in a TABLE statement to ask for a list table.

Classic formats can be used to group observations and display values of the variable, but they have no relationship with the display of cell statistics. The following program shows that SAS calculates frequency based on formatted values:

```
PROC FORMAT;
VALUE aa 1=abc 2-3=cdf;
DATA s;
INPUT a b c;
CARDS;
1 2 1
2 4 2
2 3 3
3 4 3
;
PROC FREQ;
TABLE a*b/LIST;
FORMAT a aa.;
RUN;
```

a	b	Frequency	Percent	Cumulative Frequency	Cumulative Percent
abc	2	1	25.00	1	25.00
cdf	3	1	25.00	2	50.00
cdf	4	2	50.00	4	100.00

Besides classic formats, we can also define format in a TABLE statement, which is for displaying cell values, but it is only for a crosstabulation table, and it only affects frequency, including row frequency, column frequency, expected frequency, and deviation. If we run the following program, we get the same output, which shows that it does not affect a list table:

```
PROC FREQ;
TABLE a*b/LIST format=aa.;
FORMAT a aa.;
RUN;
```

But as the following example shows, it works for a crosstabulation table:

```
PROC FREQ;
TABLE a*b/ format=aa.;
RUN;
```

a Frequency Percent Row Pct Col Pct	b 2	 3	 4	 Total
1	abc 25.00 33.33 100.00	0 0.00 0.00 0.00	cdf 50.00 66.67 100.00	cdf 75.00
2	0 0.00 0.00 0.00	abc 25.00 100.00 100.00	0 0.00 0.00 0.00	abc 25.00
Total	abc 25.00	abc 25.00	cdf 50.00	4 100.00

PROC MEANS

PROC MEANS has the following characteristics:

- It uses classic formats to group variables and shows their values.
- For numeric statistics, it uses format 12.7, 12.2, or 12, (BEST12.) depending on values.
- For discrete statistics N and NMISS, it uses format 12.
- You can see that the width is 12. It is determined by an FW= option that is called *Field width.* The FW= option affects numeric statistics, but not discrete statistics N and NMISS.
- There are no non-classic formats, but we can use a MAXDEC option in a PROC MEANS statement to adjust the numeric statistics output. Options FW=7 and MAXDEC=3 has the same effect as the format 7.3.

Let's first run the following program:

```
DATA s;
a1=1;a2=1234;
a3=123456789;
a4=1234567890123;
a5=-1234567890123;
PROC MEANS;
RUN;
```

Variable	N	Mean	Std Dev	Minimum	Maximum
a1	1	1.0000000	.	1.0000000	1.0000000
a2	1	1234.00	.	1234.00	1234.00
a3	1	123456789	.	123456789	123456789
a4	1	1.2345679E12	.	1.2345679E12	1.2345679E12
a5	1	-1.234568E12	.	-1.234568E12	-1.234568E12

Now let's run the following program:

```
PROC MEANS FW=8 MAXDEC=2;
RUN;
```

Variable	N	Mean	Std Dev	Minimum	Maximum
a1	1	1.00	.	1.00	1.00
a2	1	1234.00	.	1234.00	1234.00
a3	1	1.2346E8	.	1.2346E8	1.2346E8
a4	1	1.235E12	.	1.235E12	1.235E12
a5	1	-1.23E12	.	-1.23E12	-1.23E12

The following program shows that formats of class variables are used for group and display:

```
DATA s;
c=1;b=1;a=123;
PROC MEANS;
FORMAT c b aa.;
CLASS c;
BY b;
RUN;
```

```
------------------------------------ b=abc ---------------------------------------

                              The MEANS Procedure

                             Analysis Variable : a
```

c	N Obs	N	Mean	Std Dev	Minimum	Maximum
abc	1	1	123.0000000	.	123.0000000	123.0000000

PROC TABULATE

PROC TABULATE has the following syntax:

```
PROC TABULATE;
CLASS variable(s);
```

```
VAR variable(s);
TABLES page-dimension, row-dimension, column-dimension;
```

Classic formats for class variables are used to group observations and to display their values. The default format for numeric class variables is BEST12. The format for cell values is 12.2. To change format for cell values, we can use option FORMAT= or F= in a PROC TABULATE statement or in a TABLES statement. The former is for the whole table, and the latter is for specified rows or columns.

In the following example, there are class variables gender and grade and analysis variables sales_517 and sales_524. We define formats for gender, grade, and sales_517. The table shows formatted values for gender and grade, but not for sales_517:

```
PROC FORMAT;
VALUE $sex F=Female M=Male;
DATA student_score;
INPUT id gender $ grade sales_517 sales_524;
FORMAT gender $sex. grade sales_517 6.1;
CARDS;
1 F 4 89 78
2 F 4 78 65
3 F 5 96 87
4 M 4 77 85
5 M 5 99 88
6 M 5 87 77
7 M 5 96 88
;
PROC TABULATE;
CLASS gender grade;
VAR sales_517 sales_524;
TABLES gender*grade,sales_517 sales_524;
RUN;
```

		sales_517	sales_524
		Sum	Sum
gender	grade		
Female	4.0	167.00	143.00
	5.0	96.00	87.00
Male	4.0	77.00	85.00
	5.0	282.00	253.00

The following example uses a format= option in a PROC statement:

```
PROC TABULATE FORMAT=DOLLAR9.1;
CLASS gender grade;
VAR sales_517 sales_524;
```

```
TABLES gender*grade, sales_517 sales_524;
RUN;
```

		sales_517	sales_524
		Sum	Sum
gender	grade		
Female	4.0	$167.0	$143.0
	5.0	$96.0	$87.0
Male	4.0	$77.0	$85.0
	5.0	$282.0	$253.0

In the following example the format is only defined for the column sales_517:

```
PROC TABULATE ;
CLASS gender grade;
VAR sales_517 sales_524;
TABLES gender*grade, sales_517 *f=DOLLAR9.1 sales_524;
RUN;
```

		sales_517	sales_524
		Sum	Sum
gender	grade		
Female	4.0	$167.0	143.00
	5.0	$96.0	87.00
Male	4.0	$77.0	85.00
	5.0	$282.0	253.00

Notice that we can cross the modifier F= with any variable in page, row, and column dimension. If we cross it with a variable in a page dimension, it affects all cells in the specified table. Otherwise, it affects only specified rows or columns. In the following example, there are two concatenated statistics, N and SUM, for variable sales_517 in the column dimension that use format 4. and DOLLAR9.1 respectively.

```
TABLES grade, sales_517 *(N*F=4. SUM*F=DOLLAR9.1 );
```

The format in TABLES statement overwrites that in the PROC TABULATE statement for the specified column or row or table. Just out of curiosity, if you define one format for row and one for column, what is the format for the cell of that column and that row? SAS uses column format for that cell.

PROC SQL

PROC SQL does not have a BY statement or a FORMAT statement, and class variables are defined in a GROUP BY statement. Different from the others, PROC SQL does not show values of class variables (in GROUP BY clause). If you want to show them, you have to specify class variables in SELECT clause. Therefore, we don't have to discuss what format is needed to display values of class variables. One important difference from other procedures is that it groups rows by original value. In a SELECT clause we can use original columns, new columns that are expressions of original columns, summary results, and their combinations. A classic format applies only to an original column, but not to new columns. We can specify format in a SELECT clause for any column, original or new. It has the same functionality as a FORMAT statement in other procedures. Non-classic format will overwrite classic format if it is for the same original column.

The following program shows that PROC SQL uses original values for grouping, but it displays formatted values:

```
PROC FORMAT;
VALUE aa 1=abc 2-3=cdf;
VALUE bb 1-2=rts 3=xyz;
DATA s;
INPUT a b; FORMAT a aa.;
CARDS;
1 3
2 4
3 5
3 4
;
PROC SQL;
SELECT a,SUM(b) FROM s GROUP BY a;
```

a	
abc	3
cdf	4
cdf	9

The following program shows that we can use the option FORMAT= in a SELECT clause:

```
SELECT a,a FORMAT=bb.,a+1 AS b, a+1 AS c FORMAT=aa.,
   SUM(b) AS d, SUM(b) AS e FORMAT=aa. FROM s GROUP BY a;
```

a	a	b	c	d	e
abc	rts	2	cdf	3	cdf
cdf	rts	3	cdf	4	4
cdf	xyz	4	4	9	9

PROC REPORT

Class formats in a PROC REPORT affect everything, grouping and display, display of class variables and display of statistical result, except in calculating statistics. A format for one variable affects all summary columns of this variable. See the following example:

```
PROC FORMAT;
VALUE aa 1=abc 2-3=cdf;
DATA s;
INPUT a b; FORMAT a b aa.;
CARDS;
1 3
2 4
3 5
3 4
;
PROC REPORT NOWD HEADLINE;
COLUMN a b b,MEAN MEAN,b;
DEFINE a/GROUP;
RUN;
```

```
                            mea
                      b       n
  a     b          mean       b
 ------------------------------
abc   cdf   cdf             cdf
cdf    13   4.3333333       4.3
```

In this program, SAS uses the format of variable a to group observations and to display the values of a. Columns 2, 3, and 4, which are statistical results, use the format of variable b (The default statistic for the second column is SUM.). Notice the difference in width for these columns. They are different because the positions of the variable and the statistic are different.

Besides classic formats, PROC REPORT can define non-classic format in DEFINE statements. We can specify it for a variable or for a specified column. See the following example:

```
PROC FORMAT;
VALUE aa 1=abc 2-3=cdf;
DATA s;
INPUT A b c;
CARDS;
1 3 3
2 4 4
3 5 5
3 4 4
;
PROC REPORT NOWD HEADLINE;
COLUMN a b b,MEAN MEAN,b c c=cmin c=cmax ;
DEFINE a/GROUP;
DEFINE b/ANALYSIS F=aa.;
DEFINE cmin/MIN F=aa. "min c";
RUN;
```

```
                     mea
                b    n               min
a    b       mean    b          c     c          c
--------------------------------------------------
1  cdf  cdf        cdf          3   cdf          3
2    4         4     4          4     4          4
3    9       4.5   4.5          9     4          9
```

In the above program, we define format for variable b, which applies to three columns, and we define format for cmin, which is used only for one column.

Now we will talk about column width. SAS determines the column width according to the following conditions in order:

1. There is a WIDTH= option in a DEFINE statement.
2. There is a format defined in a DEFINE statement.
3. For a character variable, SAS uses its length attribute. For a numeric variable, if there is a COLWIDTH= option in a PROC REPORT statement, SAS uses that value; otherwise, it uses default value 9.

Notice that there is also an option SPACING=. The default is 2. You may wonder that if we already use format in an F= option, then a WIDTH= option is redundant. However, as we said above, we can use options WIDTH=9 F=5.1 CENTER. Maybe you like this style. Also for character variables, using option WIDTH=40 F=$200. FLOW can control the width and keep the value. Let's see the following example:

```
DATA student_score;
INPUT id gender $ grade test1 test2 test3 test4;
CARDS;
1 F 1 89 78 95 88
2 M 1 78 65 87 97
3 F 1 99 87 77 80
4 M 1 77 85 68 77
5 M 2 97 88 79 95
6 M 2 87 77 95 84
7 M 2 96 88 89 69
;
PROC FORMAT;
VALUE $sexx M=Male F=Female;
PROC REPORT DATA=student_score NOWD HEADLINE;
COLUMN gender grade test1 test2 test3;
DEFINE gender/GROUP F=$sexx.;
DEFINE grade/GROUP WIDTH=7 F=3. CENTER;
DEFINE test1/MEAN WIDTH=9 F=5.2 'Average Test1';
DEFINE test2/MIN 'Minimun Test2';
RUN;
```

```
                         Average    Minimun
gender    grade            Test1      Test2       test3
-------------------------------------------------------
Female      1              94.00         78         172
Male        1              77.50         65         155
```

```
                    2          93.33            77           263
```

Notice the following points:

- If a variable already has a statistic defined in a COLUMN statement, we can still define other options for the variable or for the statistic.
- Notice that if you define a variable in a DEFINE statement, attributes such as width, format, and header, are for all the columns with the variable. If we define a statistic in a DEFINE statement, then attributes apply to all items with the statistic as the second part.
- If we define a statistic in a DEFINE statement, the statistic must be explicitly defined in COLUMN statement, i.e., it does not apply to default statistic SUM.

PCTN in PROC REPORT

Now let's talk about the PCTN statistic. It is similar to statistic N.

- You can put it in a COLUMN statement together with a character variable.
- You can define it in a DEFINE statement for a numeric variable.
- Notice that SAS uses format 9. for both N and PCTN if the variable is character, i.e., it treats both N and PCTN as an integer. Let's see the following example:

```
DATA s;
INPUT a $ b p;
CARDS;
1 1 1
2 2 2
4 4 3
;
PROC REPORT NOWD headline;
COLUMN p a,N a,PCTN b,N b,PCTN;
DEFINE p/GROUP;
RUN;
```

```
                          a          a          b          b
             p            N       PCTN          N       PCTN
       ------------------------------------------------------
             1            1          0          1  0.3333333
             2            1          0          1  0.3333333
             3            1          0          1  0.3333333
```

You can see that the output for the numeric variable b is OK, but for the character variable a, it is not OK. If you use an OUT= option in a PROC REPORT statement to output to a data set, you will see that a,PCTN and b,PCTN have the same values. So the problem is format, and to fix this, we need to define format.

First, we can define the statistic or define the variable (if it is numeric) in a DEFINE statement using format. See the following example:.

```
DATA s;
INPUT a $ b p;
CARDS;
1 1 1
2 2 2
```

```
4 4 1
;
PROC REPORT NOWD HEADLINE;
COLUMN p a,N a,PCTN b,N b,PCTN PCTN,a;
DEFINE p/GROUP;
DEFINE PCTN/F=5.2 WIDTH=10 'percentage';
RUN;
```

```
                                                  percenta
                    a          a          b          b  ge
        p           N  percentage         N  percentage  a
    ------------------------------------------------------
        1           2        0.67         2        0.67          1
        2           1        0.33         1        0.33          0
```

However, this is for all items with the variable or all items with the statistic as the second part. We can see that the format we defined affects a,PCTN and b,PCTN, but not PCTN,a.

Second, we can define an alias for PCTN that is only for a specified item and then define format for the alias. See the following example:

```
PROC REPORT NOWD HEADLINE;
COLUMN p a,N a,PCTN=apc b,N PCTN,b=bpc;
DEFINE p/GROUP;
DEFINE apc/F=5.2 WIDTH=10 'percentage';
DEFINE bpc/F=5.3 WIDTH=10 'percent';
RUN;
```

```
                    a          a          b        PCTN
        p           N  percentage         N     percent
    ---------------------------------------------------
        1           2        0.67         2       0.667
        2           1        0.33         1       0.333
```

There is one more way to define format that we can use a COMPUTE block and a CALL DEFINE statement. See the following example:

```
PROC REPORT NOWD HEADLINE;
COLUMN p a,N a,PCTN b,N PCTN,b dummy;
DEFINE p/GROUP;
DEFINE dummy/NOPRINT;
COMPUTE dummy;
CALL DEFINE('_C3_', 'FORMAT','5.2');
ENDCOMP;
RUN;
```

```
                    a          a          b        PCTN
        p           N       PCTN          N           b
    ---------------------------------------------------
        1           1       0.33          1   0.3333333
        2           1       0.33          1   0.3333333
        3           1       0.33          1   0.3333333
```

Reference

Scerbo, Marge and Mic Lajiness. (2005). "PROC FREQ and MEANS – to Stat or not to Stat." *Proceedings of the Thirty Annual SAS Users Group International Conference*, Paper 263-30, Cary, NC: SAS Institute Inc.
http://www2.sas.com/proceedings/sugi30/263-30.pdf

Chapman, David D. (2003). "Using Formats and Other Techniques to Complete PROC REPORT Tables." *Proceedings of the Twenty-eight Annual SAS Users Group International Conference*, Paper 132-28, Cary, NC: SAS Institute Inc.
http://www2.sas.com/proceedings/sugi28/132-28.pdf

Formats and BY statement

Introduction

We know that in a data set, a variable has two kinds of values: original (unformatted) values and formatted values. In [III] I discussed how SAS executes a BY statement in a DATA step and in PROC. When SAS executes a BY statement, it reads the next observation and compares values of BY variables. That is for unformatted variables. In [XIV] we show that SAS uses formatted values to group observations. Now, we have a question: When some BY variables have formats defined, how does SAS execute BY statement? We have to discuss the relationship between the formats and the BY statement. Notice that SAS handles a BY statement in the same way for PROC PRINT and for statistical procedures. I usually use PROC PRINT as an example. You can replace PROC PRINT with other procedures such as PROC MEANS to verify.

Formats and BY statement

For the relationship between format and a BY statement, we consider the following three cases:

- PROC SORT uses original values to sort the data set.

```
PROC FORMAT;
VALUE aa 1=b 2-3=a;
DATA s;
INPUT a b;
FORMAT a aa.;
CARDS;
3 3
2 2
1 1
;
PROC SORT;
BY a;
PROC PRINT;RUN;
```

The following is the printout:

```
Obs    a    b

  1    b    1
  2    a    2
  3    a    3
```

- In DATA step, a BY statement uses original values to check if the data set is sorted.

```
PROC FORMAT;
VALUE aa 1=b 2-3=a;
DATA s;
INPUT a b;
FORMAT a aa.;
CARDS;
1 3
```

```
2 3
3 3
;
DATA t;
SET s;
BY a;
IF FIRST.a THEN c=1;
PROC PRINT;RUN;
```

The program is OK because the data set is sorted by original values. The following is output. We can see that FIRST.a is set according to original values.

Obs	a	b	c
1	b	3	1
2	a	3	1
3	a	3	1

- For PROC PRINT and statistic procedures, MEANS, REPORT, UNIVARIATE, and TABULATE, with a BY statement, SAS uses double standards to build groups. As I say, SAS reads the next observations when executing a BY statement.
    - SAS first compares them (BY values) with those in the current group using formatted values. If they are the same, the observation will go to the group and continues.
    - If they are different, then SAS compares them with those of the first observations in the current group using unformatted values to decide either to create a new group or to stop processing.

Let's see the following program:

```
PROC FORMAT;
VALUE aa 1,3,5=1 2,4,6=2;
DATA s;
INPUT a b @@;
FORMAT a aa.;
CARDS;
1 1 2 2 6 6 3 3 4 4 2 2 5 5 2 2 4 4
;
PROC PRINT;BY a;RUN;
```

The following is output:

```
------------------------------------------- a=1 ---------------------------------------

                                          Obs    b

                                           1     1

------------------------------------------- a=2 ---------------------------------------
```

```
                    Obs    b

                     2     2
                     3     6

------------------------------------------- a=1 ----------------------------------------

                    Obs    b

                     4     3

------------------------------------------- a=2 ----------------------------------------

                    Obs    b

                     5     4
                     6     2
```

The following is the message in the log file:

```
NOTE: The data set WORK.S has 9 observations and 2 variables.

809  PROC PRINT;BY a;RUN;

ERROR: Data set WORK.S is not sorted in ascending sequence. The current by-group has a =
1 and the next by-group has a = 2.
NOTE: The SAS System stopped processing this step because of errors.
NOTE: There were 8 observations read from the data set WORK.S.
```

I put the values of variable a, its formatted values, and the first values in each group in the following so that you can make a comparison:

Obs	Value of a	group	formatted value	first value in group
1	1	1	1	1
2	2	2	2	2
3	6	2	2	2
4	3	3	1	3
5	4	4	2	4
6	2	4	2	4
7	5	5	1	5
8	2		2	2
9	4		2	2

Now we consider how SAS processes this program. Notice that there is only one BY variable.

In the first iteration, SAS reads in two observations and compares their formatted BY values. They are different. SAS compares their original values, and they are ascending, so SAS builds the first group. The second observation begins a new group.

In the second iteration, SAS reads in the third observation and compares formatted BY values. They are the same, so the third observation will go to the second group.

In the third iteration, SAS reads in the fourth observation and compares formatted BY values. They are different. SAS compares the original value with that in the first observation in the second group. They are ascending (3>2). So SAS builds the second group, and the fourth observation will go to the third group.

In the fourth iteration, SAS reads in the fifth observation and compares formatted BY values. They are different. SAS compares original values, and they are ascending, so SAS builds the third group, and the fifth observation will go to the fourth group.

In the fifth iteration, SAS reads in the sixth observation and compares formatted BY values. They are the same, so the sixth observation will go to the fourth group.

In the sixth iteration, SAS reads in the seventh observation and compares formatted BY values. They are different. SAS compares original values, and they are ascending, so SAS builds the fourth group, and the seventh observation will go to the fifth group.

In the seventh iteration, SAS reads in the eighth observation and compares formatted BY values. They are different. Then SAS compares original values and they are descending, so SAS stops processing. There are a total of four groups built and eight observations read as you can see from the output and the log.

Now we can see the difference between a DATA step and a PROC step when using a BY statement. In the following program, the DATA step does not work, but PROC PRINT is OK:

```
PROC FORMAT;
VALUE aa 1,3,5=1 2,4=2;
DATA s;
INPUT a b @@;
FORMAT a aa.;
CARDS;
1 1 2 2 3 3 4 4 2 2
;
DATA t;
SET s;
BY a;
PROC PRINT; BY a; RUN;
```

Notice that if a BY variable is not formatted, SAS uses its original values as formatted values and follows the rules.

Types of formats

Now we discuss how a format affects analysis. There are four situations as we show in the following. Notice that situation 1 is a special case of situation 2, situation 2 is a special case of situation 3, and situation 3 is a special case of situation 4. For the first three situations, we assume that the data set is already sorted (by original values), and BY variables are formatted. Notice that a format consists of range (left side of the equal sign) and formatted value (right side of the equal sign).

1. Suppose that the format is consistent. That means if we pick any two range values a1 and a2, and they have corresponding formatted values b1 and b2, then a1>a2 implies b1>=b2. For this case, the analysis results are the same as if the data set is sorted by formatted values. Let's see the following example:

```
PROC FORMAT;
VALUE agex 5-10=1 11-50=2 51-80=3;
DATA s;
INPUT age height;
FORMAT age agex.;
CARDS;
6 48
8 52
20 70
49 68
70 65
;
PROC PRINT;
BY age;
RUN;
```

```
age=1

Obs    height

 1       48
 2       52

age=2

Obs    height

 3       70
 4       68

age=3

Obs    height

 5       65
```

2. Suppose that the format has the following property: If we pick three range values a1, a2, and a3, and they correspond to three formatted values b1, b2, and b3, respectively, where a1>a2>a3, then b1=b3 implies b1=b2. For this case, SAS does grouping the same as if the data set is sorted by formatted values, but groups may not be sorted. See the following example:

```
PROC FORMAT;
VALUE prox 1-2=Heart problem 3=Eye problem 4=Mouth problem;
DATA s;
INPUT pro index;
FORMAT pro prox.;
CARDS;
1 48
2 52
3 70
3 68
4 65
;
PROC PRINT;
BY pro;
RUN;
```

```
pro=Heart problem

Obs    index

 1       48
 2       52

pro=Eye problem

Obs    index

 3       70
 4       68

pro=Mouth problem

Obs    index

 5       65
```

3. In general, there is no restriction on format. SAS does an analysis for the data set for all observations, i.e., finishes analysis, but the grouping may be different from that sorted formatted BY values. One group of formatted BY values may have more than one group. It is the same as if the BY statement use the same variables with formatted values, but with NOTSORTED options. In the following example, the data set is divided into four groups:

```
PROC FORMAT;
VALUE mixx 1,3=a 2=b 4,5=c;
DATA s;
INPUT pro index;
CARDS;
1 48
2 52
3 70
3 68
4 65
;
```

```
PROC PRINT;
BY pro;
FORMAT pro mixx.;
RUN;
```

```
pro=a

Obs    index

 1      48

pro=b

Obs    index

 2      52

pro=a

Obs    index

 3      70
 4      68

pro=c

Obs    index

 5      65
```

4. As I already discussed in [III], suppose that the data set is not sorted. Then it is possible that SAS will not finish the analysis. If we use a NOTSORTED option, SAS will finish analysis.

Now we explain cases 1, 2, and 3. For case 1, it is easy to see that the formatted values are ascending for groups. For case 2, the same group cannot appear twice. Otherwise, it conflicts with our assumption. For case 3, the data set is sorted means that the first values in groups are ascending. Therefore, SAS can finish grouping.

Therefore, to obtain the correct results, you have to choose good formats. Don't choose formats in situation 3. For this kind of variable, it is better to create a new variable.

In many procedures, there are more than one way to do grouping. For example, in PROC MEANS, we can use CLASS statement, and in PROC REPORT, we can use DEFINE/GROUP statement. Usually, people think that different grouping methods create the same results, and the difference is that a BY statement needs the data set to be sorted. However, when the class variables are formatted, and the format is "bad", this is not the case. Let's see the following example:

```
PROC FORMAT;
VALUE aa 1,3,5=1 2,4=2;
DATA s;
```

```
INPUT a b @@;
FORMAT a aa.;
CARDS;
1 1 1 1 2 2 2 2 3 3 3 3
;
TITLE "GROUP output";
PROC REPORT NOWD;
DEFINE a/GROUP;
RUN;
TITLE "BY output";
PROC REPORT NOWD;
BY a;
RUN;
```

```
                    GROUP output

                    a          b
                    1          8
                    2          4

                     BY output

------------------------------- a=1 -------------------------------

                    a          b
                    2          2

                     BY output
------------------------------- a=2 -------------------------------

                    a          b
                    2          4

                     BY output
------------------------------- a=1 -------------------------------

                    a          b
                    6          6
```

The program is OK. There is no ERROR message, no WARNING message, but two printouts are totally different.

Data Sets and Excel Files

Introduction

In SAS applications we need to read data sets from files (import) and write data to files (export). As we know, Excel files (xls files) are very commonly used files. Therefore, many times we need to read data from an Excel file or to write data to an Excel file.

An Excel file can be saved as a text file (Tab delimited, with extension txt) or a csv file (comma delimited, with extension csv). On the other hand, the default software to open a csv file is Excel. You can also use Notepad to open a csv file. The default software to open a txt file is Notepad. Also, you can save an Excel file in different versions: Excel4, Excel5, Excel95, Excel97, and Excel2000. It is the same if you use Excel to view any of them, but when importing to SAS or exporting from SAS, there may be some differences. In this paper we will concentrate on Excel2000.

First, we will talk about methods. There are many ways to convert Excel files to SAS data sets or vice versa. How do we decide which method we should use? We have two points to consider: One is simplicity. We want methods that are easy to remember and easy to use. On the other hand, sometimes we need more choices, more options. So the choice of method depends on the situation. The most important thing is to get correct values. The other consideration is program vs. manual. Manual does not need to write code, but there is no trace. On the other hand, we may need a written document. A program is easy to run, and it keeps track for checking and debugging. So usually if we need to do only one time, we may do it manually, but if it is routing work, it is better to write a program.

When doing an import from Excel and an export to Excel, there are several situations:

1. SAS/ACCESS to PC Files installed.
2. SAS/ACCESS to ODBC installed.
3. SAS/ACCESS Interface to OLE DB installed.
4. None of above software is installed.

You can run the following program to check if these components are installed:

```
PROC SETINIT NOALIAS;RUN;
```

In this paper, we will concentrate on situations 1 and 4.

Compare an Excel file with a SAS data set

Now, we will talk about the differences between an Excel file and a SAS data set.

For the structure, an Excel file may have multiple sheets. Usually, as we will discuss in this paper, we import a data set from one sheet or write a data set to one sheet. There are some papers on handling multiple sheets. Within a worksheet, we can specify a range and assign it a name. The range is called a *named range*. Notice that when viewing an

Excel file, on the up left corner, there is a box that usually shows the cell number such as f5 if you put cursor in the cell f5. This is called the *Name Box*. We can name a range as follows:

Highlight range
Click in the Name box (or go to Insert->Name->Define)
Type the name for this range

If we type the name of a named range or a cell number, such as f5, in the Name Box, Excel will show us the range or the cell. Notice that we can use a worksheet name as a range name, but we cannot use the same range name in different worksheets.

The following table shows limitations for an Excel worksheet and a SAS data set that you may need to consider when doing import and export.

Table 1. Comparison of an Excel worksheet and a SAS data set on limitations

	Column limit	**Row limit**	**Character length limit**	**Date limit**
Excel worksheet	256	65536	32767 (only 1024 display)	1/1//1900 - 12/31/9999
SAS data set	32767 (v8)	Very big (Under 64-bit operating environments, you can create a data set with greater than 2^{31}-1 [about 2 billion] observations.)	32767	1/1/1582 – 12/31/20000

Table 1 shows that when we import data from Excel, usually we don't have to consider these limitations, but when we export data to Excel, we may need to consider them.

A SAS data set has the following attributes for each variable:

- Name: There are strict rules for names: They consist of characters, underscores, and non-beginning numerals.
- Type: character or numeric; for character variables, SAS has a length attribute that we have to care about.
- Format
- Label.

In many cases, an Excel file uses the first row as headers that show meanings of columns. In an Excel file, you can right click on a column header or on any cell to get a pull-down menu and then click on Format Cells. You can see that there is a big difference compared to formats we have learned in SAS.

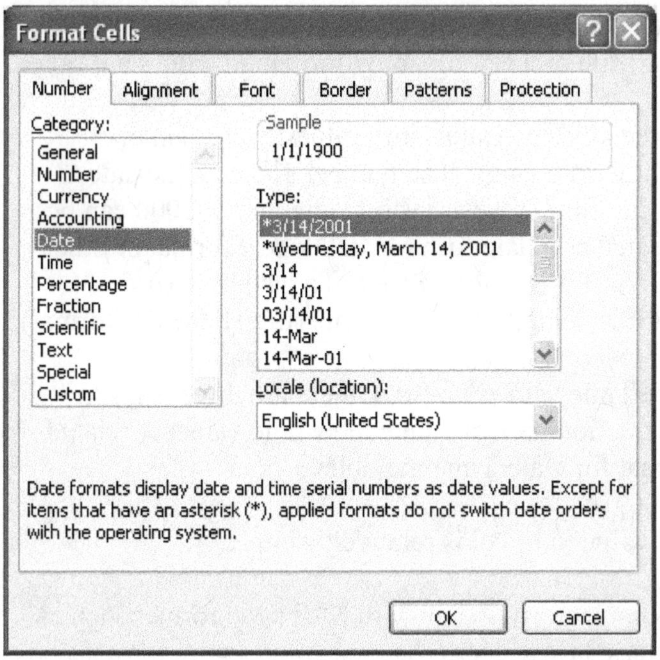

Most of these formats are symbolic, and we do not have to pay much attention to them. We have to pay attention to format General, Text, Number, and Date/Time. The default format of Excel is General, which means to treat a value as text, numeric, and Date/Time according to Excel's understanding. For example, if you type in 1/4, you will see that the value becomes '4-Jan' because Excel treats it as a Date/Time value. But we can force it to take a Text format or a Number format. Notice that when we change the format to Number, the cell will be 39451 rather than 0.25 because the date 1/4/2008 (The default year for a Date/Time value is the current year.) corresponds to the numeric value 39451. The following Excel file shows different formatting values when I first format cells and then input values the same as in the first column:

	A	B	C	D	E	F	G	H	I
1	Text	General	Number	Date 3/14	Date 3/14/01	Date 3/14/2001	Date 14-Mar-01	Date 3/14/01 13:30	Time 13:30
2	5/2	2-May	2.50	5/2	5/2/08	5/2/2008	2-May-08	5/2/08 0:00	0:00
3	2.5	2.5	2.50	1/2	1/2/00	1/2/1900	2-Jan-00	1/2/00 12:00	12:00
4	2/5/2000	2/5/2000	36561.00	2/5	2/5/00	2/5/2000	5-Feb-00	2/5/00 0:00	0:00
5	1234	1234	1234.00	5/18	5/18/03	5/18/1903	18-May-03	5/18/03 0:00	0:00

Notice that even if we format cells, if Excel cannot get its formatted value, Excel will keep it as Text value, as the first row shows.

There is only one type of value for Date/Time. Excel does not allow negative numbers for a Date/Time value. For a positive number, its integer part is for date and its fraction part is for time. 1 is 1/1/1900 12:00 AM (0 is 1/0/1900 12:00 AM, which is weird.), and 37440.625 is 3/July/2002 3:00 PM. Using Date format means to take its integer part with a specified style (7/3/02 using format 3/14/01 or 3-Jul-02 using format 14-Mar-01). Using Time format means to take its fraction part with a specified style (15:00 using format 13:30 or 3:00 PM using format 1:30 PM), and using Date/Time format means to take the whole value (7/3/02 15:00 using format 3/14/01 13:30). Notice that when we save an Excel file to a txt file or a csv file, only formatted values are saved.

In SAS, as we know, there are three kinds of Date/Time values: Date, Time, or Date/Time. It is related to what format we are using. The number 1 can be the date 1/2/1960 or 1 second depending on what format we are using. Number 392000 can be treated as 04/05/3033 if it is being treated as a date (use MMDDYY10 format or other date format), or as 05JAN1960:12:53:20 if it is being treated as a date time (use DATETIME19. format), or 108:53 if it is being treated as a time (use HHMM6. format).

Therefore, when importing a Date/Time value into SAS, there are three ways to convert: take its integer part, take its fraction part, and take the whole value. A related consideration is to determine the format for Date/Time variables.

However, exporting a Date/Time value to Excel is relatively simple.

There are type considerations. When importing data, will SAS keep format such as Text to character and Number to numeric? How does SAS treat values with format General? When exporting data, will SAS keep format, character to Text, and numeric to Number, or converts both types to General? Will a character value '1/7' become 7-Jan in Excel?

There are also header-label considerations. In Excel, usually values in the first row are headers. When importing data, will they be converted to variable labels or variable names? If they do not satisfy name requirements, how does SAS handle this? When exporting data, could we put labels or variable names in the first row?

We will consider these questions in this paper.

In general when importing data from Excel, it is better to do the following pre-processing:

- Remove empty rows and empty columns, especially the right most empty columns and bottom empty rows.
- Use the first row for variable names and other rows for values.
- Make the type and format of each column consistent.

Import data

There are many methods to import an Excel file into SAS. Mainly, we divide these methods into three categories:

1. Use SAS/ACCESS component.
2. Do not use SAS/ACCESS component, save an Excel file as a csv file or a txt file, then import data.
3. Do not use SAS/ACCESS component, use DATA step to import data.

Import Wizard for an Excel file (Category 1)

Suppose we have a file student_info.xls in c:\excel, and it has the following contents. Notice that there are two missing values.

	A	B	C	D	E	F	G	H
1	Name	age	sex	test1	test2	birthday	enroll date	enroll time
2	Jim Watson	15	M		87	1/5/1987	3-Feb-07	
3	Jerry Gates	14	M	78	89	4/4/1986	4-Feb-07	9:38
4	Jennifer Brain	15	F	88	93	5/3/1988	5-Feb-07	11:20

In Category 1, we will talk first about the Import Wizard. Click on the File -> Import Data. You will see the following window:

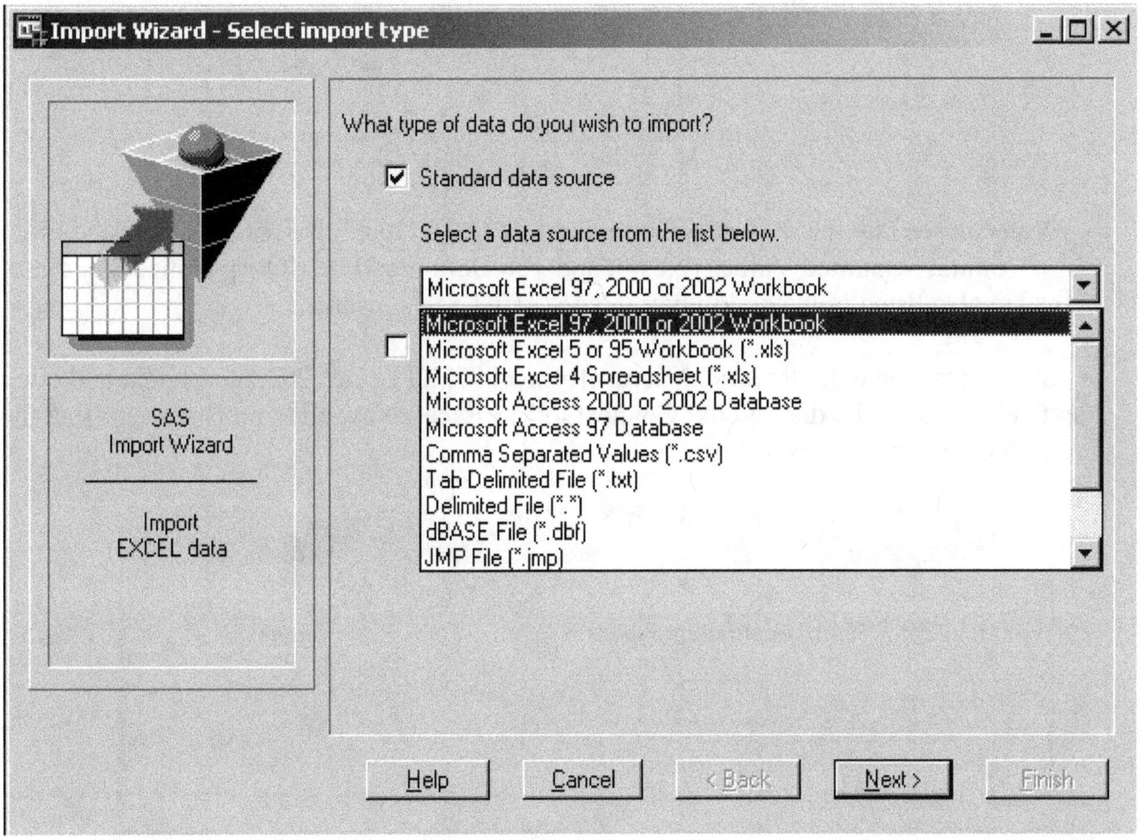

In the above window, there are two options. The default is Standard data source. The other is User-defined formats. In the text area, the content is Microsoft Excel 97, 2000, or 2002 Workbook. We click the down arrow and get the pull-down list. In the list there are plain files such as csv file, txt file, and other Delimited File and also database files such as access file, dbf file, and Excel file.

Notice that if you don't have SAS/ACCESS installed on your computer, the pull-down list will look like this:

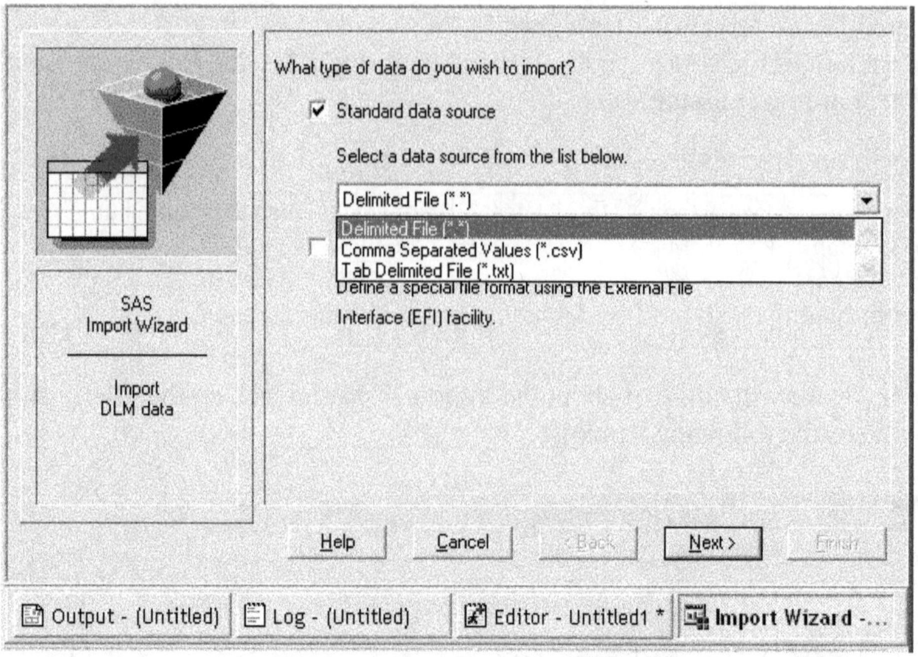

You can see that the default is Delimited File (*.*). Other choices are Delimited File (*.*), Comma Separated Values (*.csv), and Tab Delimited File (*.txt). Notice that these items are also listed in the dialog box if SAS/ACCESS is installed.

We choose the default value: Microsoft Excel 97, 2000, or 2002 Workbook, and click Next. We come to the dialog box: Connect to MS Excel. Now click on Browse to find the file or type in the path, as follows:

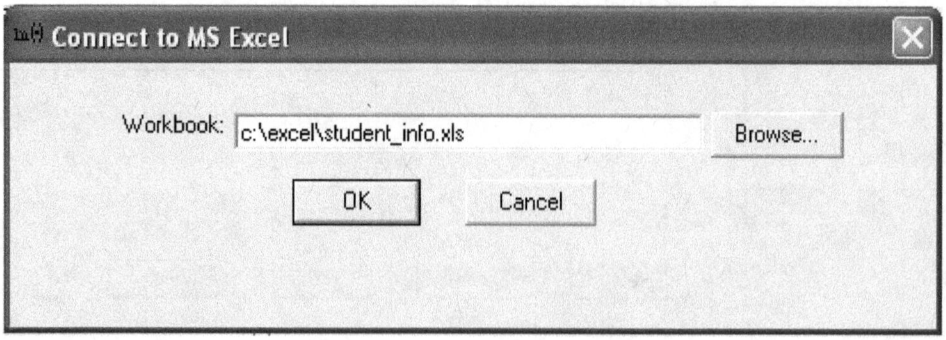

Click on OK and we get the following dialog box: Select Table.

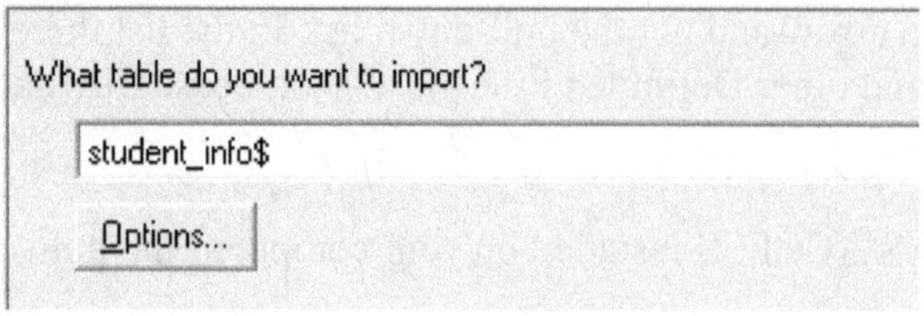

We can choose a name of a worksheet. From the pull-down list you can find table names in the Excel file. However, notice that there are names ending with a dollar sign and maybe also names not ending with a dollar sign. The former names are for worksheets, and the latter names are for name ranges. You can choose either one. Also, notice that if there is a worksheet and a range with the same name, then no matter which one you choose, one that has a dollar sign or not, SAS will treat it as a worksheet. Then click Next. We come to the dialog box: Select library and member.

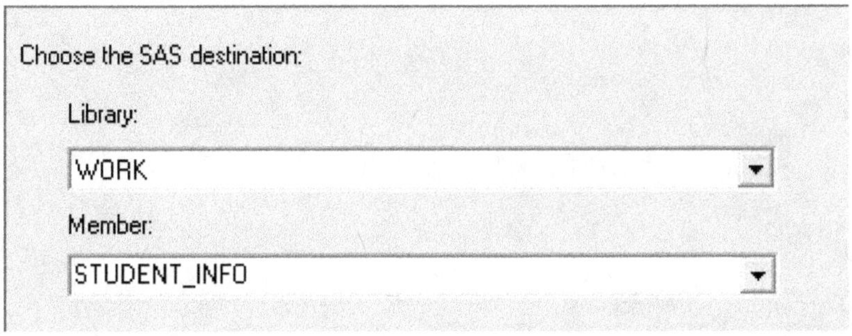

Now we put a data set name and click on Finish. You can find the following message in the log file:

```
NOTE: WORK.STUDENT_INFO was successfully created.
```

Go to the WORK library where you will find that there is the data set student_info. The data set shows labels of the variables.

VIEWTABLE: Work.Student_info

	Name	age	sex	test1	test2	birthday	enroll date	enroll time
1	Jim Watson	15	M	.	87	05JAN1987	03FEB2007	.
2	Jerry Gates	14	M	78	89	04APR1986	04FEB2007	9:38:00
3	Jennifer Brain	15	F	88	93	03MAY1988	05FEB2007	11:20:00

Notice that we can also ask SAS to create a program for this process. To do this, we click Next instead of Finish. This opens the following dialog box: Create SAS statements.

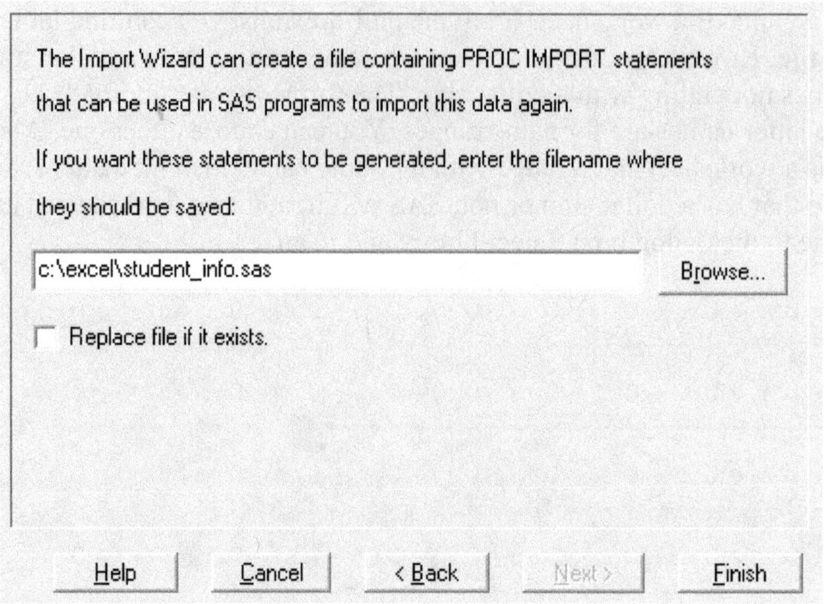

We enter the name c:\excel\stuent_info.sas and click Finish. In the directory c:\excel, you can find the SAS program student_info.sas. Open it, and we can see the following contents:

```
PROC IMPORT OUT= WORK.STUDENT_INFO
            DATAFILE= "C:\excel\student_info.xls"
            DBMS=EXCEL REPLACE;
     SHEET="student_info$";
     GETNAMES=YES;
     MIXED=NO;
     SCANTEXT=YES;
     USEDATE=YES;
     SCANTIME=YES;
RUN;
```

This program does the same thing as the Import Wizard. In order to understand the code, we go back to the Select Table dialog box. There is a button: Options, which brings the following dialog box:

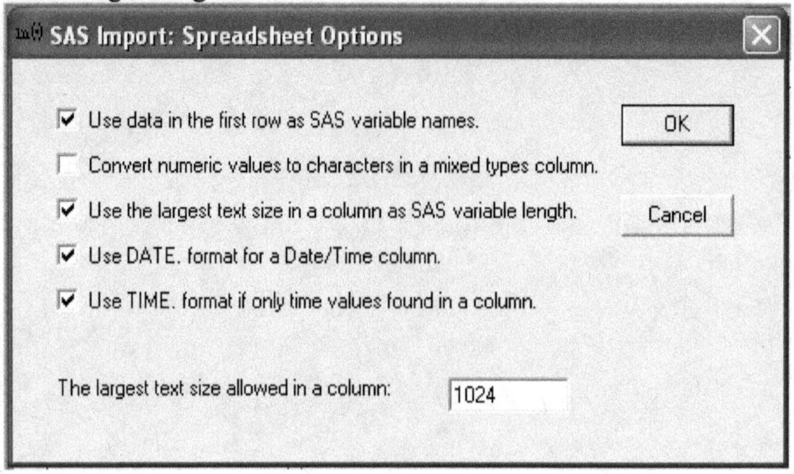

Options in the dialog box correspond to statements in PROC IMPORT. We explain what they are doing in the following table. We see that we can import data from a worksheet or a range. In the table, range can mean either a worksheet or a named range.

Table 2. Options in Import Wizard and statements in PROC IMPORT (for xls files)

Options in Import Wizard	Statement in PROC IMPORT	Value	Functionality
Use data in the first row as SAS variable names.	GETNAMES=	YES*	Treats first not-all-empty row in the range as labels, converts them to names (convert all special characters including blank and beginning digit to underscore). If all digits, use default names F1, F2 etc. If some names are same, add postfix 1,2,3 to latter ones.
		NO	Treat all values in the range as values, use default variable names F1,F2, …as the same as labels.
Convert numeric values to characters in a mixed type column.	MIXED=	YES	For any column, take the first eight rows (from the first row in the range if GETNAMES=NO or from the second row in the range if GETNAMES=YES). If all cells have the same type (character, Date or numeric), take that type, otherwise character type.
		NO*	Take the first eight rows to determine type: numeric, Date or character. Take the type as that most rows have. If there is a tie, according to the order: numeric, Date, character. No conversion between numeric and character.
Use the largest test size in a column as SAS variable length.	SCANTEXT=	YES*	Set the length attribute as the largest text size or the max size, whichever is less.
		NO	Set the length attribute as 255 or max size
The largest text size allowed in a column	TEXTSIZE=	Default 1024, max 32767	Set max size.
Use DATE. Format for a Date/Time column.	USEDATE=	YES*	Take Date part and convert, use DATE9. as format
		NO	Take whole Date/Time and convert, use DATETIME19. format
Use TIME. Format if only time values found in a column.	SCANTIME=	YES*	Scan whole column. If all values are <1, use TIME format. Otherwise see USEDATE= option.
		NO	See USEDATE= option.

* default value

Now we check the case MIXED=YES. Suppose we have the following Excel file.

	A	B	C	D	E	F	G
1	number	char_num	date	date_num	char_date	char_num	char_date_num
2	1	1	1/1/1900	1	1/1/1900	1	a
3	1	1	1/1/1900	1	1/1/1900	1	1
4	1	1	1/1/1900	1	1/1/1900	1	1
5	1	1	1/1/1900	1	1/1/1900	1	1/1/1900
6	1	1	1/1/1900	1	1/1/1900	1	1/1/1900
7	1	1	1/1/1900	1/1/1900	a	a	
8							

We run the following program and get the following data set. Notice that for the second column, the format is Text, but all cell are numeric, SAS sets its type as numeric. However, the fourth column has seven cells with format Numeric and one cell with format Date, SAS sets its type as character.

```
PROC IMPORT OUT= WORK.mixed_yes
            DATAFILE= 'c:\excel\mixed.xls'
            DBMS=EXCEL REPLACE;
  SHEET="sheet1$";
  MIXED=yes;
RUN;
```

	number	char_num	date	date_num	char_date	char_num1	char_date_num
1	1	1	01JAN1900	1	1	1	a
2	1	1	01JAN1900	1	1	1	1
3	1	1	01JAN1900	1	1	1	1
4	1	1	01JAN1900	1	1	1	1
5	1	1	01JAN1900	1	1	1	1
6	1	1	01JAN1900	1	a	a	

Next we check the case MIXED=NO. We use the following Excel file and run the following program:

	A	B	C	D	E	F	G
1	p3_4_0	p4_4	p3_3_2	p3_4_1	p2_2_3	p2_2_4	char_num
2	1	1	1/1/1900	1	1.00	1.00	1
3	1	1	1/1/1900	1	1.00	1.00	1
4	1	1	1/1/1900	1	1/1/1900	1/1/1900	1
5	1/1/1900	1	1.00	1/1	1/1/1900	1/1/1900	1
6	1/1/1900	1/1/1900	1.00	1/1	a	a	1
7	1/1/1900	1/1/1900	1.00	1/1	a	a	
8	1/1/1900	1/1/1900	a	1/1	a	a	
9		1/1/1900	a	a		a	
10		a		a			
11				a			
12		1/1/1900		a			
13		1/1/1900		a			

```
PROC IMPORT OUT= WORK.mixed_no
            DATAFILE= 'c:\excel\mixed1.xls'
            DBMS=EXCEL REPLACE;
  SHEET="sheet1$";
RUN;
```

	p3_4_0	p4_4	p3_3_2	p3_4_1	p2_2_3	p2_2_4	char_num
1	01JAN1900	1	1	01JAN1900			1
2	01JAN1900	1	1	01JAN1900			1
3	01JAN1900	1	1	01JAN1900			1
4	01JAN1900	1	1	01JAN1900			1
5	01JAN1900	1	1	01JAN1900	a	a	1
6	01JAN1900	1	1	01JAN1900	a	a	.
7	01JAN1900	1	.	01JAN1900	a	a	.
8	.	1	.	.		a	.
9	.	.	.	.			.
10	.	.	.	.			.
11	.	1	.	.			.
12	.	1	.	.			.

To understand the output, we count the value of three types in the first six columns (row 2 – row 9) as the following:

3:4:0 4:4:0 3:3:2 3:4:1 2:2:3 2:2:4

Here the default value 8 comes from TypeGuessRows registry setting. We can change this setting so SAS will check more rows. Interested readers are referring to SAS/ACCESS document.

Notice that for PROC IMPORT, there are two statements, SHEET= and RANGE=. The default for a SHEET= statement is the first sheet in the file, or the first sheet according to the alphabetic sorting order, depending on Excel versions. Also, we can specify a rectangle to input. In a SHEET= statement, we can specify sheet name, sheet name + range, or range name. If a name is for both a worksheet and a range, SAS treats it as a worksheet. In a RANGE= statement, we can specify sheet name + range or just range including absolute range or named range. If there is any conflict for the name or range, that specified in the RANGE= statement will overwrite that specified in the SHEET= statement. The following statements are all legal:

```
SHEET=sheet1;
SHEET= "sheet1";
SHEET="sheet1$";
SHEET="sheet1$"n;

SHEET="sheet1$a1:b3";

RANGE="sheet1$a1:b3";

RANGE="a1:b3";
RANGE="$a1:b3";
RANGE="abc"; (range name abc is defined in Excel)
```

The RANGE= option is only for PROC IMPORT but not for the Import Wizard. The Import Wizard cannot specify absolute range.

Suppose we have the option GETNAMES=YES. Usually, we say that SAS gets names from the first row. This is not accurate. Actually, if a range is specified, then SAS gets names from the first row in the range. And if no range is specified, then SAS gets names from the first not-all-null row.

SAS v8 also has the Import Wizard and PROC IMPORT, but it only has a GETNAMES= statement, SHEET= statement, and a RANGE= (only for range name) statement. For SAS v9, the Import Wizard that works on Excel95 or earlier is the same as the one in v8.

DIMPORT command, libref and pass-through facility

Display Manager command DIMPORT is an old tool to import data from an Excel file. Type the following command in the command line and hit return. We can see that there is a data set stuent_info created in the WORK library.

```
DIMPORT "c:\excel\student_info.xls" student_info REPLACE
```

We can put the command in a program as follows:

```
DM 'DIMPORT "c:\excel\student_info.xls" student_info REPLACE';
```

For a DIMPORT command, we need to specify only the Excel file and data set name. SAS executes the command as the Import Wizard or PROC IMPORT with default options.

However, there are two newest tools to import data from Excel files: libref and pass-through facities. They are only in SAS v9. Libref treats an xls file as a library. Notice that we can specify options here which correspond to those in PROC IMPORT. If not specified, SAS takes default options. See the following statement:

```
LIBNAME ss EXCEL 'c:\temp\date1.xls' MIXED=YES SCANTEXT=YES
   USEDATE=YES SCANTIME=YES GETNAMES=YES;
```

It is not necessary to use LIBNAME statement to create a library. We can also do this manually as follows:

- Click on Libraries->New in Explorer window.
- In New Library window, choose EXCEL in Engine box. Then fill in Name (libname), Path, and Options. Then click OK.

The following choices work the same as the above statement.

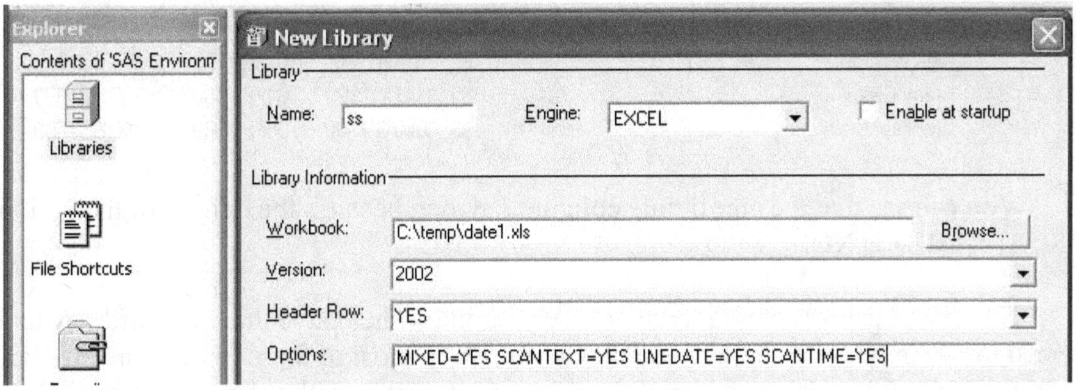

We want to talk more about LIBNAME method. From the options in the statement, we can see that this method belongs to the first category.

- In the same way as with the normal LIBNAME, it virtually moves an Excel file as a library to a SAS session. However, data sets in the library include worksheets (with a dollar sign ending) and named ranges (without a dollar sign ending). Clicking on the library we will see them both. Then we can open a worksheet or a named range to read it.
- We can open a sheet or a range in the library and save it as a SAS data set.
- The default option SCANTIME= is NO.

The following program shows you the usage of libref, where sheet1 is the name of a worksheet, and abc is the name of a named range.

```
DATA ss;
SET ss."sheet1$"n;
RUN;
DATA pp;
SET ss.abc;
RUN;
```

Notice that when using LIBNAME, we cannot open the Excel file because it is still being used in a SAS session. To open it, we have to end the SAS session or clear the libref using one of the following commands:

LIBNAME libref CLEAR;
LIBNAME _ALL_ CLEAR;

The PROC SQL pass-through facility is a SAS tool for directly connecting with a database server such as Excel, Access, or Oracle. The following program shows you how to use pass-through facility:

```
PROC SQL;
CONNECT TO EXCEL (path='c:\excel\student_info.xls' HEADER=YES);
CREATE TABLE ss AS SELECT * FROM CONNECTION TO EXCEL
(SELECT * FROM [student_info$]);
DISCONNECT FROM EXCEL;
QUIT;
```

	Name	age	sex	test1	test2	birthday	enroll date	enroll time
1	Jim Watson	15	M	.	87	05JAN1987	03FEB2007	.
2	Jerry Gates	14	M	78	89	04APR1986	04FEB2007	30DEC1899
3	Jennifer Brain	15	F	88	93	03MAY1988	05FEB2007	30DEC1899

You can see that the enroll time column is wrong because the default of the option SCANTIME= is NO.

Libref and pass-through facility are very similar. They have the same birthday and need to run in v9. They both have many options and most of these options are similar. In the following we compare some of their options, together with their default values. Notice that for a libref, some options can be put in LIBNAME statement as well as options in SET statement or suboptions in DATA= option in some PROC. When an option is in both LIBNAME statement and SET statement, the one in SET statement will overwrite that in the LIBNAME statement.

Table 3. Options in libref and pass-through facility

Statement in PROC IMPORT (default)	Options in libname (default)	Options in DATA step or PROC for libname	Options in Pass Through facility (default)
GETNAMES= (Y)	GETNAMES=|HEADER=|HDR= (YES)		GETNAMES=|HEADER=|HDR= (YES)
	DBGEN_NAME=DBMS|SAS (SAS)	DBGEN_NAME=DBMS|SAS	DBGEN_NAME=DBMS|SAS (SAS)
DBSASLABEL= (COMPAT)	DBSASLABEL=COMPAT|NONE (COMPAT)	DBSASLABEL=COMPAT |NONE	DBSASLABEL=COMPAT|NONE (COMPAT)
MIXED= (N)	MIXED=|MIXED_DATA= |MIXED_DATATYPE= (NO)		MIXED=|MIXED_DATA= |MIXED_DATATYPE= (NO)
SCANTEXT= (Y)	SCANTEXT=|SCAN_TEXT= |SCAN_TEXTSIZE= |SCANMEMO= (YES)		
TEXTSIZE= (1024)	DBMAX_TEXT= (1024)	DBMAX_TEXT=	DBMAX_TEXT= (1024)
USEDATE= (Y)	USEDATE= |USE_DATE |USE_DATETYPE (Y)		USEDATE= USE_DATE |USE_DATETYPE (NO)
SCANTIME= (Y)	SCANTIME=| SCAN_TIME=| SCAN_TIMETYPE= (NO)		

In the above table option DBSASLABEL= takes two values: COMPAT and NONE, where COMPAT sets labels and NONE does not set labels. When GETNAMES=YES and column header contains special character(s), DBGEN_NAME=DBMS converts special character to underscore and DBGEN_NAME=SAS uses name _COLn where n is the column number. The following two DATA steps create the same data set.

```
LIBNAME ss EXCEL 'c:\temp\date1.xls' DBSASLABEL=NONE;
DATA ss;
SET ss."sheet1$"n;
RUN;
LIBNAME ss clear;
LIBNAME ss EXCEL 'c:\temp\date1.xls' ;
```

```
DATA ss;
SET ss."sheet1$"n (DBSASLABEL=NONE);
RUN;
```

All methods we have talked need SAS/ACCESS component and work similarly. Actually, we can also use PROC ACCESS. The following program is an example.

```
PROC ACCESS DBMS=XLS;
   CREATE WORK.XLSA.ACCESS;
   PATH="c:\excel\student_info";
   SCANTYPE  = YES;
   GETNAMES  = YES;
   ASSIGN    = YES;
   UNIQUE    = YES;
   CREATE WORK.XLSV.VIEW;
   SUBSET WHERE birthday>='01JUN1987'd;
SELECT ALL;
FORMAT 6=DATE9.;
RUN;

DATA student_info1;
  SET WORK.XLSV;
RUN;

PROC DATASETS LIBRARY=WORK;
  DELETE XLSV / MEMTYPE=VIEW;
  DELETE XLSA / MEMTYPE=ACCESS;
RUN;
QUIT;
```

Import wizard for a plain data file (category 2)

As we have said, the above Import Wizard needs SAS/ACCESS to be installed. If this is not the case, you can still use the Import Wizard, but it needs a detour: First, save the xls file as a txt file (tab delimiter) or a csv (comma delimiter) file. Then use the Import Wizard.

We will first talk about the relationship between Excel files and csv files. Let's type in number 3.625 in an Excel file. Then we use format 3/14/01. It shows 1/03/00, but the actual date/time value is 1/3/1900 3:00:00 PM.

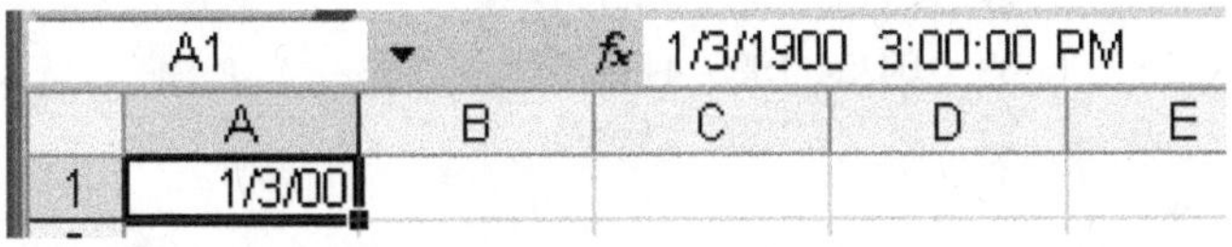

Now we save it as a csv file. We can continue and keep the same feature, but if we close it and open it again, we'll see that it changes.

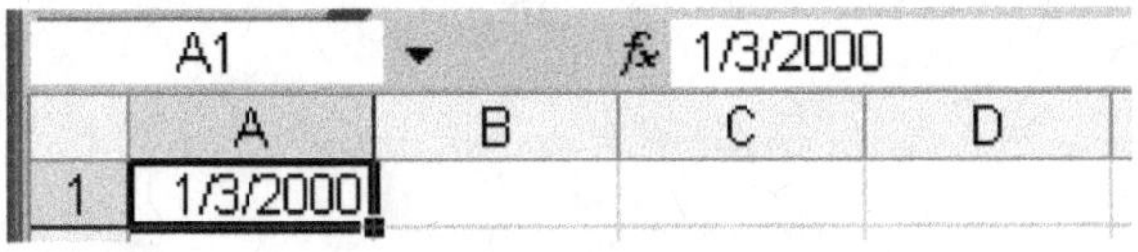

And if we use Notepad to open it, it shows 1/3/00. Why is it 1/3/2000 in Excel? Because the cut off year is 1930 in Excel. Anyway, all values in csv are just text. We can open a cvs file with Excel or Notepad. For a Date/Time value, in Excel it is a number with format, but in Notepad it is only a text value with no relationship to a number.

So let us save the student_info.xls as student_info.csv. Run the Import Wizard, and in the dialog box Select import type, select Comma Separated Values (*.csv). Afterward, steps are almost the same as that for Excel.

Notice that for a csv file, you have to close the file and then run Import Wizard.

In the Select files dialog box, there is a button: Options. Click the button, and we get the following dialog box:

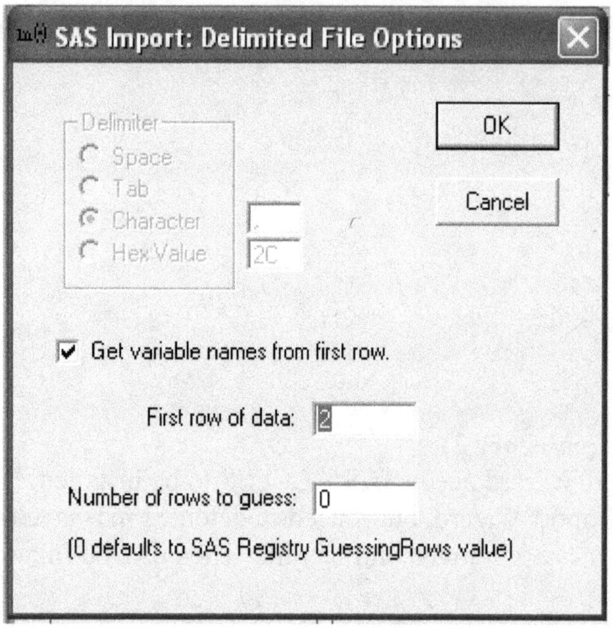

Finally, the following data set is created:

	Name	age	sex	test1	test2	birthday	enroll_date	enroll_time
1	Jim Watson	15	M	.	87	01/05/1987	3-Feb-07	
2	Jerry Gates	14	M	78	89	04/04/1986	4-Feb-07	9:38
3	Jennifer Brain	15	F	88	93	05/03/1988	5-Feb-07	11:20

The following is the code created by the Import Wizard:

```
PROC IMPORT OUT= WORK.student_info
            DATAFILE= "C:\excel\student_info.csv"
            DBMS=CSV REPLACE;
     GETNAMES=YES;
     DATAROW=2;
RUN;
```

From the data set you can see that the Import Wizard and PROC IMPORT do not have labels for variables. For Date/Time values, SAS can figure out if it is the MMDDYY format, but not other formats, as well as the time format. Therefore, SAS treats enroll_date and enroll_time as character variables but treats birthday as a numeric variable.

The following is a comparison between Import Wizard and PROC IMPORT for csv files:

Table 4. Options in Import Wizard and Statements in PROC IMPORT (for csv files)

Options in Import Wizard	Statement in PROC IMPORT	Value	Functionality
Use data in the first row as SAS variable names.	`GETNAMES=`	YES*	Treats first not-all-empty row in the range as names, see below for rules.
		NO	Treats all values as values, use default variable namesVAR1, VAR2….
First row of data	`DATAROW=`	2 – 32767 if getnames=YES 1-32767 if getnames=NO	Determines the first row to read.
Number of rows to guess (New in v9)	`GUESSINGROWS=`	Must be greater than or equal to DATAROW= value	SAS scans rows from DATAROW= value to GUESSINGROWS= value to determine the type of variables and length attribute of character variables. Default value is 0, which means to use SAS registry GUESSINGROWS setting, which usually is 20.

Although when saving an Excel file as a csv file the file has the same column number and row number as the Excel file, csv files themselves do not have column limit, row limit, and text limit. Also, for a csv file, we can specify the first row, but not a rectangle. SAS determines variable type in the same way as MIX=YES in PROC IMPORT for xls files.

To import data, the following are main differences between that for csv (txt) files and that for xls files (We will talk about values later.).

- When importing data from a csv files, there are no variable labels in the data set.
- The default variable names are VAR1, VAR2, etc., for a csv file, but F1, F2, etc., for xls files.
- For a header consisting of all digits, only the first digit is converted to an underscore for csv files, but all digits are converted to underscores for xls files.
- If there is more than one column with the same variable name, the second one will be set as the default variable name, such as VAR4 for csv files, but for xls files, SAS will add postfix for the second variable.
- For Date/Time values, SAS can figure out if it is MMDDYY format, but not other formats as well as time format for csv files.

- SAS takes the number of rows specified in the option GUESSINGROWS=. If they are all Date/Time type with format MMDDYY, then the type of the corresponding variable is Date, if they are all numeric, then the type is numerics, and otherwise the type is character.
- For a csv file, we can use the first row as variable names and read from any row after that, but the same is not true for Excel files.
- Notice that there are two important registry settings, for number of rows that used to determine the type of a variable. One is TypeGuessRows that is for methods in category 1 (for xls files, usually is 8), and the other is GuessingRows that is for methods in category 2 (for csv files, usually is 20). They have similar functionality. You may notice that for csv files, there is an option GuessingRows. That is new in SAS v9. Option GuseeingRows=0 means to use registry setting. SAS v8 does not have this option, and we have to change registry setting to change the value. The case for TypeGuessRows in v9 is similar to the case for GuseeingRows in v8. There is no such option and we have to change registry setting even for SAS v9.

We can use a DM command, too. It is the same as the Import Wizard using default options.

```
DIMPORT "c:\excel\student_info.csv " pp REPLACE
```

We can also put the DM command in the code as follows:

```
DM 'DIMPORT "c:\temp\uu.csv " pp REPLACE';
```

DATA step (category 3)

In category 2, we save an xls file as a csv file, and then we use PROC IMPORT to read it, but as we know, we can use DATA step to read a csv file or tab delimiter files. So in category 3, we use DATA step. There are three methods: use the DDE tool to work on an Excel file, save as a csv file, or save as a txt file and use DATA step.

Actually, when using the Import Wizard, you can ask SAS to generate a corresponding code of PROC IMPORT. Also, if the raw data file is a plain text file, then for Import Wizard or PROC IMPORT, SAS will generate code for DATA step. The following code is generated by SAS when importing data from the csv file student_info. Notice informats in the code:

```
238      data WORK.STUDENT_INFO2                          ;
239      %let _EFIERR_ = 0; /* set the ERROR detection macro variable */
240      infile 'C:\excel\student_info.csv' delimiter = ',' MISSOVER DSD lrecl=32767
firstobs=2
240! ;
241         informat Name $10. ;
242         informat age best32. ;
243         informat sex $1. ;
244         informat test1 best32. ;
245         informat test2 best32. ;
246         informat birthday mmddyy10. ;
247         informat enroll_date $8. ;
```

```
        informat enroll_time $5. ;
        format Name $10. ;
        format age best12. ;
        format sex $1. ;
        format test1 best12. ;
        format test2 best12. ;
        format birthday mmddyy10. ;
        format enroll_date $8. ;
        format enroll_time $5. ;
     input
                Name $
                age
                sex $
                test1
                test2
                birthday
                enroll_date $
                enroll_time $
     ;
     if _ERROR_ then call symputx('_EFIERR_',1);  /* set ERROR detection macro
variable */
     run;
```

Notice that the program is for the specified csv file. One thing I have to point out is that PROC IMPORT cannot figure out Time value. Therefore, in the program, both informat and format of the variable enroll_time are $5. It is treated as character value. But actually, we can change their informats to TIME5 in the program.

The method that saves an Excel file as a txt file and then uses DATA step is the same as saving it as a csv file. The only difference is using DLM='09'x instead of DLM=', '. Therefore, we don't have to say too much on this method.

DDE (Dynamic Data Exchange) is a method of accessing data from other applications. It does not need SAS/ACCESS to be installed or SAS v9 to be installed. When using DDE, both applications must be running, and the Excel file that is to be read from or to be written to must be active.

Now we open the file student_info.xls and then use the following SAS program to read it:

```
FILENAME ss DDE
   'excel|c:\excel\[student_info.xls]student_info!r2c1:r4c8' ;
DATA class;
   INFILE ss NOTAB DLM='09'x DSD MISSOVER;
   LENGTH name $15;
   INFORMAT birthday MMDDYY10. enroll_t TIME5.;
   FORMAT birthday MMDDYY10. enroll_t TIME5.;
   INPUT name $ age sex $ test1  test2 birthday enroll_d $ enroll_t;
OPTION NOCENTER;
PROC PRINT NOOBS;
   VAR name age sex  test1  test2 birthday enroll_d  enroll_t;
RUN;
```

The following is the corresponding printout:

name	age	sex	test1	test2	birthday	enroll_d	enroll_t
Jim Watson	15	M	.	87	01/05/1987	3-Feb-07	.
Jerry Gates	14	M	78	89	04/04/1986	4-Feb-07	9:38
Jennifer Brain	15	F	88	93	05/03/1988	5-Feb-07	11:20

Notice that similar to a common DATA step, we have to specify variables' name, type, length, format, and informat if necessary, and we can also specify label. In our case, we cannot find a suitable informat for variable enroll_d, so we treat it as a character variable. Also, because there are missing values, we have to use the DSD option. Furthermore, since there are missing values for the last variable (TEST2), we have to use the MISSOVER option.

The difference between this method and the usual DATA step is the definition of FILENAME (Compare this program and the previous one created by SAS.). Here we specify a DDE triplet (enclosed within single quotation marks). It consists of three parts:

```
Application|topic!item
```

In our example, the application is Excel, the topic is a path followed by a file name (within square brackets) and a spreadsheet name, and the item is a specification for the rows and columns to be read. Notice that the application is followed by a vertical bar and the topic by an exclamation mark. You can also ask SAS to find the triplet: On the spreadsheet, select the rows and columns to be read, and click Edit -> Copy; then in the SAS window, click Solutions -> Accessories -> DDE triplet. You will see the following pop-up window:

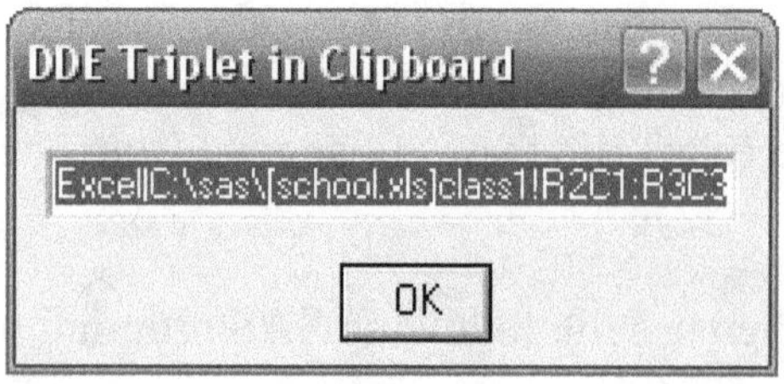

Notice that you have to open the file that you want to read. Simply opening an xls application does not work. Choose the rows and columns to be read. Don't use "Select All" if the first row is used for variable names in Excel files. If you don't want to manually open an Excel file, you can put the following statements in your program:

```
OPTIONS NOXWAIT NOXSYNC;
X '"c:\excel\student_info.xls"';
```

Here, the options NOXWAIT and NOXSYNC close the DOS window that opens Excel and let SAS proceed with the rest of the program. The default options are XWAIT and XSYNC. If the options NOXWAIT and NOXSYNC are not used, you need to close the DOS window with an exit statement before SAS can proceed.

Now we have a question. We use the DDE tool or we save an xls file as a txt file and then use DATA step. The two data steps are exactly the same. Both use DLM='09'x. So what is the difference?

- One method works on the txt file, and the other works on the Excel file itself.
- If saved as a txt file, then it is a tab delimiter file, i.e. there is a tab between two values. Using the DDE tool, the Excel file is treated as a tab delimiter file.
- When using DATA step, the default delimiter is blank, no matter whether it is for a txt file or a DDE tool. But we can use the option DLM='09'x to force SAS to use a tab as a delimiter.
- When reading the file, for a DDE tool, SAS converts a tab to a blank. Option NOTAB can prevent this. So if there is no blank within any value, we do not have to use the DLM='09'x option and do not use a NOTAB option. But when there is a blank within a value, we have to use both DLM='09'x and NOTAB options. For a txt file, SAS does not convert a tab to a blank, so we have to use DLM='09'x, but not a NOTAB option.

In this previous program, since values have embedded blanks, we have to use the options NOTAB and DLM='09'x.

Now we will make a comparison of three methods in category 3. They have common points as follows:

- They do not use SAS/ACCESS component.
- They all use INFILE + INPUT statements.
- They are working on formatted values, not original values.
- We have to specify for each variable its name, type, length, format, and informat if necessary, and we can also specify label. If necessary, we can also use DSD and MISSOVER options.

The following are differences among them:

- For DDE, the file must be open. For a txt file and a csv file, the files must be closed.
- For txt files and csv files, use FIRSTOBS=, OBS=, and KEEP= (DROP=) to specify columns and rows. DDE uses a triplet for columns and rows as well as these options.
- DDE uses the NOTAB option if necessary.

Comparison between methods in Category 1 (using SAS/ACCESS) and that in Categories 2 and 3 (not using SAS/ACCESS) when importing data

Now we will discuss differences between using SAS/ACCESS and not using SAS/ACCESS. We are already aware of some differences between these two kinds of methods. Here I want to concentrate on values because getting correct values is the most important thing. At the beginning of the paper, we have already seen the following Excel file in which I use different formats but put the same values in each column except column headers.

	A	B	C	D	E	F	G	H	I
1	Text	General	Number	Date 3/14	Date 3/14/01	Date 3/14/2001	Date 14-Mar-01	Date 3/14/01 13:30	Time 13:30
2	5/2	2-May	2.50	5/2	5/2/08	5/2/2008	2-May-08	5/2/08 0:00	0:00
3	2.5	2.5	2.50	1/2	1/2/00	1/2/1900	2-Jan-00	1/2/00 12:00	12:00
4	2/5/2000	2/5/2000	36561.00	2/5	2/5/00	2/5/2000	5-Feb-00	2/5/00 0:00	0:00
5	1234	1234	1234.00	5/18	5/18/03	5/18/1903	18-May-03	5/18/03 0:00	0:00

Now we will run the following program:

```
DM 'DIMPORT "c:\excel\format1.xls" format1 REPLACE';
PROC CONTENTS VARNUM;
RUN;
```

```
#     Variable              Type    Len    Format     Informat    Label

1     Text                  Char      8    $8.        $8.         Text
2     General               Num       8                           General
3     Number                Num       8                           Number
4     Date_3_14             Num       8    DATE9.     DATE9.      Date 3/14
5     Date_3_14_01          Num       8    DATE9.     DATE9.      Date 3/14/01
6     Date_3_14_2001        Num       8    DATE9.     DATE9.      Date 3/14/2001
7     Date_14_Mar_01        Num       8    DATE9.     DATE9.      Date 14-Mar-01
8     Date_3_14_01_13_30    Num       8    DATE9.     DATE9.      Date 3/14/01 13:30
9     Time_13_30            Num       8    DATE9.     DATE9.      Time 13:30
```

The following is data set created:

Text	General	Number	Date 3/14	Date 3/14/01	Date 3/14/2001	Date 14-Mar-01	Date 3/14/01 13:30	Time 13:30
5/2	39570	2.5	02MAY2008	02MAY2008	02MAY2008	02MAY2008	02MAY2008	02MAY2008
2.5	2.5	2.5	02JAN1900	02JAN1900	02JAN1900	02JAN1900	02JAN1900	02JAN1900
2/5/2000	36561	36561	05FEB2000	05FEB2000	05FEB2000	05FEB2000	05FEB2000	05FEB2000
1234	1234	1234	18MAY1903	18MAY1903	18MAY1903	18MAY1903	18MAY1903	18MAY1903

We already talked about how SAS determines types for variables. Here we concentrate on Date/Time columns. We can see that SAS uses original values to convert. As Table 2 indicated, because of default option USEDATE=YES, SAS takes only Date values from Excel and uses DATE9 as the format. If we want to get Date/Time values, we can run the following program (set option USEDATE=NO), but this will set format to DATETIME19. for all Date/Time columns:

```
PROC IMPORT OUT= format1
            DATAFILE= "C:\excel\format1.xls"
            DBMS=EXCEL REPLACE;
      USEDATE=NO;
RUN;
```

Methods in categories 2 and 3 do not use SAS/ACCESS. We first save the Excel file as a csv file. Notice that when we save it and open it again, some values change because when saving it, all values become text values, and when we open it again, Excel uses its own way to understand the values. The following is the saved csv file that opens with Excel:

	A	B	C	D	E	F	G	H	I
1	Text	General	Number	Date 3/14	Date 3/14/01	Date 3/14/2001	Date 14-Mar-01	Date 3/14/01 13:30	Time 13:30
2	2-May	2-May	2.5	2-May	5/2/2008	5/2/2008	2-May-08	5/2/2008 0:00	0:00
3	2.5	2.5	2.5	2-Jan	1/2/2000	1/2/1900	2-Jan-00	1/2/2000 12:00	12:00
4	2/5/2000	2/5/2000	36561	5-Feb	2/5/2000	2/5/2000	5-Feb-00	2/5/2000 0:00	0:00
5	1234	1234	1234	18-May	5/18/2003	5/18/1903	18-May-03	5/18/2003 0:00	0:00

Anyway, I use the following program to import data from the csv file:

```
DM 'DIMPORT "c:\excel\format1.csv" format2 REPLACE';
PROC CONTENTS VARNUM;RUN;
```

```
#    Variable              Type    Len    Format        Informat

1    Text                  Char     10    $10.          $10.
2    General               Char     10    $10.          $10.
3    Number                Num       8    BEST12.       BEST32.
4    Date_3_14             Char      5    $5.           $5.
5    Date_3_14_01          Num       8    MMDDYY10.     MMDDYY10.
6    Date_3_14_2001        Num       8    MMDDYY10.     MMDDYY10.
7    Date_14_Mar_01        Char     10    $10.          $10.
8    Date_3_14_01_13_30    Num       8    MMDDYY10.     MMDDYY10.
9    Time_13_30            Char      6    $6.           $6.
```

The following is the data set that we get:

Text	General	Number	Date_3_14	Date_3_14_01	Date_3_14_2001	Date_14_Mar_01	Date_3_14_01_13_30	Time_13_30
5/2	2-May	2.5	5/2	05/02/2008	05/02/2008	2-May-08	05/02/2008	0:00
2.5	2.5	2.5	1/2	01/02/2000	01/02/1900	2-Jan-00	01/02/2000	12:00
2/5/2000	2/5/2000	36561	2/5	02/05/2000	02/05/2000	5-Feb-00	02/05/2000	0:00
1234	1234	1234	5/18	05/18/2003	05/18/1903	18-May-03	05/18/2003	0:00

For methods in category 3, as we have discussed before, we have to specify variable names and informats. We have to do this for the DDE tool even though it is working on an xls file rather than a csv file, but it is working on formatted values.

We can see that the drawback of methods in category 2 is that it cannot figure out the informats for columns 4, 7 and 9, so SAS treats them as character values. For column 9, I already indicated that we can use the TIME informat in DATA step if we use methods in category 3, but we cannot find an informat for column 4, and 7.

Compare data sets format1 and format2. Format1 has correct data in column 4 and 7, because methods in category 1 have no relationship with formats. Also notice the date values in the last row on both data sets. In format1, they are all 18MAY1903, but in format2, some become 05/18/2003 because of formats.

Now we will discuss if there is no SAS/ACCESS installed, how we handle the Date/Time issue. As we have learned, each Date/Time in Excel is a Date/Time value, i.e., it includes date and time. There is no pure Date value or pure Time value. If we want to catch its Date part, it is better to use format 3/14/2001. Then we can use the informat MMDDYY10. (DATA step) to read it, or use PROC IMPORT or a DM command and SAS will figure out the informat. If we want to catch its Time part, we have to use DATA step and use the informat TIME. to read it. See the following csv file, program, and data set:

A	B	C	D	E	F	G
number	Time 13:30	Time 1:30 PM	Time 13:30:55	Time 1:30:55 PM	Time 30:55.2	Time 37:30:55
0.137	3:17	3:17 AM	3:17:17	3:17:17 AM	17:16.8	3:17:17
3.45	10:48	10:48 AM	10:48:00	10:48:00 AM	48:00.0	82:48:00

```
DATA s;
INFILE 'c:\excel\time.csv' DLM=',' ;
INFORMAT b  c  d e f g TIME.;FORMAT b c d e f g TIME.;
INPUT a  b  c  d e f g;
option nocenter;
PROC PRINT noobs;
RUN;
```

b	c	d	e	f	g	a
.	.	.	.	.	.	.
3:17:00	3:17:00	3:17:17	3:17:17	.	3:17:17	0.137
10:48:00	10:48:00	10:48:00	10:48:00	.	82:48:00	3.450

However, to catch both a Date part and a Time part does not seem easy. First, since these methods work on formatted values, we have to save a value using some Date/Time format. There are two such formats: 3/14/01 1:30 PM and 3/14/01 13:30. As we have said, to read data correctly, we have to use informat. (PROC IMPORT figures out informat by itself if it can.) There are two informats that can read a Date/Time value: DATETIME and EURDFDT, but neither of them can read values formatted in Excel. Therefore, we have to read them in as character values and manipulate them in DATA step.

Notice that this difference not only affects Date/Time values but also other values. The following Excel file has formatted values:

1	Text	Fraction	Percentage	Currency	Accounting
2	2.5	2 1/2	250.00%	$2.50	$ 2.50

We run the following program and get the following resultant data set:

```
DM 'DIMPORT "c:\excel\format3.xls" format3 REPLACE';
```

	Text	Fraction	Percentage	Currency	Accounting
1	2.5	2.5	2.5	$2.50	$2.50

You can see that SAS determines that the last two columns are currency values and keeps others as numeric values.

Now save the Excel file as a csv file and run the following program:

```
DM 'DIMPORT "c:\excel\format3.csv" format3 REPLACE';
PROC CONTENTS DATA=format3;RUN;
```

	Text	Fraction	Percent	Currency	_Accounting
1	2.5	2 1/2	250	3	3

#	Variable	Type	Len	Format	Informat
4	Currency	Num	8	COMMA12.	COMMA32.
2	Fraction	Char	5	$5.	$5.
3	Percentage	Num	8	COMMA12.	COMMA32.
1	Text	Num	8	BEST12.	BEST32.
5	_Accounting	Num	8	COMMA12.	COMMA32.

I don't think this is what you need.

Summary

Now it is time for a summary. First, why do I categorize methods into three categories? Below we can see their common points:

- For category1, SAS figures out names, type, labels, and length attributes. Formats in xls file are used to determine the type. SAS converts original values to data set, and no informats are needed.
- For category 2, SAS figures out names, types, informats, and converts formatted values to data set.
- For category 3, we have to specify names, types, lengths, and informats and work on formatted (saved) values.

Methods to read data from Excel files are in the following table:

Table 5. Comparison of ways to read data from an Excel file

	Method	How works	Comments
SAS/ACCESS installed (working on Excel file, and working on original values)	Import wizard	manual	SAS figures out name, label, type, and length, see Table 2. One program suitable for different Excel files. Import Wizard cannot specify absolute range. DIMPORT only has default option. LIBNAME uses default SCANTIME=NO. PROC SQL uses default SCANTEXT=NO and SCANTIME=NO.
	PROC IMPORT	coding	
	DIMPORT command	command	
	DIMPORT code	coding	
	PROC ACCESS	coding	
	Use LIBNAME to create a libref	coding	

	Manually create a libref	manual	LIBNAME and PROC SQL need v9.
	Proc SQL pass-through facility	coding	
SAS/ACCESS not necessarily installed (working on csv or txt file, and working on formatted values)	Import wizard	manual	See Table 4. DIMPORT only has default options. Can generate code for DATA step. Cannot not figure out informat for Time values. No label. Words on formatted values. One program suitable for different csv files.
	PROC IMPORT	coding	
	DIMPORT command	command	
	DIMPORT code	coding	
SAS/ACCESS not necessarily installed (DATA step, working on formatted values)	DATA step (Excel) DDE	coding	Have to specify variable names, types, informats, and lengths for character variables. Can use TIME informat. Dirrerent files need different programs.
	DATA step (csv or txt)	coding	

Output to Excel file

Limitations

Now we will talk about outputting a data set to an Excel file. First, as Table 1 shows, we have to consider the limitations. The following program shows column limitations for Excel files:

```
DATA s;
   ARRAY ab(*) ab1-ab300;
   DO i=1 TO 300;
   ab(i)=i;
   END;
RUN;
PROC EXPORT DATA= WORK.s
            OUTFILE= "C:\excel\test1.xls"
            DBMS=EXCEL REPLACE;
     SHEET="tbl1";
RUN;
```

```
ERROR: Error attempting to CREATE a DBMS table. ERROR: Execute: Too many fields defined..
WARNING: File deletion failed for _IMEX_.tbl1.DATA.
ERROR: Export unsuccessful.  See SAS Log for details.
```

But the following program is OK.

```
PROC EXPORT DATA= WORK.s(drop=ab250-ab300)
            OUTFILE= "C:\excel\test1.xls"
            DBMS=EXCEL REPLACE;
     SHEET="tbl1";
RUN;
```

For row limitation, if there are more than 65536 rows, you will get the following message:

```
ERROR: Execute: Unable to insert row
WARNING: File deletion failed for _IMEX_.tbl1.DATA.
ERROR: Export unsuccessful.  See SAS Log for details.
```

```
NOTE: The SAS System stopped processing this step because of errors.
```

The following program shows date limit:

```
DATA s;
*a=-21000;
a=-21918;
FORMAT a MMDDYY10.;
PROC PRINT;
RUN;
DM 'DEXPORT s "c:\temp\temp\tem2.xls" ';
```

```
NOTE: New file "c:\temp\temp\tem2.xls" will be created if the export process succeeds.
ERROR: During insert: _
WARNING: File deletion failed for _IMEX_.S.DATA.
ERROR: Export unsuccessful.  See SAS Log for details.
```

As we compared an SAS data set with an Excel file in section 1, we can see that output to an Excel file is relatively easy. We can divide these methods into five categories.

1. Use SAS/ACCESS component.
2. Do not use SAS/ACCESS component, export data to a csv file.
3. Do not use SAS/ACCESS component, use DATA step and FILE + PUT statements to write data to a csv file or an Excel file (DDE).
4. Use ODS tools, and do not use SAS/ACCESS component.
5. Use some other methods, and do not use SAS/ACCESS component.

Export Wizard and PROC EXPORT (Category 1)

In a way similar to Import Wizard and PROC IMPORT, we can use the Export Wizard and PROC EXPORT to write a data set to an Excel file. Notice that when exporting data, there are no options. After learning Import Wizard, it is easy to understand Export Wizard. First, we create the following data set:

VIEWTABLE: Work.Student_info

	Name	age	sex	test1	test2	birthday	enroll date	enroll time
1	Jim Watson	15	M	.	87	05JAN1987	03FEB2007	.
2	Jerry Gates	14	M	78	89	04APR1986	04FEB2007	9:38:00
3	Jennifer Brain	15	F	88	93	03MAY1988	05FEB2007	11:20:00

The data set has the following attributes:

#	Variable	Type	Len	Format	Informat	Label
1	Name	Char	14	$14.	$14.	Name
2	age	Num	8			age
6	birthday	Num	8	DATE9.	DATE9.	birthday
7	enroll_date	Num	8	DATE9.	DATE9.	enroll date
8	enroll_time	Num	8	TIME8.	TIME8.	enroll time
3	sex	Char	1	$1.	$1.	sex
4	test1	Num	8			test1

```
5     test2          Num      8                      test2
```

We run Export Wizard according to the following steps:

- File->Export Data and choose the data set to be exported.
- Choose the type of file you want to export: Microsoft Excel 97, 2000, or 2002 Workbook.
- Choose the workbook: c:\temp\test1.xls.
- Assign a name to the exported table: tbl1.
- Click Finish.

The following is the Excel file that has been created:

	A	B	C	D	E	F	G	H
1	Name	age	sex	test1	test2	birthday	enroll_date	enroll_time
2	Jim Watson	15	M		87	1/5/1987	2/3/2007	
3	Jerry Gates	14	M	78	89	4/4/1986	2/4/2007	1/0/1900
4	Jennifer Brain	15	F	88	93	5/3/1988	2/5/2007	1/0/1900

We can see that the only thing that may be wrong is column H, but if we change the format in Excel to show the Time part, we can see that the column is correct.

The following program is created by SAS.

```
PROC EXPORT DATA= WORK.Student_info
            OUTFILE= "C:\temp\test1.xls"
            DBMS=EXCEL REPLACE;
      SHEET="tbl1";
RUN;
```

For SAS v8, PROC EXPORT does not have a sheet= statement. It just uses the data set name as the sheet name.

For export, the same as import, if both SAS/ACCESS and v9 are installed, we can use LIBNAME (Use LIBNAME statement or manually assign libname.) to directly write data to an Excel file as the following program shows:

```
LIBNAME ss EXCEL 'c:\excel\test1.xls' ;
DATA ss.sheet1;
   SET student_info;
RUN;
LIBNAME _ALL_ clear;
```

Notice that using this method, we can put labels in the xls file, as the following code shows:

```
DATA ss.sheet1 (DBLABEL=YES);
   SET student_info;
RUN;
```

As we can see, for import, we can read data from a sheet or from a named range. Therefore, we have to differentiate sheets and named ranges using a dollar sign. If sheet1 is a worksheet name, and we use ss.sheet1 to import data, we will get the following message:

```
ERROR: File SS.sheet1.DATA does not exist.
```

For export, we only export a data set to a sheet, not to a named range. Therefore, we should specify a sheet without a dollar sign. If we specify ss."sheet1$"n to export data, we will get the following message:

```
ERROR: Execute: 'sheet1$' is not a valid name.
       Make sure that it does not include invalid characters or punctuation and that it
is not too long..
```

Actually you can see that SAS creates a worksheet with the same name as the data set that is also a named range. As we already discussed in importing data, when using libname to assign an Excel file, we cannot open it. To open it, you have to end the SAS session or clear the library.

We can also use the Display Manager command to export data, such as the following:

```
DEXPORT student_info "c:\excel\temp.xls"
```

Here, `student_info` is the data set name, which is also the worksheet name in the xls file, as well as a range name. You can also put the DM command in a SAS program.

```
DM 'DEXPORT student_info "c:\excel\temp.xls" ';
```

Export Wizard and PROC EXPORT without SAS/ACCESS (Category 2)

If we don't have SAS/ACCESS installed, we cannot use the above method, but we can still use Export Wizard to export a data set to a csv file. Then we can use Microsoft Office Excel to open it and save it as an xls file. In order to do this, we have to choose Comma Separated Values (*.csv) in Export Wizard, instead of Excel.

We can also use PROC EXPORT to do this, as the following program created by Export Wizard shows.

```
PROC EXPORT DATA= WORK.student_info
            OUTFILE= "C:\excel\test1.csv"
            DBMS=CSV REPLACE;
RUN;
```

We can also use the Display Manager command to export a data set to a csv file.

```
DEXPORT student_info "c:\excel\temp.csv "
```

We can also put the command in a SAS program.

```
DM 'DEXPORT student_info "c:\excel\temp.csv" ';
```

The following is the Excel file that is created:

	A	B	C	D	E	F	G	H
1	Name	age	sex	test1	test2	birthday	enroll_date	enroll_time
2	Jim Watson	15	M		87	5-Jan-87	3-Feb-07	
3	Jerry Gates	14	M	78	89	4-Apr-86	4-Feb-07	9:38:00
4	Jennifer Brain	15	F	88	93	3-May-88	5-Feb-07	11:20:00

DATA step (Category 3)

Of course, we can use DATA step to output data to a csv file. Notice that whenever you run Export Wizard or PROC EXPORT for a csv file, SAS will create code for corresponding DATA step. The following code is created by SAS:

```
data _null_;
set  WORK.STUDENT_INFO                              end=EFIEOD;
%let _EFIERR_ = 0; /* set the ERROR detection macro variable */
%let _EFIREC_ = 0;     /* clear export record count macro variable */
file 'C:\excel\test1.csv' delimiter=',' DSD DROPOVER lrecl=32767;
   format Name $14. ;
   format age best12. ;
   format sex $1. ;
   format test1 best12. ;
   format test2 best12. ;
   format birthday date9. ;
   format enroll_date date9. ;
   format enroll_time time8. ;
if _n_ = 1 then        /* write column names */
 do;
   put
   'Name'
   ','
   'age'
   ','
   'sex'
   ','
   'test1'
   ','
   'test2'
   ','
   'birthday'
   ','
   'enroll_date'
   ','
   'enroll_time'
   ;
 end;
 do;
   EFIOUT + 1;
   put Name $ @;
   put age @;
   put sex $ @;
```

```
        put test1 @;
        put test2 @;
        put birthday @;
        put enroll_date @;
        put enroll_time ;
        ;
       end;
     if _ERROR_ then call symputx('_EFIERR_',1);  /* set ERROR detection macro
variable */
     if EFIEOD then call symputx('_EFIREC_',EFIOUT);
     run;
```

We can also use the DDE tool to export data to an Excel file. Notice the following points:

- SAS treats an Excel file as a tab separated file and converts a blank to a tab when using the DDE tool. So whenever there is a tab or a blank, SAS separates its two sides into two values.
- If there are no values containing blanks, you don't have to use the NOTAB option and '09'x between two values. Instead, just put a blank (or a tab='09'x) between two values. Otherwise, you have put '09'x between two values in the PUT statement and use the NOTAB option to prevent SAS from converting a blank to a tab. Let's see what is in an Excel file created by the following program. Notice that if you use some formats in a PUT statement, and the formatted values contain blanks, you have to use the NOTAB option and `'09'x` delimiter as well.

```
FILENAME ss DDE 'excel|c:\sas\[school.xls]sheet1!r1c1:r5c8' ;
DATA _NULL_;
   FILE ss ;
   PUT 'Name abc' '99' '09'x 'test1' ' test2';
RUN;
```

The program creates the following Excel file:

	A	B	C	D
1	Name	abc99	test1	test2

In the above program, notice that in the PUT statement, there is a blank between Name and abc, no blank or tab between abc and 99, a tab between 99 and test1, and a blank between test1 and test2. We can understand the results. Now let's use a NOTAB option (either in the FILENAME statement or in the FILE statement). We get the following Excel file because blanks are not converted to tabs anymore:

	A	B
1	Name abc99	test1 test2

The following program shows the usual usage of this method:

```
FILENAME ss DDE 'excel|c:\excel\[school.xls]sheet1!r1c1:r5c8' ;
```

```
DATA _NULL_;
   SET  student_info ;
   FILE ss NOTAB;
   FORMAT birthday enroll_date DATE9. ;
   FORMAT enroll_time TIME8. ;
   IF _N_ = 1 THEN  DO;
      PUT 'Name' '09'x 'age' '09'x 'sex' '09'x 'test1' '09'x 'test2'
      '09'x 'birthday' '09'x 'enroll_date' '09'x 'enroll_time';
   END;
   PUT Name $ '09'x  age '09'x  sex $ '09'x test1 '09'x test2
      '09'x birthday '09'x enroll_date '09'x enroll_time ;
RUN;
```

Now we open the Excel file in Microsoft Excel.

	A	B	C	D	E	F	G	H
1	Name	age	sex	test1	test2	birthday	enroll_date	enroll_time
2	Jim Watson	15	M	.	87	5-Jan-87	3-Feb-07	.
3	Jerry Gates	14	M	78	89	4-Apr-86	4-Feb-07	9:38:00
4	Jennifer Brain	15	F	88	93	3-May-88	5-Feb-07	11:20:00

We can see, same as we categorize methods when importing from an Excel file to a data set, DDE and csv are in the same category. They both use FILE + PUT. However DDE can update a rectangle of the Excel file.

ODS tools (Category 4)

We can also use the ODS tool to output a data set to an Excel file. ODS does not need SAS/ACCESS to be installed. There are several destinations and tagsets to do this. Most of them are similar. In the following, HTML works for SAS v8, csv, csvall, markup, and tagset.msoffice2k are experimental for v8, and msoffice2k and excelxp work for v9. Besides exporting a data set, we can also output statistical results of procedures such as PROC FREQ, PROC MEANS, and others.

These methods all use PROC PRINT or PROC REPORT or PROC SQL to fulfill this. Values are formatted values. You can specify labels for column headers. They capture title and footnote except csv and excelxp. Let's see the following example:

```
ODS CSV FILE='c:\excel\csv.CSV';
PROC PRINT DATA=student_info l NOOBS;
RUN;
ODS CSV CLOSE;

ODS CSVALL FILE='c:\excel\csvall.CSV';
PROC PRINT DATA=student_info l NOOBS;
RUN;
ODS CSVALL CLOSE;

ODS HTML FILE='c:\excel\html.xls';
PROC PRINT DATA=student_info l NOOBS;
RUN;
```

```
ODS HTML CLOSE;

ODS MSOFFICE2K FILE='c:\excel\office2k.xls';
PROC PRINT DATA=student_info l NOOBS;
RUN;
ODS MSOFFICE2K CLOSE;

ODS TAGSETS.MSOFFICE2K FILE='c:\excel\office2k1.xls';
PROC PRINT DATA=student_info l NOOBS;
RUN;
ODS TAGSET.MSOFFICE2K CLOSE;

ODS MARKUP TAGSET=MSOFFICE2K FILE='c:\excel\office2k2.xls';
PROC PRINT DATA=student_info l NOOBS;
RUN;
ODS MARKUP CLOSE;

ODS markup tagset=excelxp FILE='c:\excel\excelxp.xls';
PROC PRINT DATA=student_info l NOOBS;
RUN;
ODS MARKUP CLOSE;
```

The following two outputs are csv and HTML. You can see their difference.

1	Name	age	sex	test1	test2	birthday	enroll date	enroll time
2	Jim Watson	15	M	.	87	5-Jan-87	3-Feb-07	.
3	Jerry Gates	14	M	78	89	4-Apr-86	4-Feb-07	9:38:00
4	Jennifer Brain	15	F	88	93	3-May-88	5-Feb-07	11:20:00

	A	B	C	D	E	F	G	H
1	The SAS							
2								
3	**Name**	**age**	**sex**	**test1**	**test2**	**birthday**	**enroll date**	**enroll time**
4	Jim Watson	15	M	.	87	5-Jan-87	3-Feb-07	.
5	Jerry Gates	14	M	78	89	4-Apr-86	4-Feb-07	9:38:00
6	Jennifer Brain	15	F	88	93	3-May-88	5-Feb-07	11:20:00

When we use an ODS tool, we can pick variables, arrange variables, and of course we can pick a subset by FIRSTOBS=, OBS=, or even a WHERE option or a WHERE statement). The advantage is that we can use formatted values, labels, or even titles or footnotes.

Other methods (Category 5)

When we open a data set in the SAS Explorer window, we cannot copy the data set in a VIEWTABLE window to the clickboard, but we can directly copy it if we have SAS v9 installed. Right click on the data set in the Explorer window, and you will get the following pop-up list:

You can see that there are two buttons: Copy Contents to Clipboard and View in Excel. Click on Copy Contents to Clipboard, and then you can paste it to an Excel file. Click on View in Excel, and then you can save the file as an xls file.

We can also use the SAS System Viewer to open a data set if you have SAS System Viewer installed. This method is usually for a permanent data set. Open the data set using the SAS System Viewer, and then we can click Select All or highlight a rectangle and click Copy, and then paste the data set to an Excel file.

Compare methods in Category 1 (using SAS/ACCESS) and those in Categories 2, 3, 4, and 5 (not using SAS/ACCESS) when exporting data

From the above example it looks like the methods in categories 2, 3, 4, and 5 are better that those in category 1. Don't be fooled by appearance. Actually, the situations are the same for exporting data as they are for importing data. The example shows that when we use the TIME format in a data set and then export the data set using methods in categories 2, 3, 4, and 5, Excel accepts this format. However, with SAS/ACCESS installed,

- SAS keeps variable types.
- SAS works on original values in the data set, The Date/Time formats only determines their types.

Let's see the following example:

```
PROC FORMAT;
   VALUE aa 5=ab;
   VALUE $aa '5'=ab;
DATA conv;
   char='1/23/2001';OUTPUT;
   char='1234';OUTPUT;
   char='1/6 ';OUTPUT;
   char='abc';
   a=5;b=5;c1=5;c2=5;d=360;e=5;f=5;g='5';OUTPUT;
```

```
    FORMAT a YYMMDD6.  b MMDDYY6.  c1 MMDDYY8. c2 YYMMDD8. d HHMM5.
    e DATE9.;
    FORMAT f aa. g $aa.;
PROC PRINT;RUN;
```

char	a	b	c1	c2	d	e	f	g
1/23/2001	.	.	.	.	.	.	.	
1234	.	.	.	.	.	.	.	
1/6	.	.	.	.	.	.	.	
abc	600106	010660	01/06/60	60-01-06	0:06	06JAN1960	ab	ab

Let's run the following program:

```
DM 'DEXPORT conv "c:\excel\conv.xls" REPLACE';
```

We get the following Excel file:

	A	B	C	D	E	F	G	H	I
1	char	a	b	c1	c2	d	e	f	g
2	1/23/2001								
3	1234								
4	1/6								
5	abc	1/6/1960	1/6/1960	1/6/1960	1/6/1960	1/0/1900	1/6/1960	5	5

We can see that SAS converts numeric values to numeric and character values to character. For Date/Time values, SAS uses original values in a SAS data set to convert. In other words, values to be converted have no relationship with their formats. Formats determine only their types, numeric or Date/Time. SAS uses their formats to determine their types and then uses their original values to convert. Notice that for column F, the actual value is 1/0/1900 12:06:00 AM, but it shows 1/0/1900 because of format. As we discussed at the beginning of this paper, we know that this is correct.

Now let's see how methods in other categories handle this data set:

```
DM 'DEXPORT conv "c:\excel\conv.csv" REPLACE';
```

	A	B	C	D	E	F	G	H	
1	char	a	b	c1	c2	d	e	f	g
2	1/23/2001								
3	1234								
4	6-Jan								
5	abc	600106	10660	1/6/1960	60-01-06	0:06	6-Jan-60	ab	ab

You can see that in column A, the first three values are treated as numeric values and the fourth value as character value. Also '1/6' becoming '6-Jan' may not be what you want. The values in columns B and C are pure numbers, rather than Date/Time values, but values in columns D, F, and G are treated as Date/Time values. Value in column E is treated as a character value. From this example, we can draw the following conclusions:

- They are working on formatted values in a SAS data set.
- They don't care about the type, or we could say that they treat character values and numeric values the same: as text values.
- Excel determines if a value is numeric, character, or a Date/Time value according to its own rules.

The following program shows that the DDE tool works in the same way:

```
FILENAME ss DDE 'excel|c:\excel\[conv1.xls]sheet1!r1c1:r9c9' ;
DATA _NULL_;
   SET conv;
   FILE ss ;
   PUT char a b c1 c2 d e f g;
RUN;
```

	A	B	C	D	E	F	G	H	
1	1/23/2001	.	.	.	.	.	.	.	
2	1234	.	.	.	.	.	.	.	
3	6-Jan	.	.	.	.	.	.	.	
4	abc	600106	3/8/1929	1/6/1960	60-01-06	0:06	6-Jan-60	ab	ab

We can use any methods in categories 4 and 5, and they all work the same way.

Now we will discuss how to handle a Date/Time situation if SAS/ACCESS is not installed. To export Date values, we can use format mmddyy10 (Notice that the cutoff date of SAS is 1920 and that of Excel is 1930.). To export Time values, we can use format TIME, but there is trouble for Date/Time values. There are three formats to express Date/Time values: DATETIME, DATEAMPM, and EURDFDT. However, none of them has a corresponding format in Excel. We have to manipulate the data in DATA step to get character values like those formatted in Excel, as in the following example:

```
FILENAME ss DDE 'excel|c:\excel\[temp.xls]sheet1!r1c1:r5c8' ;
DATA ss;
   a='1/14/04 2:24 PM';b='1/14/04 14:24';
DATA _NULL_;
   SET ss;
   FILE ss NOTAB;
   PUT a '09'x b;
RUN;
```

When exporting data to Excel, you also have to pay attention to format. Let's see an example. In SAS, the value -21841 represents the date 3/15/1900, and 14684 represents the date 3/15/2000. So if you use format mmddyy8., these dates will become 3/15/00 or 3/15/1900 in an Excel file if SAS/ACCESS is not installed. You have to use format mmddyy10. But methods in category 1 will be OK no matter what formats you use.

Summary

Table 6 gives a comparison of different methods of converting a data set to an Excel file.

Table 6. Comparison of ways to export data to an Excel file

	Method	Comments	
SAS/ACCESS installed (working on Excel file)	Export Wizard	Work on original values	No labels.
	PROC EXPORT		
	DEXPORT command		
	DEXPORT code		
	Use LIBNAME to create a libref		Opetion DBLABEL=YES will add labels.
	Manually create a libref		
SAS/ACCESS not necessarily installed (working on csv file)	Export Wizard	Work on formatted values	No labels.
	PROC EXPORT		
	DEXPORT command		
	DEXPORT code		
SAS/ACCESS not necessarily installed (FILE + PUT)	DATA step (Excel) DDE		Specify variable names or labels or formats in a PUT statement.
	DATA step (csv or txt)		
ODS tool (PROC PRINT, PROC REPORT or PROC SQL)	HTML		Labels or names. Can use the feature of ODS such as color setting. May use default VAR statement in PROC PRINT, or default COLUMN statement in PROC REPORT or a SELECT * clause in PROC SQL. Capture title and footnote except CSV and HTML.
	CSV		
	CSVALL		
	MSOFFICE2K		
	EXCELXP		
Other methods	Copy to clipboard		v9 installed, whole data set, no label
	View in Excel		
	SASview		Labels or names, rectangle, system-formatted values

References

Andrews, Rick. (2008) "Printable Spreadsheets Made Easy: Utilizing the SAS® Excel XP Tagset." *Proceedings of the NorthEast SAS Users Group Conference (NESUG 2008)*, Paper AP06, Cary, NC: SAS Institute Inc.
http://www.nesug.org/Proceedings/nesug08/ap/ap06.pdf

"Base SAS Try This Demo: The ExcelXP Tagset and Microsoft Excel. "
http://support.sas.com/rnd/base/ods/odsmarkup/excelxp_demo.html

Churchill, Alan. (2007). "How to Generate 10,000 Excel Spreadsheets in 10 Minutes (Or Less)." *Proceedings of the SAS Global Forum Conference (NESUG 2008)*, Paper 001-2007, Cary, NC: SAS Institute Inc.
http://www2.sas.com/proceedings/forum2007/001-2007.pdf

Cranford, Keith. (2007). "How to Excel with SAS®."
http://www.scsug.org/SCSUGProceedings/2007/papers/how/HOW-Cranford.pdf

"DATA TRANSFER TO AND FROM EXCEL WITH DYNAMIC DATA EXCHANGE (DDE). "
http://darkwing.uoregon.edu/~robinh/data_trnsf_dde.txt

"Excel specifications and limits. "
http://office.microsoft.com/en-us/excel/HP051992911033.aspx

"How to Import an Excel File into SAS. "
http://www.ciser.cornell.edu/FAQ/SAS/excel2sas.shtml

Hunter, Tim. (2005). "What's New and Upcoming in ***SAS*** 9 ***ODS***." *Proceedings of the Midwest SAS Users Group Conference (MWSUG 2005)*, Paper TS1200, Cary, NC: SAS Institute Inc.
www.mwsug.org/Conference/2005/Tutorials/TS1200.pdf

"Moving Data between SAS and EXCEL, SAS version 6.12. "
http://www.stat.ncsu.edu/sas/faq/excel.html

Parker, Chevell. "Using ODS to Generate Excel Files. "
http://support.sas.com/rnd/base/ods/templateFAQ/Excel1.pdf

Perry, Joe. (2008). "SAS to MS-Excel, Auto-Loading a Full SAS Library into a Multi-Tabbed, Labeled Column, Excel Spreadsheet" *Proceedings of the Pharmaceutical SAS Users Group Conference (PharmaSUG 2008)*, Paper AD09, Cary, NC: SAS Institute Inc.
http://www.lexjansen.com/pharmasug/2008/ad/ad09.pdf

Qi, Hong, Liping Zhang, & Jiannan (Jane) Kang. (2006). "Approaches to Data Transfer from Microsoft Excel® to SAS® V9." *Proceedings of the NorthEast SAS Users Group Conference (NESUG 2006)*, Paper IO04, Cary, NC: SAS Institute Inc.
http://www.nesug.org/proceedings/nesug06/io/io04.pdf

SAS/ACCESS interface to PC files. 2004. Cary, NC: SAS Institute Inc.
http://support.sas.com/documentation/onlinedoc/91pdf/sasdoc_91/access_pcfiles_7056.pdf

TS325: The SAS System and DDE
ftp://ftp.sas.com/techsup/download/pc/ts325.pdf

TS589A: Using PC SAS/ACCESS Software to Read and Write to the DBF File Format,
http://support.sas.com/techsup/technote/ts589a.pdf

TS589B: Use PC-SAS 8.x and Higher to Read and Write Excel Files,
http://support.sas.com/techsup/technote/ts589b.pdf

SAS and File Editing

Introduction

Many people know that SAS can manipulate data sets and do statistical analysis. However, SAS can do file edit as well. SAS can search text, insert text, and replace text.

Mainly, we are going to talk about plain text files that have extensions txt, log, or sas, and RTF files and HTML files that have extensions RTF, HTM, or HTML. We can use Notepad to view and edit text files, use Microsoft Word to open and edit RTF files, and use Internet Explorer to read an HTML file. We can also use Notepad to edit HTML and RTF files. We can do Search, Replace, and Replace All when editing. So why should we write programs? The following cases show that sometimes it is convenient to run programs:

- We have several keywords to search if a file contains any one of them.
- We have a bunch files to search.
- We repeatedly create a file that needed to search.
- We want to insert a page number or replace a page number x with Page x of y, where y is the number of total edges.

In this paper we will concentrate on plain text files that have extensions txt or log. We will also talk about RTF files briefly. RTF files and HTML files are both code files that can be opened with Notepad. However, RTF files are much more complicated than HTML files. Many people use Notepad to write HTML files, but I wonder how many people use Notepad to write RTF files.

CHKLOG program

As an SAS programmer, you know that checking log files is very important in programming. How can a log file be checked? Open the log file and search for special text such as `ERROR, WARNING, ALERT, uninitialized,` where upper case or lower case depends on SAS. As we know, we can put a message in the log file to debug, such as the following:

```
IF id>100 THEN PUT "USER INFO: ID is greater then hundred";
```

Then we can check the log file to find useful information.

However, sometimes we may execute a bunch of SAS programs. To open these log files one by one and to search for these words one by one is tedious and boring. Therefore, it is better to write a program that can check a log file or a bunch of log files. Actually, this is a common thing that many programmers do. Many companies have their own version of programs. Suppose we are working in Windows, and we want to check all log files that are in c:\project\log. The following is my SAS program CHKLOG. You can modify it according to your need, for example, if you want to check more or fewer keywords:

```
OPTIONS NOXWAIT NOXSYNC;
```

```
%LET path=c:\project\log;
x "dir /b &path\*.log > &path\temp.dat";
FILENAME loglst "&path\temp.dat";

%MACRO readlog(logfile);
DATA temp; LENGTH line $ 200 fname $ 20;
   INFILE "&path\&logfile" MISSOVER PAD;
   INPUT LINE $ 1-200;
     *if scan(line,1,':') in ('WARNING','ERROR', 'ALERT');
   IF INDEX(line, 'WARNING') | INDEX(line, 'ERROR')
      | INDEX(line,  'ALERT')
      | INDEX(line, 'uninitialized')
      /*
      | INDEX(line, 'repeats of BY values')
      | INDEX(line, 'Invalid numeric data');
      | INDEX(Line, 'values have been converted')
        | INDEX(Line,'Missing values were generated')
        | INDEX(Line,'Division by zero')
        | INDEX(Line,'Mathematical operations could not')
        | INDEX(Line,'Invalid argument to function')
        | INDEX(Line,'No observations')
        | INDEX(Line,'There were 0 observations')
        | INDEX(Line,'The data set') and
         INDEX(Line,'has 0 observations');
      */
   fname="&logfile";
     RUN;
%IF &logfile=&file1 %THEN %DO;
DATA chklog;
   SET temp;
RUN;
%END;
%ELSE %DO;
PROC APPEND BASE=CHKLOG DATA=temp;
RUN;
%END;
%MEND;

%MACRO logfile;
DATA _NULL_;
   INFILE loglst END=end;
   LENGTH fname $20;
   INPUT fname $;
   IF SUBSTR(fname, 1,6)^='CHKLOG';
   CALL SYMPUT('file'||left(_n_), fname);
   IF end THEN CALL SYMPUT('tot',_n_);
RUN;

%DO i=1 %TO &tot;
   %readlog(&&file&i);
%END;
%MEND;
%logfile;
PROC PRINTTO PRINT="&path\chklog.txt" NEW;
PROC PRINT DATA=chklog;
RUN;
PROC PRINTTO;
```

```
RUN;
```

The program is fairly easy to understand. First, we get a list of log files in a specified directory. Then for each file in the list, we search for keywords that we need. The option /b in the DIR command lists only file names. The following is output in CHKLOG.txt:

```
Obs    line                                                    fname

 1     ERROR: Expecting page 1, got page -1 instead.          temp1.log
 2     ERROR: Page validation error while reading
SASUSER.PROFILE.CATALOG.    temp1.log
 3     ERROR: Expecting page 1, got page -1 instead.
temp2.log
 4     ERROR: Page validation error while reading
SASUSER.PROFILE.CATALOG.    temp2.log
 5     a=5 b=. _ERROR_=1 _N_=1
temp2.log
```

However, the program does not always work. I have seen one case. We know that for macro variables, the statement %PUT _USER_; (or _GLOBAL_ or _ALL_ or _LOCAL_) will print out values of corresponding macro variables to the log file. If a value has been masked, SAS will add some special characters around the value. In my case, I have a value which is a greater than sign (>), it is masked by some quoting function, and SAS prints it out as an arrow. Then, when I run the program, SAS reads the log file and treats the arrow as an end of file symbol and will stop at the symbol. I will talk about this soon.

We can also write a similar SAS program for UNIX. Due to the different nature between PC Windows and UNIX, I will give the whole program:

```
%LET path=/project/prg;
x ls -t1 &path/%QUOTE(*.log) > &path/temp.dat;
FILENAME loglst "&path/temp.dat";

%MACRO readlog(logfile);
DATA temp;
   LENGTH line $ 200 fname $ 100;
   INFILE "&logfile" MISSOVER PAD;
   INPUT line $ 1-200;
   IF INDEX(line, 'WARNING') | INDEX(line, 'ERROR') |INDEX(line,
   'ALERT');
   fname="&logfile";
   PUT fname=;
RUN;

%IF %QUOTE(&logfile)=%QUOTE(&file2) %THEN %DO;
DATA chklog;
   SET temp;
RUN;
%END;
%ELSE %DO;
PROC APPEND BASE=CHKLOG DATA=temp;
RUN;
%END;
```

```
%MEND;

   %MACRO logfile;
   DATA _NULL_;
      INFILE loglst END=end;
      LENGTH fname $100;
      INPUT fname $;
      IF _N_^=1;
      CALL SYMPUT('file'||LEFT(_n_), fname);
      IF end THEN CALL SYMPUT('tot',_n_);
   RUN; '

   %DO i=2 %TO &tot;
   %readlog(&&file&i);
   %END;
   %MEND;
   %logfile;
   PROC PRINT DATA=chklog;
   RUN;
```

We have to explain several points for this program. In UNIX, it is not necessary to use quotes for UNIX commands, and it uses the slash (/) rather than the backslash (\). When we execute the program, UNIX creates the corresponding log file in the directory. So no matter if there is a file CHKLOG in the directory before execution of the program, CHKLOG.log will be in the directory and in the file temp.dat. (UNIX creates a log file and a lst file in the directory when running a sas program, but DOS does not. The default for DOS output is Windows.) Since we want to exclude CHKLOG.log in our program, we use option t in a LS command; then the file CHKLOG.log will be the first one, and we can delete it. Option 1 in the LS command lists only file names.

Another application using SAS to read a file is to capture title and footnote information in a table shell. In pharmaceutical industry, programmers need to create tables, listings, and graphs according to table shells provided by statisticians. In table shells, there are table numbers, titles, footnotes, and contents. Programmers need to write SAS programs to get contents. However, for titles and footnotes, programmers need to manually type them into programs. An easy way is copy + paste, but this is also time-consuming. Furthermore, the table shell may be updated time by time. Therefore, to keep titles and footnotes accurate, it is better to read them directly from table shell. There are several works on this topic and we will not discuss further.

Other programs

We can see that in the CHKLOG program, we use DOS commands. Actually, DOS commands are easier than the SAS program. So why don't we directly use DOS commands to check log files? The DOS command to search text is FIND. The following are DOS commands. Put them in a batch file CHKLOG.bat. Then every time we want to check log files, we only need to double click the batch file:

```
CD c:\procject\log
FIND "ERROR" *.log>chklog_dos.txt
FIND "WARNING" *.log>>chklog_dos.txt
FIND "ALERT" *.log >>chklog_dos.txt
```

```
FIND "uninitialized" *.log>>chklog_dos.txt
```

The following is output:

```
---------- TEMP1.LOG
ERROR: Expecting page 1, got page -1 instead.
ERROR: Page validation error while reading SASUSER.PROFILE.CATALOG.

---------- TEMP2.LOG
ERROR: Expecting page 1, got page -1 instead.
ERROR: Page validation error while reading SASUSER.PROFILE.CATALOG.
a=5 b=. _ERROR_=1 _N_=1

---------- TEMP1.LOG

---------- TEMP2.LOG

---------- TEMP1.LOG

---------- TEMP2.LOG
```

We know that we can put DOS commands in a SAS file. Suppose the batch file is in directory c:\project\pgm. We can put the following statement in a SAS program:

```
X 'c:\project\pgm\CHKLOG.bat';
```

We can also directly put the above DOS commands in a SAS file. However, as indicated in Li (2005), some DOS commands may not work appropriately when they are used as the X statement, such as FC and FIND commands. Putting COMMAND/C (start a new DOS command processor) before the DOS command can usually resolve the problem. Therefore, we can write the following program and save it as CHKLOG.sas:

```
option noxwait noxsync;
x 'cd c:\project\temp\temp';
x 'command/c find "ERROR" *.log>chklog.txt';
x 'command/c find "WARNING" *.log>>chklog.txt';
x 'command/c find "ALERT" *.log >>chklog.txt';
x 'command/c find "uninitialized" *.log>>chklog.txt';
```

As we know, search is usually case sensitive. We write the above programs because we know cases of these keywords in the log file. If we don't know their cases or want to be cautious, we can use function UPCASE or LOWCASE in a SAS program. However, in a DOS command, we only need to add option /i.

As we have discussed, SAS program CHKLOG has one shortcoming. It may treat some special characters as an end of file symbol, but a DOS command does not treat any special characters as end of file symbols. To verify this point, we can run the following program and save the log file. (Thanks to Michael Snyder for pointing this out.) The log file for the data set t contains the word 'uninitialized', but we cannot use the SAS CHKLOG program to find it (Some computers can, due to different settings.). However, the above program using DOS commands can do it.

```
%LET s=%QUOTE(a > b);
DATA s;
   a=3+b;
RUN;
%PUT _ALL_;
DATA t;
   a=4+c;
RUN;
```

In UNIX, we can write a shell program to fulfill this task. Notice that the command in UNIX corresponding to FIND in DOS is GREP. Suppose we want to search log files in the directory /project/log. Write the following program and save it in a shell program. Then we only need to call this program.

```
Cd /project/log
grep ERROR *.log>CHKLOG.txt
grep WARNING *.log>>CHKLOG.txt
grep ALERT *.log >>CHKLOG.txt
```

Suppose the file is CHKLOG.sh. We can also call it in a SAS program by using the following statement:

```
X CHKLOG.sh;
```

We can also directly put these codes in a SAS program, but we have to use quoting functions.

As we know, many people are accustomed to using the awk facility to search for special patterns, so we can use the following commands:

```
Cd /project/log
awk /ERROR/ *.log>chklog1.txt
awk /WARNING/ *.log>>chklog1.txt
awk /ALERT/ *.log >>chklog1.txt
```

Notice that usually the awk facility is installed in UNIX but not in Windows. If you want to use it in Windows, you have to install it.

Of course, the above methods work not only for SAS log files but also for general text files.

Wrapped text

Notice that the above methods have one shortcoming. Because SAS reads a document line by line, if one phase, such as `'No observations'`, is wrapped, i.e., separated into two lines, then SAS cannot find it. This is true not only for the SAS program but also for a DOS command or a UNIX command. Using Microsoft Word, we can search for wrapped text but not for a DOS command or a UNIX command. However, we can write a SAS program to do this. Now suppose we have a txt file with the following contents:

```
MPRINT(__GSLIST):   select distinct __varname, __varid into:vlist
separated by ' ', :tmp separated by ' ' from __varinfo order by
__varid;
```

Here the sentence is wrapped after "order by", so if we run the following DOS command, the phase 'order by __' cannot be found.

```
Find 'order by __' c:\project\chk\ae_listing.log
```

The following program provides a way to solve this issue:

```
%MACRO find_text(source,except);
FILENAME warp "&source";
DATA temp;
   LENGTH line line1 $ 200 line2 $400;
   INFILE wrap MISSOVER PAD;
   INPUT line $ 1-200;
   RETAIN line1;
   line2=TRIM(line1)||' '||line;
   IF INDEX(line2,"&except")>0 THEN OUTPUT;
   line1=line;
RUN;
PROC PRINT;VAR line2;RUN;
%MEND;
%find_text(c:\project\chk\ae_listing.log,order by __);
```

You can see from the printout that SAS finds the wrapped text.

More than one word

Now we consider the case in which we want to search for two or more words. If you search on a Web site, such as Google and input words such as "text search," Google will return a lot of Web sites that contain both the word "text" and the word "search," but they are not necessarily one word right after the other (contiguous). Can we do this same thing in a SAS program? Yes. It just looks like using a pipe in DOS or UNIX. But this "pipe" is not easy in DOS or UNIX. However, it is easy in SAS because SAS is a program language. The following program finds a file that contains the words "ERROR" and "_N_":

```
OPTIONS NOXWAIT;
%LET path=c:\temp\temp;
x "dir /b &path\*.log > &path\temp.dat";
FILENAME loglst "&path\temp.dat";

%MACRO readfile(logfile,text,out);
DATA temp; LENGTH line $ 200 fname $ 20;
INFILE "&path\&logfile" MISSOVER PAD;
INPUT line $ 1-200;
IF INDEX(line, "&text");
fname="&logfile";
RUN;

%IF &logfile=&file1 %THEN %DO;
DATA &out;
SET temp;
RUN;
%END;
```

```
%ELSE %DO;
PROC APPEND BASE=&out DATA=temp;
RUN;
%END;
%MEND;

%MACRO logfile(text1,text2);
DATA _NULL_;
INFILE loglst END=end;
LENGTH fname $20;
INPUT fname $;
CALL SYMPUT('file'||left(_N_),fname);
IF end THEN CALL SYMPUT('tot',_n_);
RUN;

%DO i=1 %TO &tot;
%readfile(&&file&i,&text1,out1);
%END;

PROC SORT DATA=out1(KEEP=fname) NODUPKEY;
BY fname;
RUN;

DATA _NULL_;
SET out1 END=end;
CALL SYMPUT('file'||LEFT(_N_), fname);
IF end THEN CALL SYMPUT('tot',_N_);
RUN;

%DO i=1 %TO &tot;
%PUT &i;
%readfile(&&file&i,&text2,out2);
%END;
%MEND;
%logfile(ERROR,_N_);
PROC PRINTTO PRINT="&path\files.txt" NEW;
PROC PRINT DATA=out2;
RUN;
PROC PRINTTO;
RUN;
```

Text edit

Look at the file chklog_dos.txt, and you will see that there are many lines for the file names and without messages following them. If we want these lines to be removed, we can use the following program to edit it:

```
DATA s;
INFILE 'c:\temp\temp\chklog_dos.txt';
FILE 'c:\temp\temp\chklog_dos1.txt';
INPUT;
RETAIN file ;
IF SUBSTR(_INFILE_,1,1)='-' THEN file=SUBSTR(_INFILE_,12);
ELSE messa=_INFILE_;
IF messa ^='';
label file='File name' messa='Message';
PUT file @20 messa;
```

```
PROC PRINT l;RUN;

    Obs     File name     Message

      1     TEMP1.LOG     ERROR: Expecting page 1, got page -1 instead.
      2     TEMP1.LOG     ERROR: Page validation error while reading
SASUSER.PROFILE.CATALOG.
      3     TEMP2.LOG     ERROR: Expecting page 1, got page -1 instead.
      4     TEMP2.LOG     ERROR: Page validation error while reading
SASUSER.PROFILE.CATALOG.
      5     TEMP2.LOG     a=5 b=. _ERROR_=1 _N_=1
```

Text count

SAS can also do text count. Suppose we want to know how many times the text "SAS" appears. We can use SAS to do the count. First, there are two kinds of count. How many substring "SAS" are in the word "SASAS"? 1 or 2? Below we have a program that counts it as 1, but it is easy to modify this so that you can count it as 2. Suppose that each line has at most 10 "SAS".

```
DATA count;
   LENGTH a $200;
   INFILE 'c:\temp\temp\count.txt' EOF=g;
   INPUT a;
   c=a;
   DO i=1 TO 10;
   b= INDEX(c,'SAS');
   IF b=0 THEN LEAVE;
   k+1;
   c=SUBSTR(c,b+3);
   END;
   G:OUTPUT;
PROC PRINT;VAR k;RUN;
```

Page x of y

Replacing or inserting text is pretty easy for both manually replacing and program replacing. When using a SAS program to do the replacement, the replacement text should not be longer than the text to be replaced. Otherwise, there may be a linesize problem. However, the most common and difficult replacing is page number replacing. There are several situations:

- There is a page number "x", and we want to change it to "x of y" or "x/y" or "Page x of y", where y is the number of total pages.
- There is no page number "x", and we want to insert it. Following are three cases:
  - We don't want to change the page break and structure of the file. There is space to insert a page number.
  - We don't want to change the page break. We add one or two lines in each page, where one line is for page number.
  - We want to keep the same pagesize, but the page break may change.

When using a SAS program to do this, we may have the following things to do:

- Set the PAGESIZE option.
- Set NUMBER option (print page number, default) and PAGENO=1 option.
- Count the number of pages.
- Count the maximum number of lines on each page.
- Remove the original page break.
- Insert a new page break and a page number.

Let's create a file that has no page number but has page breaks. Notice that for a plain text file, the page break (form feed) symbol is '0c'x.

```
DATA ss;
   DO i=1 TO 200;
   OUTPUT;
   END;
RUN;
OPTIONS NONUMBER NODATE PAGESIZE=50 NOCENTER LINESIZE=64;
TITLE;
PROC PRINTTO FILE='c:\temp\temp\ss.txt' NEW;
PROC PRINT;RUN;
PROC PRINTTO;RUN;
```

The following is the part of the file at the page break. Notice that there is no page number:

```
                              47    47
                              48    48
♀                             Obs    i

                              49    49
                              50    50
                              51    51
```

Now we want first to insert a page number at the break line so that we can keep the structure and page breaks of the file. Run the following program:

```
DATA pp;
   INFILE 'c:\temp\temp\ss.txt' LENGTH=len TRUNCOVER;
   FILE 'c:\temp\temp\ss1.txt';
   LENGTH record $200;
   INPUT   record $VARYING200. len;
   IF _N_=1 OR SUBSTR(record,1,1)='0c'x THEN DO;
      len=len+20;
      page+1;
      record=SUBSTR(record,1,44)||'Page'||PUT(page,6.);
   END;
   PUT   record $VARYING200. len;
RUN;
```

The following is part of the file:

```
                    47    47
                    48    48
♀                   Obs     i        Page      2

                    49    49
                    50    50
```

Next, we want to add two more lines for a page number, but keep the PAGESIZE setting.

```
DATA _NULL_;
   SET SASHELP.VOPTION;
   IF optname='PAGESIZE' THEN CALL SYMPUT('pgs',setting);
RUN;

DATA pp;
   INFILE 'c:\temp\temp\ss.txt' LENGTH=len TRUNCOVER;
   FILE 'c:\temp\temp\ss2.txt';
   LENGTH record1 $200;
   INPUT   record $VARYING200. len;
   IF SUBSTR(record,1,1)='0c'x THEN record=SUBSTR(record,2);
   IF _N_=1 THEN DO;
      len=10;
      page+1;
      record1=PUT(page,10.);
      PUT   record1 $VARYING200. len;
      record1=' ';
      PUT   record1 $VARYING200. len;
   END;
   IF MOD(_N_+2*page,&pgs)=0 THEN DO;
      len=50;
      page+1;
      record1='0c'x||put(page,10.);
      PUT   record1 $VARYING200. len;
      record1=' ';
      PUT   record1 $VARYING200. len;
   END;
   PUT   record $VARYING200. len;
RUN;
```

The following is part of the file at a page break:

```
                    44    44
                    45    45
♀         2


                    46    46
                    47    47
                    48    48
                   Obs     i

                    49    49
                    50    50
```

Finally, we want to count the total number of pages. In TS-548 and TS-549, there is a way to count the total number of pages, but it is only for SAS output. The point is, for SAS output, the page number is accumulating. If an output file has 5 pages starting from 1, then the next output file will begin from page number 6. So you can create a temporary output after the original output file and get the starting page number and minus 1. It is not necessary to do so. The following program finds the total number of pages for a file either created by SAS or not created by SAS:

```
DATA _NULL_;
   INFILE 'c:\temp\temp\ss.txt' TRUNCOVER EOF=g;
   INPUT   record $1-200;
   IF _N_=1 OR SUBSTR(record,1,1)='0c'x THEN cnt+1;
   g: CALL SYMPUT('tot', cnt);
RUN;
DATA _NULL_;
   INFILE 'c:\temp\temp\ss.txt' LENGTH=len TRUNCOVER;
   INPUT  record $VARYING200. len;
   FILE 'c:\temp\temp\ss3.txt';
   IF _N_=1 OR SUBSTR(record,1,1)='0c'x THEN DO;
      page+1;
      len=50;
      record=SUBSTR(record,1,40)||PUT(page,6.)||'/'||LEFT(&tot);
   END;
   PUT  record $VARYING200. len;
RUN;
```

```
                           47    47
                           48    48
♀                          Obs      i          2/5

                           49    49
                           50    50
```

In the above program, we count the total number of pages. If there is already a page number in the file, we can also catch it by repeatedly assigning the page number to a macro variable, as the following code shows. We suppose that page number is the last one in the line.

```
IF _N_=1 OR SUBSTR(record,1,1)='0c'x THEN DO;
   cnt=SCAN(record,-1);
   CALL SYMPUT('tot', cnt);
END;
```

Search in RTF files

Now we will briefly talk about RTF files. RTF files and HTML files consist of text, tags (HTML files), and control words (RTF files). We can use Notepad to open and read them. Using the SAS program to read them is like using Notepad to read them. Notice that we can use FIND (a DOS command) and GREP (a UNIX command) to search text in RTF files and HTML files. Suppose in a directory there are some RTF files. Among them, some are for the ITT population, and some are for the randomized population. The following program checks to see if an RTF file contains the word "ITT":

```
%MACRO find_text(source,except);
FILENAME wrap "&source";
DATA temp;
   LENGTH line line1 $ 200 line2 $400;
   INFILE wrap MISSOVER PAD;
   INPUT line $ 1-200;
   RETAIN line1;
   line2=TRIM(line1)||' '||line;
   IF INDEX(line2,"&except")>0 THEN OUTPUT;
   line1=line;
RUN;
PROC PRINT;VAR line2;RUN;
%MEND;
%find_text(c:\project\chk\adid3.RTF,ITT);
```

```
1     \s22 Table(8.1.2.1)7 - Mean change from baseline in HbA1c at endpoint (LOCF)
\par\s0 \s22 ITT population - Patients without Regular insulin \par\s0
 2     \s22 ITT population - Patients without Regular insulin \par\s0 }
```

Now we will look at an HTML file to see if it contains word "test."

```
%find_text(c:\sas\gra.HTML,test);
```

```
Obs    line2

  1      this is a test
  2     this is a test <!DOCTYPE HTML PUBLIC "-//W3C//DTD HTML 3.2 Final//EN">
  3     <TD ALIGN=CENTER>Obs</TD> <TD ALIGN=CENTER>test1</TD>
  4     <TD ALIGN=CENTER>test1</TD> <TD ALIGN=CENTER>test2</TD>
  5     <TD ALIGN=CENTER>test2</TD> </TR>
  6     </HTML> this is a test
  7     this is a test <!DOCTYPE HTML PUBLIC "-//W3C//DTD HTML 3.2 Final//EN">
  8     <TR> <TD ALIGN=LEFT>test1<br>
  9     <TD ALIGN=LEFT>test1<br> test2</TD>
 10     test2</TD> <TD ALIGN=RIGHT>2<br>
```

You can see that for RTF files and HTML files, search cannot differentiate text and control words (or tag in HTML). However, for RTF files, control words follow a backslash, and texts follow a blank. This may be helpful to know. Sometimes a string in an RTF file may be separated by control words when the file is viewed in Notepad.

Page number in RTF

Although we can use SAS to edit RTF files, it is not a good idea for the following reasons:

- Editing an RTF file using Microsoft Word is easy, but it is complicated when viewing in Notepad.
- Two RTF files that look the same in Microsoft Word may have different RTF code. So it is very possible that a SAS program works for one RTF file but not

for another RTF file. For example, the font Symbol can be defined as f1 or f3. So most likely, if you write a program to edit an RTF file, you have to open it using Notepad and find out where to modify it.

- Microsoft Office is so powerful. You can insert a page number at the left, right, center, inside and outside, header or footer. For page numbers, you can also use format – x – and page x of y (Office 2003), although these two can only be at the center, header, or footer.
- In SAS ODS RTF output, for SAS v9, we can use {THISPAGE}, {LASTPAGE} and {PAGEOF} to insert page numbers using different styles. We can also do this in SAS v8 although the code is a little bit complicated.

In the following we use a page number as an example to show how to edit RTF files using a SAS program. We use the following program to create an RTF file:

```
DATA ss;
DO i=1 TO 200;
OUTPUT;
END;
RUN;
ODS RTF FILE='c:\temp\temp.RTF';
OPTION NODATE;
PROC REPORT NOWD;
DEFINE i/DISPLAY;
RUN;
ODS RTF CLOSE;
```

The following is the top of a page:

If we open the RTF file with Notepad, we can see the following contents:

\b\sb0\sa0\qr\f1\fs20\cf1{{\field{*\fldinst { PAGE }}}}

Suppose the file has 5 pages. In order to change the number to 1/5, we have to change the code to the following:

\b\sb0\sa0\qr\f1\fs20\cf1{{\field{*\fldinst { PAGE }}}/5}

If we don't know how many pages the file has, we have to find out. There is no page break symbol. Hence, we can find the number of pages manually. When we open the file, we can see that it has 5 pages. Then we run the following program:

```
DATA pp;
    INFILE 'c:\temp\temp.RTF' TRUNCOVER;
    FILE 'c:\temp\temp1.RTF';
```

```
    INPUT    record $1-200;
    record=TRANWRD(record,'PAGE }}}', 'PAGE }}}/5');
    PUT record;
RUN;
```

The following is the page number part of the new file:

1/5

The SAS System

Of course, this is not a good idea. If we open the file to find the number of pages, why don't we open the file with Notepad and insert "/5"? Notice that number of total pages is denoted as NUMPAGES in an RTF file, so we can also use the following program. Then we don't have to count the number of pages manually:

```
DATA pp;
INFILE 'c:\temp\temp.RTF' TRUNCOVER;
FILE 'c:\temp\temp2.RTF';
INPUT  record $1-200;
record=TRANWRD(record,'PAGE }}}', 'PAGE }}}/{\field{\*\fldinst
{NUMPAGES }}}');
PUT record;
RUN;
```

1/5

The SAS System

In other words, I substitute the second line of text below for the first line of text below:

{\field{*\fldinst {\b\cf1 PAGE }}}

{\field{*\fldinst {\b\cf1 PAGE }}}/{\field{*\fldinst {NUMPAGES }}}

But when I tried to apply this code to another RTF file, it did not work. I opened the RTF file, and there was no such line. Actually, I have to substitute the second line of text below for the first line of text:

{\field{*\fldinst {\b\cf1 PAGE }}{\fldrslt {\b\cf1\lang1024\langfe1024\noproof 2}}}

{\field{*\fldinst {\b\cf1 PAGE }}{\fldrslt {\b\cf1\lang1024\langfe1024\noproof 2}}}
/{\field{*\fldinst {NUMPAGES }}}

You can see that the above code is not so smooth, and we have to adjust it for different RTF files. There is also another keyword, SECTIONPAGES, in RTF files. These keywords give you more choices to modify RTF files.

If you are using v8, using ODS to output and want to use page of, you may remember the following code:

```
.j=r "{Page }{\field{\*\fldinst {\b
PAGE }}}\~{\b\ of}\~{\field{\*\fldinst {\b\ NUMPAGES }}}";);
```

Zhang (2005) and Zhang and Li (2006) did some work gluing tables using SAS and VBS programs. You can see that using a SAS program with RTF is not so smooth, but it works. For different RTF files, maybe you need to modify their programs.

References

"Check the log. "
http://sastricks.wikidot.com/base:checklog

Chung, Chang and Toby Dunn. (2005) "Page X of Y with Proc Report." *Proceedings of the Pharmaceutical SAS Users Group Conference (PharmaSUG 2005)*, Paper CC31, Cary, NC: SAS Institute Inc.
http://www.lexjansen.com/pharmasug/2005/coderscorner/cc31.pdf

Felty, Kelly and Diane Nicholson. (1999) "The Power of PAGEOF (A Valuable Page Numbering Macro)." *Proceedings of the Twenty-fourth Annual SAS Users Group International Conference*, Paper 081-24, Cary, NC: SAS Institute Inc.
http://www2.sas.com/proceedings/sugi24/Coders/p081-24.pdf

Huang, Daniel, and Lois Lynn. (2008) "Read Titles and Footnotes from a Table Shell into a SAS Dataset." *Proceedings of the Pharmaceutical SAS Users Group Conference (PharmaSUG 2008)*, PaperPO07, Cary, NC: SAS Institute Inc.
http://www.lexjansen.com/pharmasug/2008/po/po07.pdf

Kirkpatrick, John. "How can I get Page <x> of <y> into my document? "
http://www.isc-ltd.co.uk/faqs/rtf/rtf_faq0003.htm

Li, Na (2005) "Applications for Running DOS Commands within SAS." *Proceedings of the Twenty-eighth Annual SAS Users Group International Conference*, Paper PO13, Cary, NC: SAS Institute Inc.
http://www.lexjansen.com/pharmasug/2005/posters/po13.pdf

Shannon, David, (2005) "To ODS RTF and Beyond, Third Edition." *Proceedings of the Pharmaceutical Users Software Exchange (PhUSE 2005)*, Paper TS01, Cary, NC: SAS Institute Inc.
http://www.lexjansen.com/phuse/2005/ts/ts01.pdf

Smoak, Carey G. (2002) "A Utility Program for Checking SAS® Log Files. " *Proceedings of the Twenty-fourth Annual SAS Users Group International Conference*, Paper 096-27, Cary, NC: SAS Institute Inc.
http://www2.sas.com/proceedings/sugi27/p096-27.pdf

"TS-548 Page 1 of n: Customizing Page Numbers."
http://support.sas.com/techsup/technote/ts548.html

"TS-549 Is there a way to return the last page number generated by a SAS procedure? "
http://support.sas.com/techsup/technote/ts549.html

Worley, Jim. (2007). "Combining RTFs While Retaining Each Original Document's Page Numbering." *Proceedings of the Pharmaceutical SAS Users Group Conference (PharmaSUG 2007)*, Paper CC12, Cary, NC: SAS Institute Inc. *Proceedings of the Pharmaceutical SAS Users Group Conference (PharmaSUG 2005)*, Paper AD16, Cary, NC: SAS Institute Inc.
http://www.lexjansen.com/pharmasug/2007/cc/cc21.pdf

Zhang, Lei (2005) "Constructing Stack Tables With Proc Report and ODS RTF." *Proceedings of the Pharmaceutical SAS Users Group Conference (PharmaSUG 2005)*, Paper AD16, Cary, NC: SAS Institute Inc.
http://www.lexjansen.com/pharmasug/2005/applicationsdevelopment/ad16.pdf

Zhang, Lei, and George Li. (2006) "Constructing Stack Tables with Magic %GluePlus (Another User-Defined Macro for Creating Stack Tables)." *Proceedings of the Thirty-first Annual SAS Users Group International Conference*, Paper 089-31, Cary, NC: SAS Institute Inc.
http://www2.sas.com/proceedings/sugi31/089-31.pdf

RTF Output and Special Characters

Introduction

Note: This paper is based on my experience. Therefore, some conclusions may be not applicable to others due to factors such as computer settings and language settings. Also, when we say finding hex value or Unicode in Microsoft Word, we mean version 2003. Version 2000 does not have this function.

RTF output is probably the most commonly used output for SAS programmers. However, many people have difficulty inserting special characters such as †, ‡, ±, ½, ≤, and ≥ as well as Greek symbols. This paper will provide several methods to insert special characters. I suppose you already know about escapechar. Escapechar works for PDF, RTF, and HTML ODS output. It tells SAS that the following symbol has special meaning.

How many ways are there to insert a dagger into an ODS RTF output?

Often we need to use special characters in an RTF file, and there are many ways to create special characters to do this. Where do we use these special characters? Usually the following places need special characters: title, footnote, data value, variable label (column header), and LINE statement in PROC REPORT. The following program shows that we can use different methods to insert special characters in an ODS RTF output. We use a dagger (†) and a superscript 2 (^{2}) as examples. Notice the relationship between numbers in the program as follows:

86 (hex) =134 (decimal) = 8*16+6
B2 (hex) = 178 (decimal)=11*16+2
2020 (hex) =8224 (decimal) = 2*4096+2*16
8224 + 57312 = 65536 = 16**4
178 + 65358 = 65536

```
ODS ESCAPECHAR='^';
%LET x1=%BQUOTE(^R/RTF"\'86");
%LET y1=%BQUOTE(^R/RTF"\'b2");
%LET x2=%BQUOTE(^R/RTF"\u8224*");
%LET y2=%BQUOTE(^R/RTF"\u178*");
%LET x3=%BQUOTE(^R/RTF"\u-57312*");
%LET y3=%BQUOTE(^R/RTF"\u-65358*");
%LET x4=%NRSTR({\u8224*});
%let y4=%NRSTR({\u178*});
TITLE1 '86'x 'first title1 hex value';
TITLE2 '† second title copy character';
TITLE3 '^{dagger} third title symbol name';
TITLE4 "&x1 fourth title rtf format";
TITLE5 "&x2 fifth title Unicode";
TITLE6 "&x3 sixth title Unicode (negative)";

DATA s;
LENGTH a $30 c $60 d $20;
b=2;e=5;
a='86'x||'Text';
   c='a'||'b2'x||'=b'||'b2'x||'+c'||'b2'x;
```

```
      d='hex value';output;
a=BYTE(134)||'Text';
   c='a'||BYTE(178)||'=b'||BYTE(178)||'+c'||BYTE(178);
      d='BYTE function';OUTPUT;
a='† Text';
   c='a²=b²+c²';
      d='copy character';OUTPUT;
a='^{dagger} Text';
   c='';
      d='symbol name';OUTPUT;
a="&x1 Text";
   c="a&y1=b&y1+c&y1";
      d='RTF format';OUTPUT;
a=INPUT('86',$hex2.)||" Text";
   c="a"||INPUT('b2',$HEX2.)||"=b "||INPUT('b2',$HEX2.)||"+c
"||input('b2',$HEX2.);
      d='input function';OUTPUT;
a=INPUT('2020'x,$UCS2l.)||" Text";
   c="a"||INPUT('00b2'x,$ucs2b.)||"=b "||INPUT('00b2'x,$UCS2b.)||"+c
"||INPUT('00b2'x,$UCS2b.);
      d='big-endian';OUTPUT;
a=INPUT('2020'x,$UCS2l.)||" Text";
   c="a"||INPUT('b200'x,$ucs2l.)||"=b "||INPUT('b200'x,$UCS2l.)||"+c
"||INPUT('b200'x,$UCS2l.);
      d='little-endian';OUTPUT;

a="&x2 Text ";
   c="a&y2=b&y2+c&y2";
      d='unicode ';OUTPUT;
a="&x3 Text ";
   c="a&y3=b&y3+c&y3";
      d='unicode (negative)';OUTPUT;
a="&x4  ";
   c="&y4";
      d='unicode direct';OUTPUT;
RUN;
ODS RTF FILE='c:\rtf\tbl1.rtf';
PROC REPORT DATA=s NOWD split='|';
COLUMN a b c d e;
DEFINE a/DISPLAY '† copy character';
DEFINE b/DISPLAY '^{dagger} symbol name';
DEFINE c/DISPLAY "&x1 RTF format";
DEFINE d/DISPLAY "&x2  unicode ";
DEFINE e/DISPLAY "&x3 unicode (negative)";
COMPUTE AFTER;
x=BYTE(134);
y=INPUT('86',$HEX2.);
z=INPUT('2020'x,$UCS2B.);
ww=INPUT('2020'x,$UCS2L.);
LINE '86'x 'first line hex value';
LINE '† second line copy character';
LINE '^{dagger} third line symbol name';
LINE x $1. " fourth line BYTE function";
LINE y $1. " fifth line INPUT function";
LINE z $1. " sixth line big-endian";
LINE ww $1. " seventh line little-endian";
ENDCOMP;
```

```
RUN;
ODS RTF CLOSE;
```

The following is output:

†first title1 hex value
† second title copy character
† third title symbol name
† fourth title rtf format
† fifth title Unicode
† sixth title Unicode (negative)

† copy character	† symbol name	† RTF format	† unicode	† unicode (negative)
†Text	2	$a^2=b^2+c^2$	hex value	5
†Text	2	$a^2=b^2+c^2$	BYTE function	5
† Text	2	$a^2=b^2+c^2$	copy character	5
† Text	2		symbol name	5
† Text	2	$a^2=b^2+c^2$	RTF format	5
† Text	2	$a^2 =b^2 +c^2$	input function	5
† Text	2	$a^2=b^2+c^2$	big-endian	5
† Text	2	$a^2=b^2+c^2$	little-endian	5
† Text	2	$a^2=b^2+c^2$	unicode	5
† Text	2	$a^2=b^2+c^2$	unicode (negative)	5
†	2	^{2}	unicode direct	5

†first line hex value
† second line copy character
† third line symbol name
† fourth line BYTE function
† fifth line INPUT function
† sixth line big-endian
† seventh line little-endian

You can see that there are many ways to insert a dagger symbol. In the following, we explain these methods as well as a macro using FILE+PUT.

Use hex value for special characters

As we said in [IX], there are 256 characters. They are catalyzed as regular characters, special characters, and unprintable characters. Suppose we are using the Times New Roman font. You may be interested in the following special characters:

†, ‡, ™, §, ©, ®, £, ¢, ¥, ^{1}, ^{2}, ^{3}, ¼, ½, µ, ±, ÷

You cannot directly type them in, but you can use their hex values, as the above program shows. You can find their hex values from Microsoft Word -> Insert -> Symbol -> Times New Roman. On the right lower corner, you can choose ASCII (hex) and ASCII (decimal). They correspond to its hex value and decimal value. For example, find the dagger and click on it. If you choose ASCII(hex), the Character code shows 0086. Here 86 is the hex value of the dagger. If you choose ASCII(decimal), the Character code shows 134 which is the decimal value of the dagger.

The following table gives you a summary. We will talk about Unicode later.

Table 1. Comparison of ways to insert special characters into ODS RTF
P1: Use escapechar? P2: HTML /PDF too?

	example	restriction	P1	P2
Hex value	'86'x	Not work for line statement in PROC REPORT for SAS V8	n	y
BYTE function	BYTE(134)	Cannot be in title and footnote statements	n	y
INPUT function	INPUT ('86',$HEX2.)	Cannot be in title and footnote statements	n	y
Character copy	†	That in code may look different from SAS output.	n	y
Hex value with RTF format	^R/RTF"\'86"	Not for line statement in PROC REPORT.	y	n
Decimal value with RTF format for unicode	^R/RTF"\u8224*	Not for line statement in PROC REPORT.	y	n
hex value with $UCS2B informat for Unicode	INPUT('2020'x, $UCS2B.)	Cannot be in title and footnote statements	n	y
Unicode directly input	%NRSTR({\u8224*})	Cannot combine with other characters	n	n
Symbol name	^{dagger}	Only for dagger, sigma etc.	y	y

In the above program, in some places we used functions such as BYTE or INPUT. They cannot be used in titles, footnotes, or headers, but we can use them in variable values. To use functions in LINE statements of PROC REPORT, we have to assign them to a variable first.

Notice that 'character copy' means that you copy the special character to your program. You have three ways to do this.

- Copy from a Word document (Use Insert->Symbol to find it, and then use copy+paste).
- Use the Character Map.
- Copy from output created from your SAS program such as function BYTE(). When copying from SAS output, some characters may seem strange in output because the default font for output is SAS Monospace. For example, a dagger in SAS Monospace is ┐, but it is OK to copy it to your program. The default font for the program is Courier New.

Symbol characters

There are several characters that are not in a specified font, say Times New Roman, such as the following:

Greek characters (only one character μ is in Times New Roman), ≤, ≥, ∞, ≡, and ≠.

These characters are used very often, especially ≤ and ≥. They are not in the Times New Roman font, but they are in the font Symbol. You can go to Microsoft Word -> Insert -> Symbol or Character Map -> Symbol to find them. Notice that the Symbol font does not have a dagger, a double dagger, or English characters.

Therefore, we can "borrow" them from the Symbol font. In other words, we can ask rtf file to display them using the Symbol font in a specified location. In Microsoft Word, we can highlight any text and change its font. Now we want to do this in the SAS program.

To do this, we have to tell SAS the beginning and the ending where we need to borrow the Symbol font. In ODS, the beginning is specified by `|S={font_face=symbol}`, and the ending by `|S={}`, `(escapechar='|')`. In the following program, we use four ways to borrow the Symbol font: hex value, BYTE function, character insert, and PUT function. Notice that the hex value B3 equals the decimal value 179, which corresponds to `³ (superscript 3)` in the Courier New font (the default SAS editor font) and to ≥ in the Symbol font.

We can use them in variable values as well as in TITLE, FOOTNOTE, LABEL, and LINE statement in PROC REPORT. Notice that we can use other fonts in addition to the Symbol font. In the following program, we use the Symbol font and the Wingding font:

```
DATA s;
INPUT id grade;
LENGTH grade1-grade4 $60;
IF grade<90 then GRADE1='<90';
ELSE DO;
grade1='|S={FONT_FACE=SYMBOL}'||'B3'x||'90 |S={}';
grade2='|S={FONT_FACE=SYMBOL}'||BYTE(179)||'90 |S={}';
grade3='|S={FONT_FACE=SYMBOL}³90 |S={}';
grade4='|S={FONT_FACE=SYMBOL}'||INPUT('B3', $HEX2.)||'90 |S={}';
END;
CARDS;
1 90
2 86
3 97
;
RUN;
TITLE 'Listing of students with grade ' '|S={font_face=symbol}' 'B3'x
'90 |S={}'
      '|S={font_face=wingdings} Œ |S={}' ;
TITLE2 FONT="Times New Roman" "Listing of students with grade  "
```

```
    FONT="Symbol"      'B3'x
    FONT="Times New Roman" " 90 " FONT="wingdings" '8d'x font="Times
New Roman";

ODS ESCAPECHAR='|';
ODS RTF FILE='c:\rtf\tbl2.rtf';
PROC REPORT NOWD;
COLUMN id grade grade1 grade2 grade3 grade4;
*DEFINE grade1/DISPLAY '|S={font_face=symbol}³90 |S={}';
compute after;
line '|S={font_face=wingdings} Œ |S={}' 'Note1';
line '|S={font_face=wingdings}' '8d'x ' |S={}' 'Note2';
endcomp;
RUN;
ODS RTF CLOSE;
```

Listing of students with grade ≥90 ❶

Listing of students with grade ≥ 90 ❷

id	grade	grade1	grade2	grade3	grade4
1	90	≥90	≥90	≥90	≥ 90
2	86	<90			
3	97	≥90	≥90	≥90	≥ 90
		❶·Note1 ❷·Note2			

How does RTF work?

RTF is a document format. Similar to an HTML file, it consists of elements that you can code, although it is complicated. Let us run the following program first:

```
DATA s;
name="abc"; test=88;OUTPUT;
name="ab"; test=90; OUTPUT;
TITLE;
OPTION NOCENTER NONUMBER NODATE;
ODS RTF FILE='c:\rtf\tbl3.rtf';
PROC REPORT NOWD;
RUN;
ODS RTF CLOSE;
```

Go to the directory c:\rtf and double click the file tbl3.rtf. The file will open in Microsoft Word, as follows:

name	test
abc	88
ab	90

Now use Notepad instead of Microsoft Word to open the file (right click File -> Open With -> Notepad). You will see the following contents:

```
{\rtf1\ansi\ansicpg1252\uc1\deff0\deflang1031\deflangfe1031
{\fonttbl
{\f1\froman\fprq2\fcharset0 Times New Roman;}
}{\colortbl;
\red0\green0\blue0;
\red0\green0\blue255;
\red0\green255\blue255;
......
```

The {\rtf1 at the beginning of the file means the start of an rtf file, Version 1. \ansi means the document is in the ANSI character set. {\f1\froman\fprq2\fcharset0 Times New Roman;} defines font, and \colortbl defines a color table. The book *RTF pocket guide* and online documents are good references for readers interested in detailed information. But one important point is the following:

Each rtf file begins with {\rtf1 and ends with }.

Notice that different codes (open with Notepad) may create the same rtf file (open with Microsoft Word). In the above example, if we remove color definition, there is no affection, because we never use it.

Write a macro (FILE + PUT) to create RTF files

In an RTF file, we can define nicknames for different fonts. As you have seen, in the above program, the nickname for the Times New Roman font is f1. Similarly, we can define, for example, f0=Times New Roman, f1=Symbol, and f3=Courier New. Then every time we want to invoke a specified font, we can just specify its nickname. It looks like it is hard to define a nickname for fonts in a style template. In other words, it is hard to define nicknames for fonts in ODS.

As we have seen, we can create an RTF file in Microsoft Word, but actually the created file is a coded file. However, we can directly create a coded RTF file using FILE + PUT in SAS programming. Code using FILE + PUT to create RTF output is tedious, but we can write a macro. It is tedious too. However after the macro is defined, it is easy to call the macro. Defining nicknames for some fonts in a FILE+PUT macro is easy. Then it is easy to specify a font that we want to use.

Using FILE + PUT to create an RTF file has its own advantages, not just to define nicknames for different fonts. For example, in ODS, it is hard to glue two tables together, up and down, but it is not so hard using the FILE+PUT technique. Some companies have their own macros for their output, so all outputs will follow their standard.

The following is a simplified example to show how to create an RTF file that contains a table:

```
DATA _NULL_;
FILE "c:\rtf\tbl4.rtf" NEW;
PUT "{\rtf1\ansi
\deff0\deflang1033{\fonttbl{\f0\froman Times New
Roman;} {\f1\froman\fcharset2\fprq2 Symbol;}}";
RUN;
DATA _NULL_;
FILE "c:\rtf\tbl4.rtf" MOD;
PUT '\trowd \trgraph180\cellx1440\cellx2880
\pard\intbl{name}\cell\pard{test}\cell\row';
PUT '\trowd \trgraph180\cellx1440\cellx2880
\pard\intbl{abc}\cell\pard{88}\cell\row';
PUT '\trowd \trgraph180\cellx1440\cellx2880
\pard\intbl{ab}\cell\pard{90}\cell\row';
DATA _NULL_;
FILE "c:\rtf\tbl4.rtf" mod;
PUT '}';
RUN;
```

name	test
abc	88
ab	90

You can see that tbl4.rtf is almost the same as the tbl3.rtf. The difference is that tbl3.rtf is fancier than tbl4.rtf. We did not set the margins, color, adjustment, etc.

Now we will try to write a macro to accomplish this task.

```
%MACRO rtf(data=, output=,col_no=,column=,obs=);
DATA _NULL_;
FILE "&output" ;
PUT "{\rtf1\ansi
\deff0\deflang1033{\fonttbl{\f0\froman Times New Roman;}
{\f1\froman\fcharset2\fprq2 Symbol;}}";
RUN;

DATA _NULL_;
SET &data;
FILE "&output" MOD;
IF _N_=1 THEN DO;
PUT '\trowd \trgraph180';
%DO i=1 %TO &col_no;
%LET tem&i=%SCAN(&column,&i,' ');
%LET wid&i=%EVAL(1440*&i);
PUT "\cellx&&wid&i";
```

```
%END;
PUT "\trowd \trgraph180";
%DO i=1 %TO &col_no;
PUT "\cellx&&wid&i";
%END;
PUT "\pard\intbl{&tem1}\cell";
%DO i=2 %TO &col_no;
PUT "\pard{&&tem&i}\cell";
%END;
PUT "\row";
END;
RUN;

%DO j=1 %TO &obs;
DATA _NULL_;
SET &data;
IF _N_=&j THEN DO;
%DO i=1 %TO &col_no;
CALL SYMPUT("var&i",&&tem&i);
%END;
END;
RUN;
%PUT _USER_;

DATA _NULL_;
SET &data;
FILE "&output" MOD;
IF _N_=1 THEN DO;
PUT "\trowd \trgraph180";
%DO i=1 %TO &col_no;
PUT "\cellx&&wid&i";
%END;
PUT "\pard\intbl{&var1}\cell";
%DO i=2 %TO &col_no;
PUT "\pard{&&var&i}\cell";
%END;
PUT "\row";
END;
RUN;
%END;

DATA _NULL_;
FILE "&output" MOD;
PUT '}';
RUN;
%PUT _USER_;
%MEND;

DATA s;
INPUT a $ b;
CARDS;
abc 88
ab 90
;
%rtf(data=s,output=c:\rtf\tbl5.rtf,col_no=2,column=a b,obs=2);
```

a	b
abc	88
ab	90

Of course, this program is not very simple, but it shows you how this method works. You can write your own macro to create fancy output, add a title, a footnote, align elements, use color, etc.

As the program shows, we first define f0 as a nickname for Times New Roman font and f1 for the Symbol font. Then, whenever we want to use the Symbol font, we only need to specify its nickname, and after that, we can go back to the regular font. See the following example and output:

```
DATA s;
a='\f1 abc\f0';b=88;OUTPUT;
a='\f1 ab\f0';b=90; OUTPUT;
RUN;
%rtf(data=s,output=c:\rtf\tbl6.rtf,col_no=2,column=a b,obs=2);
```

a	b
αβχ	88
αβ	90

For a FILE+PUT macro, it is easy to insert Unicode. See the following example:

```
DATA s;
LENGTH a $40;
a='\u8224* abc';b=88;OUTPUT;
a='\f1 abc\f0';b=90; OUTPUT;
a='\u945*\u946*\u947';OUTPUT;
%rtf(data=s,output=c:\rtf\tbl7.rtf,col_no=2,column=a b,obs=3);
```

a	b
† abc	88
αβχ	90
αβγ	90

Notice that the order of Greek characters in the Symbol font is different from that in Unicode.

Unicode characters

Up till now we have used Unicode several times. Unicode works for both ODS and a FILE+PUT macro. It is easier for a FILE+PUT macro than for ODS. Now we will talk about it. The Symbol font has a limited number of characters. It has only ACII code. Therefore, including unprintable characters, there are a total of 256=16**2 characters.

However, Unicode opens a wild door for us. The range for Unicode is from 0 to 65,535 (16**4 in total). You can even input different languages, such as Chinese. See the following example:

```
DATA s;
LENGTH company $40;
company='\u22823* \u22887';revenue=25830;OUTPUT;
company='abc';revenue=34180; OUTPUT;
company='\u945*\u946*\u947';revenue=33240;OUTPUT;
RUN;
%rtf(data=s,output=c:\rtf\tbl8.rtf,col_no=2,column=company
revenue,obs=3);
```

company	revenue
大 奧	25830
abc	34180
αβγ	33240

Notice the difference between borrowing the Symbol font and using Unicode.

- When borrowing from the Symbol font, the characters use the Symbol font. You can highlight them and change the font to, say, Times New Roman. But for Unicode, these characters are using the Times New Roman font.

The following is a summary for Unicode. Suppose that the font of the file is Times New Roman, the font that people generally use:

- If the character has ASCII code 255 (hex value ff) or under, you can use a hex value, such as \'86.
- When the character has ASCII code 255 (hex value ff) or under, and it is not between 80 – 9f (hex value), ASCII code and Unicode are the same.
- You can find hex value and decimal value for ASCII and hex value for Unicode in Microsoft Word (Insert -> Symbol-> Times New Roman).
- You can also find hex value for Unicode in Character Map (Start ->All Programs -> Accessories -> System Tools -> Character Map, and select). The 4-digit Unicode displays at the bottom left corner of the window after the "U+". For example, if you click dagger, it will show "U+2020", so 2020 is Unicode of the dagger in hex value.
- We can use the informat $UCS2B. to convert hex value to character for Unicode, as the first program shows.
- Both methods (Microsoft Word -> Insert and Character Map) show only the hex value of Unicode. We can also use a RTF format to insert a character using decimal value. You have to convert hex value to a decimal value by yourself. The decimal value of Unicode for a dagger is 2*4096+2*16=8224.
- Many special characters can be displayed using the RTF format, but not the $UCS2B format.

- You can use a negative number in Unicode. If two numbers with different signs have a sum of absolute values equal to 65536, they correspond to the same character. For example, 8224 and -57312 correspond to the same character: dagger.
- If the Unicode of a character is over 65535 (16**4-1), we cannot express it in RTF.
- Both Microsoft Insert and Character Map do not provide a complete list of Unicode. There are many Web sites to find Unicode, such as the following:

http://www.alanwood.net/unicode/index.html
http://www.unicode.org/

- Although we can find Unicode using the above methods and Web sites, if you use Unicode often, it is better to create a Unicode table for yourself, the same as we do for the ASCII table [IX]. The following code shows you how to do this. It also gives a comparison between $USC2B informat and RTF format of a hex value.

```
ODS ESCAPECHAR='^';
%LET HEX=0 1 2 3 4 5 6 7 8 9 a b c d e f;
%MACRO ss;
DATA s;
%DO a1=5 %TO 5;
%DO b1=8 %TO 8;
%DO c1=6 %TO 9;
%DO d1=1 %TO 16;
%LET a=%SCAN(&hex,&a1);
%LET b=%SCAN(&hex,&b1);
%LET c=%SCAN(&hex,&c1);
%LET d=%SCAN(&hex,&d1);
%LET aa=%EVAL(&a1*4096+&b1*256+&c1*16+&d1);
%LET w=%BQUOTE(^R/RTF"\u&aa*");
a="&a&b&c&d";
b=&a&b&c&d.x;
c=INPUT("&a&b&c&d"x,$UCS2B.);
w="&w";
OUTPUT;
%END;
%END;
%END;
%END;
RUN;
%MEND;
%ss;
ODS RTF FILE='c:\rtf\tbl9.rtf';
PROC REPORT DATA=s NOWD;
RUN;
ODS RTF CLOSE;
```

Let's talk about one point. In our programs, when we use Unicode to represent a character, we always put an asterisk. What is that for? Now let's do the following:

- Open Microsoft Word.

- Open the Character Map and insert four characters: an English character a, a dagger (Unicode 2020), and two omegas (one with Unicode 3A9[957] and the other with Unicode 2126[8486]). The content of the file is: a†ΩΩ.
- Save the file as an RTF file.
- Open the file with Notepad. You can see the following elements in the file:

```
\f0 a\'86
\f325 \'d9
 \f0 \u8486\'3f
```

This piece of RTF code corresponds to four characters. F0 is the nickname of Times New Roman. a is character a itself. Although we put Unicode 2020 for a dagger, it saves as ASCII \'86. f325 is the Times New Roman Greek font. You may never have become acquainted with the Times New Roman Greek font (me neither). Suppose it is OK. Unicode 957 corresponds to d9 in Times New Roman Greek, similar to Unicode 2020 corresponding to 86 in Times New Roman. Then we come back to use the f0 font for Unicode \u8486. We already know \u8486, but what is \'3f? Where does it come from? The hex value 3f corresponds to a question mark. Actually, this is a separating symbol that does not show if the file is open using Microsoft Word. It is created by RTF itself. You can change 3f to any number and then save and open. The output is the same, but you cannot delete it. When we write a SAS program using Unicode input, we have to put a separating symbol after a Unicode. The easiest way is just to use an asterisk (*).

SAS 9.2 will have a new feature to designate Unicode symbols in RTF, PDF, and HTML output.

References

Burke, Sean M. 2003. *RTF Pocket Guide*. O'Reilly Media, Inc.

Carpenter, Arthur L. 2007. *Carpenter's complete guide to the SAS macro language.* Cary, NC: SAS Institute Inc.

Gianneschi, Dennis. 2006. "General Methods to Use Special Characters." *Proceedings of the Pharmaceutical SAS Users Group Conference (PharmaSUG 2006)*, Paper CC06, Cary, NC: SAS Institute Inc.
http://www.lexjansen.com/pharmasug/2006/coderscorner/cc06.pdf

"How can I get special Greek characters into my tabular output? "
http://www.sas.com/offices/europe/uk/newsletter/feature/5oct_nov03/ht1.html

Huntley, Scott. "How to Add a Little Spice to Your PDF Output."
http://support.sas.com/resources/papers/sgf2008/odspdf.pdf

Parsons, Lori S. 2007. "Enhancing RTF Output with RTF Control Words and In-Line Formatting. " *Proceedings of the SAS Global Forum (global Frum 2007)*, Paper 151-2007, Cary, NC: SAS Institute Inc.

http://www2.sas.com/proceedings/forum2007/151-2007.pdf

Rowell, Richard and Lenihan, Jim. 2004. "MORE CUSTOMIZATION?: CREATING SYMBOLS IN RTF FILES USING ODS." *Proceedings of the Pharmaceutical SAS Users Group Conference (PharmaSUG 2004)*, Paper TT12, Cary, NC: SAS Institute Inc.
http://www.lexjansen.com/pharmasug/2004/technicaltechniques/tt12.pdf

Song, Cindy. 2000. "Producing Special Characters in SAS® Output in RTF." *Proceedings of the Pharmaceutical SAS Users Group Conference (PharmaSUG 2000)*, Paper CC02, Cary, NC: SAS Institute Inc.
http://www.lexjansen.com/pharmasug/2000/coders/cc02.pdf

Word 2007: Rich Text Format (RTF) Specification, version 1.9.1,
http://www.microsoft.com/downloads/details.aspx?FamilyID=dd422b8d-ff06-4207-b476-6b5396a18a2b&displaylang=en

Zhang, Liping, Eric Qi and Weifeng Xu. 2002. "%Rtfsymbl – An Easy Solution for Defining Special Symbols in RTF File-Generating SAS® Programs." *Proceedings of the NorthEast SAS Users Group Conference (NESUG 2002)*, Paper CC010, Cary, NC: SAS Institute Inc.
http://www.nesug.org/proceedings/nesug02/cc/cc010.pdf

www.ingramcontent.com/pod-product-compliance
Lightning Source LLC
LaVergne TN
LVHW060444061126
851857LV00016B/1723